KING ALFRED'S COLLEGE

GOLD CAMP DESPERADOES

GOLD CAMP

A STUDY OF VIOLENCE, CRIME, AND

University of Oklahoma Press
Norman and London

DESPERADOES

PUNISHMENT ON THE MINING FRONTIER

R. E. Mather
and
F. E. Boswell

By R. E. Mather and F. E. Boswell

Hanging the Sheriff: A Biography of Henry Plummer (Salt Lake City, 1987)
John David Borthwick: Artist of the Gold Rush (Salt Lake City, 1989)
Gold Camp Desperadoes: Violence, Crime, and Punishment on the Mining Frontier (San Jose, Calif., 1990; Norman, 1993)
Vigilante Victims: Montana's 1864 Hanging Spree (San Jose, Calif., 1990)

Library of Congress Catalog Number: 92-50724

ISBN: 0-8061-2521-7

The paper in this book meets the guidelines for permanence and durability of the Committee on Production Guidelines for Book Longevity of the Council on Library Resources, Inc.∞

Published by the University of Oklahoma Press, Norman, Publishing Division of the University, by arrangement with History West Publishing Company, San Jose, California. Copyright © 1990 by History West Publishing Company. All rights reserved. Manufactured in the U.S.A. First printing of the University of Oklahoma Press edition, 1993.

1   2   3   4   5   6   7   8   9   10

To Leona Mather, Granddaughter of Increase,
And
To Pioneer Orrin Tallman

CONTENTS

ILLUSTRATIONS

MAP

ACKNOWLEDGMENTS

We are grateful to the following libraries and historical societies for their help with this study:

Idaho Historical Society

Luna House Museum, Nez Perce County Historical Society, Idaho

California State Library

National Archives, San Bruno, California, Branch

Bancroft Library, Berkeley

Stanford University Libraries

San Jose State University Libraries

California State Archives

The Church of Jesus Christ of Latter-day Saints Genealogical Library, Salt Lake City

Oregon Historical Society

Missouri State Archives

Montana Historical Society

A special thanks also goes to Dr. Merle Wells and Dr. Brigham D. Madsen for their contributions to the manuscript.

INTRODUCTION

A desperado, Webster's tells us, is a "bold or violent criminal," especially "of the western U.S. in the 19th century."[1] California's turbulent gold rush society proved a hotbed for the germination of such criminals. During the 1850s, the newly established San Quentin prison unwittingly unleashed upon the state more than one hundred fifty such convicts, destined either to roam the remote California camps or to flee to unsettled territories beyond the state.[2] Public fascination for these reckless wanderers soon developed into a mystique that lured impressionable western youth. A "terrible curse," the newspaper editor of a now-vanished mining town lamented, "has taken possession of so many young men on the Pacific Coast, the desire to be a desperado."[3]

The following desperado stories confirm the finding of a 1969 study of frontier violence. Outlaws, the report stated, "were often men of good background who . . . were alienated from the values of the community."[4] Promising sons of prominent families joined the gold rush with high ideals and higher hopes, but on the frontier underwent a transformation which estranged them from traditional moral codes. They committed crimes, escaped justice, became wanted men. Because of arrest warrants, or tarnished reputations that sometimes led to unwarranted arrests, they literally could not "go home again"; they could only keep moving. As they fled to the relative safety of each new El Dorado, most could not even afford the luxury of looking back.

Their lives were usually violent; however, on the mining frontier, violence was not peculiar to the outlaw world. After the outbreak of the Civil War, sectional hostilities created continual conflicts in the West, such as the Confederate raid on the mining camp

1

of Florence, Idaho. In addition, there were sporadic skirmishes with Indians, who, as one early historian complained, "seemed to think the country belonged to them."[5] And the international character of the mining communities also caused clashes: "A Chinaman hates a negro as the devil does holy water," one miner wrote from Sonora. "I witnessed a fight between about ten darkeys and about a hundred Chinamen."[6] Sailor William Shaw reported similar aggression on any placers worked by men of "coloured" skin, adding that "ejections constantly occurred" and that "conflicts were often serious in their results."[7]

Besides sectional and racial dissension, those representing law and order contributed to the violence by responding to nonviolent crimes with brutal punishment. "If a man was caught doing anything wrong," pioneer Henry Maize explained, "we just killed him, that's all!"[8] William Shaw agreed that "hanging was sometimes resorted to for theft," though the usual punishment for petty larceny was "loss of both ears."[9] Miner David Augustus Shaw described an incident in which a convicted thief was "fastened by his hands to the branch of a tree, and the duly appointed officers proceeded to shave his head. . . . His feet were then tied to the foot of a tree, and a doctor cut off his ears, from the stumps of which he bled freely while receiving his flogging." But the punishment did not have the desired effect on the thief's morals, for when "about a mile away, he stole a mule and rode to the Calaveras diggings."[10]

It was not only the informal courts which meted out such barbaric justice. As late as 1853, California statutes decreed that theft of property valued at less than fifty dollars would be punished by "any number of lashes not exceeding fifty upon the bare back," or by "fine or imprisonment and lashes, in the discretion of the jury."[11]

But in the California gold camps there was at least a state government to set up courts and formulate laws. As the desperadoes spread to the settlements where formal justice systems had not yet been implemented, some felt safe in committing savage crimes — and some were lynched. Yet the raw camps did not exist in a state of anarchy; miners quickly united by electing officers and holding courts to settle disputes. Since the saloons were the gathering places, within their realm professional gamblers armed themselves to enforce the code of their fraternity. And adventurers who had preceded the gamblers into the wilderness also had their rules for survival — the Mountain Code, by which an individual had the right to immediately defend himself should an antagonist make a motion toward a weapon. As Thomas Dimsdale of the *Montana Post* made clear, the Mountain Code went beyond preservation of life to include the right to defend honor and dignity. In regard to the quarrels and bloodshed resulting from such defenses, Dimsdale commented, "The unwritten code of the miners, based on a wrong view of what constitutes manhood, teaches them to resent by force what should be answered by silent contempt."[12] Dimsdale's phrasing is felicitous, for "what constitutes manhood" lies at the very heart of the desperado mystique.

The young outlaws, newly dislodged from moral and social bases and by nature daring and reckless, were particularly vulnerable to potentially self-destructive portions of the frontier codes. In the stories presented in succeeding chapters, certain words and phrases recur, reflecting the image a desperado was expected to uphold: "He assumed the role of 'chief' " (meaning "top gun"); "Either he or I must die"; "He got his man"; and "He died game."

These statements lay bare the attitudes which the previously quoted editor labeled the "curse" of the Pacific coast. Since many of the outlaws described in following pages were handsome young men who displayed both generosity and bravery, it is not surprising that even during their lifetimes they assumed mythical dimensions. Dimsdale marveled at their courage in facing death: "The desire to die game, so common to desperadoes," he wrote, "frequently robs death of half its terrors."[13] And Mark Twain painted his memorable portrait of the "desperado of wide reputation," dressed in an "excessively long-tailed frock-coat, shiny stump-toed boots, and with dainty little slouch hat tipped over left eye," swaggering along the boardwalk as "small-fry roughs made room for his majesty. . . . They killed each other on slight provocation, and hoped and expected to be killed themselves."[14]

In writing about desperadoes, Dimsdale and Twain had their reasons for exaggerating; the former was justifying vigilance activities and the latter was employing literary license. Yet many of the outlaws covered in this study did indeed "die game," and if they did not actually hope to die, they should have at least expected to. It would not be unfair to say that most were addicted to alcohol, gambling, and the excitement of gold stampedes. Their reckless habits produced continual scrapes with the law, and exaggerated reports of their encounters enhanced their reputations.

The developing mining frontier—with its string of burgeoning main streets emanating the sounds of braying pack mules, the clatter of carpenters' hammers, and the wail of the violin—presented the ideal environment for notorious fugitives.[15] Here they found the companionship of other outcasts, satisfied their craving for excitement, and postponed the inevitable moment when their past would catch up to them. Most took the same route: on leaving California, they either crossed the high Sierra to the 1859 gold and silver discoveries in what is now Nevada, or rushed to the 1860–61 strikes along Washington Territory's Clearwater River. In the late spring of 1862, they stampeded to the Salmon River mines. Then a few months later, they challenged the rugged trails leading over the Bitterroots to reach Gold Creek or Bannack, and some drifted as far south as the Boise Basin. June 1863 brought the Alder Gulch stampede, and those who had not already been killed in a gunfight or hanged by that date were on hand to participate.

Despite the thousands of international participants, the mining stampedes generated their own small world; therefore, characters and events in the following stories often overlap. The first five chapters follow a chronology of mining discoveries with a story to depict a historic event in each major mining area.

Most biographies in this volume contain unresolved mysteries, instances in which needed information is missing or in which sources contradict each other. Ascertaining the truth about incidents which took place more than a hundred years ago is no simple matter. We have relied on public documents where available—wills, census schedules, prison registers, trial records, and pardon files—but such sources are not free of error or contradiction. Trial testimony, for example, depends upon the acuity and honesty of each witness. Naturally it is distressing to learn, as in the trial recreated in the second chapter, that the key witness who sent three men to the gallows was regarded by his acquaintances as dull witted and dishonest. So public records drawn upon for this study may sometimes leave the final decision with the reader.

A second source for desperado biography was contemporary newspapers. Valuable though early articles are, they run the gamut from stirring eyewitness accounts to rumors picked up in saloons. Chapter three provides an example of an outlaw accused in print of committing highway robbery at the very time he was incarcerated in the high-security section of San Quentin.

A third source—early histories and pioneer reminiscences—
presents the most serious problems. Such sources blend clear images
of the past with hazy memories or valid accounts with tall tales, yet
provide few clues to help distinguish between the two. Also, they
employ misleading language, labeling untried men "robbers" and
"murderers," rather than "alleged" or "accused" criminals. Out of
deference to unenforced laws prohibiting gambling, some writers
referred to all who gathered around a gaming table as "outlaws."
Among these writers was historian Nathaniel Langford, who considered gambling to be a "species of robbery."[16]

But most hazardous to a search for truth is the peculiar bias of
each account, as dictated by its author's personal leanings. A Unionist is apt to write disparagingly of a Secessionist. And pro-vigilantes
Langford, Dimsdale, and McConnell depicted desperadoes as presenting so great a danger to society that the populace had no choice
but to unite and destroy them. Mark Twain disagreed, stating that
"these long-tailed heroes of the revolver" did "their killing princi-
pally among themselves, and seldom molested peaceable citizens."[17]

Despite biases and inaccuracies, early histories and memoirs
contain much valuable information. By recognizing a bias, the reader
can neutralize its deleterious effect. And it is often possible to detect
when a writer was reporting an event he could not have witnessed
or recording a conversation he could not have heard. However, even
the dubious passages of the memoirs have a special value: they dis-
close the writer's way of thinking, expose false rumors in circulation, and illustrate the process of romanticizing history. Therefore,
they will be included in this work, but with commentary regarding
trustworthiness. The reader will bear the ultimate responsibility for
judging the accuracy and veracity of the many witnesses we will
now summon to retell the desperado stories.

Though it may seem unconscionable to make outlaws, rather
than respectable citizens, the focus of a book, the outlaws' lives
reveal their times. By examining each outlaw's heritage, we can
relate West to East and one generation to the previous one, rather
than attempting to study the frontier in a vacuum. By resting the
spotlight on each individual desperado and his family background,
we hope to illuminate the entire historical drama.

Having discussed sources and painted the backdrop of sectional,
racial, and judicial violence against which desperadoism flourished
in the 1850s and 60s, we will allow Langford—known for his color-

ful descriptions and "lively imagination"[18] — to introduce the main actors. The bold horsemen have just robbed five miners of their gold-laden purses and, Robin-Hood-like, flipped a five-dollar coin to a penniless boy:

They galloped furiously on towards Florence. Thundering into the town, they drew up before the first saloon, fired their pistols, and urged their horses into the establishment. Without dismounting they ordered liquor for the crowd. All the by-standers partook with them. Harper ostentatiously threw one of the purses he had just seized upon the counter, telling the barkeeper to weigh out the amount of the bill, and after a few moments they left the saloon, "to see," as one of them expressed himself, "whether the town was big enough to hold them."[19]

But like the lucky recipient of the five-dollar coin, each desperado was himself once an unstained lad, and as we shall see, each trod his own rocky pathway to notoriety.

THE MINING FRONTIER

ONE

CALIFORNIA GOLD COUNTRY

THE STORY OF ED RICHARDSON,
ALIAS CHARLEY FORBES

GRASS VALLEY, CALIFORNIA, 1852. *Courtesy California State Library*

CALIFORNIA GOLD COUNTRY

The Fourth of July 1860 was not a holiday, the local newspaper reported, but business as usual for Grass Valley courts. Justice S. C. Richardson heard the typical cases: "Charles Burdett . . . on complaint of striking and kicking Mrs. Mary Smith, — Plead guilty and was sentenced to pay a fine of $15 and 7 1/2 days in jail. Sent up." Next came Tripe Charley for assault and battery, and then there was the ongoing feud between the Jessell brothers and a merchant named Berwin. The Jessells had first charged Berwin with assault and battery, to which he pleaded guilty and paid a fine of $24.75. But the same three parties were soon back in court, this time with roles reversed. Justice Richardson ordered the Jessells to pay for the decanters, water pitcher, and tumbler they had hurled at Berwin, but the brothers then accused Berwin of having struck one of them "with his fist in the face." The justice put an end to the volley by persuading the plaintiffs to withdraw all complaints. Thus several days of disturbances ended on a harmonious note.[1] For Richardson, it had been an ordinary week of attempting to keep the peace in a small mining town reputed to surpass Mexico in its number of "banditti."[2]

The local press covered not only the court cases heard by the two justices, but also a hodgepodge of activities that ran the gamut from civic progress to barbaric sports events and murderous assaults. For example, when not engaging the Jessells in legal battle, merchant Berwin was packing his stock to move to an elegant new brick building; miners had extracted $100,000 from a recent gold strike in the canyon; shooting matches at Gallows Flat offered live turkeys and chickens as both targets and marksmanship prizes; combatants at the last dogfight had delighted the audience by ripping at each other's ears for nearly an hour; an unknown assailant had fired a ball at a man strolling down the street, striking the victim just above the hip; and all the while, the project of planking Grass Valley streets "marched bravely on."[3]

The paper also kept citizens up to date on national events. At the Baltimore political convention, a Democratic party split had left the door wide open for the Republican candidate, Abraham Lincoln. The *National*'s editor dreaded the thought of Lincoln becoming president because he considered Abe too prone to violence himself to resolve the conflict brewing between the states. If there was a scarcity of national items in the overland mail, the weather always made a good topic: July 1860 had been one of the soggiest summers on record, with one period of steady rainfall lasting for thirty-six hours. And, as a last resort, Editor Roberts could always fill a gaping column with an edifying poem, such as "Woodsman Spare That Tree," or "The Last Leaf."[4]

Though Justice Richardson read about the savage sports enjoyed by the citizenry and daily handled numerous incidents of violence, he was optimistic. As a magistrate and devout Catholic, he was doing his part to civilize the community. Despite the unstable environment, he and Sarah provided a secure home for their six children. As a symbol of cultivating the wilderness, the family had planted a small pear tree, whose delicate spring blossoms brightened the drab yard about their modest cottage. Amidst such promise, Richardson could not possibly have foreseen that the damp weeks of July 1860 would provide the last peaceful moments he would ever know. In fact, had someone informed him that during the blistering hot days of August just ahead, his family's snug little world would turn completely topsy-turvy, warned him that his two handsome, intelligent, lovingly reared teenage sons would enter San Quentin, he would have found the prediction inconceivable.[5]

Juvenile delinquency had been a problem from California's inception. Prior to December 1862, teenage offenders served sentences alongside hardened international criminals. It was not unusual for the names of sixteen or seventeen year olds to appear on the state prison register: one page, for example, lists four entrants under the age of twenty-one; another notes admittance of a boy of fourteen years; and from January 1855 to July 1858, San Quentin accepted thirty-seven minors.[6]

Most notorious of these youthful inmates was skinny, freckle-faced Bobby Durkin, convicted of grand larceny. The Grass Valley paper had carried a tongue-in-cheek article warning residents that the little "thief" was paying the county a visit. "Bobby is a great rogue for a little fellow (13 or 14 years of age) and is better acquainted with the old prison brig than almost any other person in his line of operation. — Look out for the little scamp."[7]

Being the second child of San Francisco policeman Anthony Durkin, Bobby would have appeared an unlikely candidate for crime. When the boy had gotten into trouble, his father had sanctioned Bobby's imprisonment on the brig, thinking it might teach his son a lesson. Instead, Bobby departed the prison ship as a habitual criminal who committed crime after crime, served on county and state chain gangs, and escaped and received additional time as punishment.[8]

As Justice Richardson was about to learn, the immorality so rampant in the new mining society could make inroads into even the best of homes. In his own upbringing, he had been protected from negative influences. He was born in 1806 into a prosperous Virginia family, who removed to Kentucky. There Richardson grew to manhood and studied law. Handsome, intelligent, and sensitive, he seemed destined to become a great lawyer, but he tired of the profession. He returned to school, then at age thirty-three wed a young lady thirteen years his junior, and embarked upon a second career in the more exciting field of civil engineering.[9]

Richardson's projects kept the young couple on the move. Their first son, Edward, was born in 1841 in Louisiana; three more children were born in Canada, and the last two in Indiana. Then, while working at a new site in Iowa, Richardson was taken with the urge to participate in the building of the Far West. Since the couple's brood of six ranged from Ed, age twelve, to a babe in arms, the adventuresome engineer arranged for his unwed sister to stay with Sarah while he explored California alone. If he decided to stay, he said, he would send for the family. Taking the Panama route, he left that country on March 31, 1851, on the steamer *Republic*. On April 19, the ship passed through the Golden Gate, but it would be more than two years before the Richardsons would be reunited.[10]

On their arrival, Sarah, her sister-in-law, and the children found Grass Valley a thriving town. In the fall of 1848, prospectors had crossed Bear River and stumbled upon the lush, uninhabited valley, waist high with waving grass and sprawling, crimson-blossomed peas. The first residence appeared a year later, a log cabin atop Badger Hill. The following year, James Walsh established a sawmill, a merchant set up a tent store, and a third entrepreneur constructed a log hotel. The settlement burst into prominence when a prospector discovered rich quartz on Gold Hill, setting off a rush which increased the cabins to one hundred fifty.[11]

The grassy valley was on its way to becoming the second largest settlement in the newly formed county of Nevada when Sarah settled into a cottage at the north end of Auburn Street. The town boasted a variety of businesses, daily mail service, and a stage line whose coaches departed precisely on schedule. And most important to Sarah, her family could attend mass at St. Patrick's, a small frame building on Chapel Street. She could send the four older children to either a public or private school.

True, the community's entertainments were oriented toward the predominantly male population — gambling, billiards, bowling, and wrestling matches. There were also sports such as chaining a bull and bear together or turning hundreds of rats into a pavilion and awarding a prize to the dog who killed the greatest number. A race between the white mare Jenny and the gray mare Dolly, along with accompanying betting, would create a stampede that left the streets manless. "Every horse, mule and jackass," the local editor quipped, "will be trotted out to-day to convey the large number of people to the race course." In contrast, the Alta Theater offered lectures and musical recitals for the entire family, though the editor complained in print about "the little brats" kicking up "a d——l of a muss, althrough the performance."[12] Inside the theater was a noisy audience, while outside, the banging of eight ore-crushing mills reverberated day and night.

Yet there was much natural beauty for the Richardsons to enjoy in their valley home. The local Wells Fargo agent, who wrote under the pen name Old Block, described the view as follows:

Look eastwardly and you will see beyond the house a charming valley, a quarter of a mile wide and a mile long, enclosed by beautiful rounded hills which are covered by the magnificent evergreen pines of the mountains, and in the midst of this grassy flat, through which Wolf Creek winds its way, you will see thrown up heaps of earth, whose black or grey surface contrasts strongly with the green grass of the valley . . . for you are in the mines and among the mountain moles. It is a beautiful spot, . . . the pure mountain air, the deep pine shades at noon.[13]

Colonel Richardson, as his new neighbors called him, quickly distinguished himself as an asset to the community. He constructed several buildings on Main Street and became the first county road commissioner. But realizing his career had prevented the family from putting down roots, he decided to return to his former profession. He placed an ad in the *National*: "S. C. Richardson. Attorney & Counsellor at Law. Will promptly attend to all business committed to his care in Nevada and adjoining counties."[14]

But just as the transplants were beginning to adjust to their first permanent home, they experienced firsthand one of the disasters common to frontier settlements. "Most of the mining towns in California," the *National* expounded, "are composed of pitch pine boards, paper and cloth. . . . The summer makes tinder of them."[15] To combat the hazard presented by the wooden town, volunteers formed a fire company, but after a year without a serious conflagration, members gradually disbanded. Town trustees required each building owner to keep handy a fifty-gallon barrel of water and four buckets, but failed to enforce the regulation. The scene was set for Grass Valley's "great fire."[16]

It was nearing midnight on September 13, 1855. Most residents, including the Richardsons, had retired for the night. But at the United States Hotel on Main Street, candles still burned. One careless gesture, and a room was suddenly ablaze, then the entire hotel, and then the adjoining buildings. A cry of "fire! fire!" rang through the dark streets, bringing the town to life. While their father rushed to join the fire fighting, their mother and aunt herded the Richardson children into the street, ready to flee if the wind shifted. The air was heavy with smoke, the town lit bright as day. A maze of frantic people scurried in all directions with a few precious possessions clutched in their arms while behind them raging orange flames leaped so high they tinted the black hills beyond a rosy hue. "All was confusion," an early history recorded,

the flames were crackling and roaring, licking up the tinder dry buildings in their pathway, and all the undirected efforts of the excited people were futile to stay their onward march. Buildings were pulled down, buckets of water by the hundreds were thrown upon the burning houses, wet blankets and other devices . . . but to no avail, for the frame buildings, dried in the long summer sun, burned too fiercely for the flames to be subdued. All night they fought with tireless energy, and never ceased the struggle until the flames expired for want of food to live upon. In that one dreadful night over three hundred buildings, occupying thirty acres of ground, were swept away.[17]

The fire did not reach the Richardson's home. Like the churches, it lay just beyond the scorched area. But the Main Street property, valued at $12,000, represented Richardson's life savings. At age forty-nine, the newly reestablished lawyer with eight dependents was obliged to start over. Though he may have felt despair, he wasted no time bemoaning the loss. Old Block set the example for Richardson and other downhearted merchants. At daylight, the Wells Fargo agent hauled a frame shanty from the hills and propped it against his company's brick vault, one of the few objects to survive the fire. Next, he tugged out a charred slab, scrawled "Express Office" on it, and tacked it to the wobbly building. Then with the ground beneath his feet still warm, Old Block proceeded to wait on customers, trampling through the ashes of his former building. His good spirits and energy inspired others to get on with their own lives in a similar manner.[18]

The Richardson parents used the "great fire" as a valuable lesson for their offspring: worldly goods do not endure, but faith brings a will to continue. Richardson's law practice was soon flourishing in a rebuilt office, and he also found time to raise funds for the church and participate in the incorporation of the town and the selection of officials. From the first day, the marshal was kept busy issuing citations: one to a pair of brawlers, another to a man riding his horse too fast through town, and two more to women "parading the streets in male attire."[19] In 1856, voters chose Colonel Richardson as one of their town trustees and also named the lane where he kept his law office Richardson Street in his honor. As a trustee, the Colonel soon learned that bringing neatness to the town was an uphill battle. Uncaring inhabitants refused to abandon the practice of tossing rubbish into the streets including "old boots, shoes, hats, gunny-bags, barrels, boxes."[20] A second problem that defied resolution was "fast riding" in the downtown area. More than once such reckless-ness resulted in an accident. "The Grass Valley stage went out on Tuesday last with twenty-four passengers—fifteen of them outside," the paper reported. "Near Weiss' brewery the balance was lost and the stage upset; . . . Mrs. Randall of Rough and Ready received a severe cut on the forehead." But Richardson's unsuccessful war against traffic accidents and filth in the streets did not detract from his popularity. In 1857, and again in 1859, he won election as one of the town's two justices of the peace.[21]

The hectic 1859 election did not augur an easy term ahead. "A free fight came off at Hornbrook's a day or two before the election," according to the *National*, and "during the scuffle one of the combatants drew a knife but before he could use it, it was wrested from him, and his face considerably spoiled." Bystanders interceded to effect a reconciliation, buying drinks all around. "Queer world this," mused the reporter.[22]

On assuming the duties of a peace official in this queer world, the Colonel moved to a new office on Mill Street. Though the 1859 silver discoveries on the other side of the Sierra had drained away a third of the town's population, those who remained behind disturbed the peace sufficiently to keep both justices busy. Since his duties included serving as a judge to the circuit court, Richardson also dealt with robberies and murders, but the most common case brought before him was assault and battery.[23]

In one instance, he had the unpleasant duty of passing judgment on a housewife who had become annoyed because her husband invited friends home for a drink. When the party turned rowdy, the irate woman picked up a chair and struck down a drunken man. "Intoxication," the justice noted, was a frequent factor in the cases of violence he arbitrated. A second factor was racial hostility. Due to "whiskey and the too free use of an axe handle," one Mr. Roach "nearly knocked out a Chinaman's eyes." Richardson fined the offender seventy-five dollars, trusting that Roach would be "learnt a lesson." For the times, the sum constituted stern punishment. By way of comparison, another judge fined a wife beater only fifteen dollars.[24]

Justice Richardson's sentences were not intended to be punitive. His goal was that plaintiff and defendant return to the community with resolution to live together in harmony. His court manner was not one of stern superiority, but of courteous firmness. Though his impartiality and dignified deportment won him admirers, he did not always take the popular side of an issue. When a controversial murder case in the district court split the community into two warring factions, he supported the lower-class minority. After listening to testimony, he had concluded that the jury had condemned an innocent man; he therefore wrote the governor requesting a pardon for Francis Moore. The governor however aligned himself with the upper-crust majority, who had petitioned for an immediate hanging.[25]

Though that particular moral battle was lost, Richardson did enjoy some civic victories. He banded with other businessmen to plank Mill Street, thus sparing customers the necessity of wading ankle deep in mud. And in November 1859, he organized a grand ball to benefit the Catholic church, serving on two committees himself. Despite a snowstorm, the ball at the Hamilton Theater drew a good crowd. "The fine band of music," the press announced, as well as the "excellent supper" and "array of beautiful ladies," made the occasion the social highlight of the year. Thus 1859 closed on a festive note.[26]

The grand ball was one of the last occasions at which the Richardsons could appear in public without a deep sense of shame. Since their arrival in California, their concern had been the welfare of their children, and the threat presented by the frontier environment caused them constant worry. The *National* editor, however, reassured parents that "as for raising children in the mines, they can be raised here as well as anywhere else" since "intelligence, virtue and good breeding, . . . the elements of good society" are as "good" in the mining society as "anywhere else."[27]

In receiving an education, the Richardson children were a minority in their community. The four older siblings attended school, while Sarah tutored the two younger sons at home, and the Colonel provided Ed with training in law. But two thirds of Grass Valley's five hundred children received no schooling at all. One California visitor had described boys of ten or twelve, "smoking cigars as big as themselves, . . . and losing their hundred dollars at a pop with all the nonchalance of an old gambler." The presence of such precocious scamps did not make it easy for the Richardsons to keep tight controls on their own youngsters.[28]

Their eldest son was their pride and joy. Ed was witty, gregarious, and intelligent, and like his father a "capital talker." One acquaintance described the youth as a "splendid looking fellow — straight as a ramrod, . . . agile as a cat in his movements." Though slender and only five foot seven, Ed was still growing. His hair was bushy and dark brown, but a fair complexion made thick, black brows arched over clear gray eyes even more striking. Though his nose was prominent, its aquilinity added to rather than detracted from his handsomeness.[29]

Ed studied during the day and in the evening worked as a printer for the *National*. Since he demonstrated a certain flair for writing, the editor allowed him to contribute an occasional item. Though the teenage printer may have fancied himself a mature professional, his articles — drawn from the small world of the Richardson household — are distinguishable for a boyish wide eyedness:

In the garden of Col. S. C. Richardson, of this place, there is a pear tree measuring at the ground one and a half inches in diameter, three feet six inches high, which is at present bearing no less than twelve pears averaging seven inches in circumference, and not of the dwarf species either, but a regular standard pear. This is certainly a precious and prolific specimen in pomological history.

FIRE — Fire Department were called out . . . Wednesday last by an alarm which proved to come from Col. Richardson's cottage on the north end of Auburn Street. The fire took from a defective junction of a stove pipe, where it passed through the attic. . . . But little damage was done, the fire being extinguished by a few buckets of water.[30]

Night work at the paper allowed Ed to acquire a new independence, and temptation to drop in at the lively entertainment houses proved irresistible. He could assuage his guilt somewhat by reasoning that his visits were educational, a source of material for articles. The Chinese theater, for example, provided a peek into a strange, fascinating culture. The painted-faced actors with flowing beards wore "artificial ears of exceptional proportions" and dressed in "gawdy garments of silk, embroidered with colors of dazzling brightness." Though their music was "almost entirely on minor scale" and therefore "not particularly attractive to English ears," there was something haunting about the "pitiful dolorousness of their chants."[31]

There was also much to be learned in the gambling halls, but in this regard Ed would have done well to consider, while he was setting type, a timely warning:

GAMBLING. . . . We cannot repress a shudder at the thought of the inevitable consequences which must attend its victims, and the certain doom which must sooner or later overtake its infatuated votaries. . . . How many a young man full of hope, and giving promise of a useful future, has fallen into the lowest depths of degradation solely through the one vice of gambling.[32]

It was almost as though the editor had in mind a certain young man "full of hope, and giving promise of a useful future," who was drifting toward irreversible "degradation."

Of course Ed was not the only person in Grass Valley teetering on the edge of firm morality, and others had already taken the plunge. Early 1860 had seen a decided increase in criminal activity. Ed's editor grumbled that "petty thieves, pick pockets, and highwaymen" were becoming "too thick to thrive."[33]

Given the abundance of vice in the community and Ed's anxiousness to break free of parental control, it was not surprising that he should fall in with bad company. He was the sort of associate certain men were seeking — a naive youth eager to join the fraternity of the initiated, yet respectable enough himself to avoid suspicion.

In sharp contrast to the jubilant air with which 1859 had closed, 1860 had opened on the ominous note of a rash of housebreakings, holdups, and burglaries. Then at midyear came an event that would nearly destroy the Richardson family. Naturally Ed's paper covered the story of a daring robbery in nearby Mountain Spring. Authorities arrested a high-living, flashily dressed suspect named Daniel "Curley" Smith and placed him in the Auburn jail. When Madam Julia Moore (the widow of the condemned man the Colonel had tried to save from the gallows) paid Curley a visit, the jailer discovered that her companion was actually a male disguised in female's clothing. The two visitors were taken into custody, but due to lack of evidence they, along with Curley, were later released. Curley returned to Grass Valley and began a discreet search for a partner ingenuous enough to dispose of stolen goods.[34]

When the census taker visited the Richardson home on June 8, 1860, his report gave no hint of the trouble brewing in the family. A census record preserves a moment in time, depicts a family as distinctly as if its members were once again gathered about the hearth: Justice Richardson, age 54 and worth $4,000 (one third of the fortune lost in the "great fire"); his wife Sarah, 41; his sister, 40; and six children, ranging from Ed, 19, to the youngest son, 9. The illusion of security was deceptive. Though the parents could not guess that Ed had befriended Curley Smith, perhaps they were remiss in not heeding one warning. The youth had acquired several tattoos, including his initials and some printing symbols on the inside of his left forearm, a cross on the back of his left hand, and the markings of a ring on one finger.[35]

In July, the unsuspecting justice optimistically moved his family to a new residence and set himself up in a more attractive office. Taking the role of impartial judge seriously, he refused to join local Democrats in their campaign against Abraham Lincoln. And despite the silver stampede to Virginia City (in what is now Nevada), the court caseload remained the same with several disturbances to handle per day.[36]

July brought the strange rainy days and an even stranger robbery. While a local jeweler was busy with a customer, an unseen thief made off with a gold breast pin and two bracelets. Since police had no suspects, the newspaper had to concentrate on the weather, commenting that the heavy downpour was "a thing without a parallel in the written history of the country." With prolonged storms continuing to move in from San Francisco, it scarcely seemed like summer. August, however, restored normalcy — days of unrelenting sun that crisped wooden buildings on Main Street to blaze-inviting tinder. When the second fateful fire broke out, it was to consume much more than Justice Richardson's corruptible buildings.[37]

On the night of August 9, residents of nearby Nevada City noticed a rosy glow hovering over Grass Valley. Volunteers, with carriages and hoses trundling noisily behind them, ran the entire four miles to join the battle against the conflagration. United efforts limited destruction to a few blocks on Main Street. As during the 1855 disaster, the justice's home lay just beyond the limits of the fire. But when the flames were at last subdued, events took a bizarre turn. Unknown persons stealthily approached the Richardson residence and ignited it. Firemen rushed to extinguish the new flames, but the house had already sustained some damage, estimated at $250. Fortunately all members of the household escaped harm.

Daylight revealed that all of Richardson's downtown property — a row of wooden buildings squeezed between two brick structures and the outhouses directly behind — was nothing more than a bed of ashes. Convinced the fire had been the work of arsonists (presumably enemies the justice had made in court), officials appointed a committee to investigate the incident. The fire, it was discovered, had erupted in an abandoned bowling alley, which two men had fled moments before it exploded in flame.[38]

Police rounded up the usual suspects, among them Curley Smith and Julia Moore. Though Julia had never been convicted of a crime, she was accustomed to being taken into custody any time authorities were under pressure to solve a troubling case. After questioning, the police released all suspects, except Curley, Julia, and, shocking though it was to the townspeople, "Ed. Richardson, a son of Col. S. C. Richardson." The three retained suspects were committed to the county jail in Nevada City. Though devastated by the disgrace, the Colonel and Sarah had faith their son was innocent and equal faith in the justice system.

The county jail did not need any more prisoners since it was already bulging at the seams. Due to the surplus of cases, the three newcomers would have to wait several weeks for trial. But now that the Richardsons' problems with their wayward son had been brought to light, the pace of impending doom accelerated at an alarming rate. With parents still reeling in shock over the upcoming arson case, a complainant came forth charging Ed with selling stolen jewelry. On September 6, the district court indicted Ed, Curley, and Julia for arson, while the court of sessions indicted Ed alone for grand larceny. To his parents' distress, Ed admitted that he had acted as fence for a thief. The trial was set for five days after the indictment.[39]

Battling humiliation at his son's moral weakness, the justice hired two attorneys, instructing them that Ed must acknowledge his crime. The case of *The People vs. Richardson* commenced on the morning of September 11, with several witnesses testifying that the defendant had sold jewelry stolen from a local merchant. The twelve male jurors could not help feeling sympathy for the clean-cut, young defendant. For all the manliness he was trying to display, he had the appearance of a mere boy — slightness of build, pale face, and clear gray eyes accentuated by dark brows; and then there was the childish ink drawing of a ring on his finger. It was obvious to everyone in court, except the defendant, that he had been duped. Guided by a sense of honor imbued in him from childhood, Ed insisted on taking sole responsibility for the crime, steadfastly refusing to name the jewel thief. At 4:30 P.M., the case went to the jury. Within the hour it returned, and the foreman pronounced the verdict "Guilty," recommending the defendant "to the mercy of the Court." The judge regretfully sentenced the nineteen year old to eighteen months of labor at San Quentin.[40]

Hoping the punishment would jolt their son back to the straight and narrow path, his parents quietly accepted the sentence. Still ahead lay the arson trial. Since Curley and Ed were charged as accomplices to a crime Julia had instigated, it was necessary to first establish her guilt, but at the November 12 trial, the prosecution could produce no evidence she had laid plans to burn the bowling alley or the Richardson home. After an absence of only fifteen minutes, the jury returned with an acquittal, and the prosecutor dismissed charges against Ed and Curley.[41]

Though Ed was no longer doing the printing, the *National* brought out an issue proclaiming Lincoln's election as president. National news held little interest for the heartsick Richardsons. Despite their sterling example of reverence for the laws of man and God, the son in whom they had taken an intense pride was soon to dishonor the family name by entering it on the state prison register.[42]

Edward Richardson passed behind the twenty-foot walls of San Quentin early on the morning of November 28, 1860, the first admission of the day. A guard conducted him inside the six-year-old prison structure, called the Stones, and deposited him at the turnkey's office. Here, an official assigned the new prisoner number 2041 on the register and then ordered him to strip off his clothing. During the measurement and physical examination, a clerk recorded Ed's features — every scar, mole, or other marking no matter where located — for identification in case of escape.[43]

High-risk prisoners were sent to the top floor — two rows of cells equipped with cots, night bucket, and a foot-long slit in the plate-iron door — but the turnkey handed Ed a coarse, fraying blanket and directed him to the "long room" of the bottom floor, which he would share with hundreds of criminals, the dregs of the gold rush population. They were a mixture of callow youth like himself and recidivists hardened by years of crime and ensuing punishment. Since no prisoner was allowed to remain in his bed during the day, the guard ordered Ed to drop his blanket on the assigned cot and hurry off to his work detail.[44]

The typical day of the new San Quentin inmate can best be imagined through a perusal of the "Rules to be observed by Convicts":

1. At the first ringing of the Bell in the morning each Convict shall *arise* and *dress himself*, and *be in readiness to issue forth from his room* at the second ringing of the Bell.
2. When the doors are opened each Convict will march out of his room in *regular order*, one behind the other. Those working *outside* the Prison Wall shall form in a line two deep, and move

in close order to the Gate from whence they will be conducted to their labor by an Officer. Those working *inside* the Prison Walls will form in a separate line two deep . . . from whence they will be moved off to their respective places of labor.

3. When the Bell rings in the Morning and at Noon, the Convicts will *cease labor*, and will fall in line two deep . . . and march to the eating room. Those *inside* the Prison Wall will march to within five paces of the door of the dining room, there halt and there await the arrival of those working outside. After all have got into one line they will move off and as they enter the door, will *take off their hats and caps*, break off to the right and left, and take their places at the table *standing* and there remain until the small Bell rings, when they will take their seats and proceed to eating; at the second ringing of the small Bell *they will rise* and upon the order being given, march out and form in their respective lines, when they will be taken to their labor by the Overseers.

4. At Table when anything is required, the convicts must make known their wants by the following signs.

For Soup or Coffee they must present their cups to the waiter *with the handle foremost.*

For Water the *reverse*, and under no consideration must a word *be spoken at Table*.

5. At the ringing of the Bell in the Evening all will cease labor, form into double line, and at the command March, will move off to the Eating room, and whilst there will observe the same regulations as at Morning and Noon meals.

6. On leaving the Eating room in the Evening, *those prisoners* confined in the *cells* will move off forming in double file and march to the stairs *in close order*, where they will *halt*, until the word is given them to proceed to their cells; Any convicts found *conversing* in the corridor or *in another's cell* will be severely punished.

7. Prisoners sleeping in the *Long Room* will form in line in front of the Prison, . . . and there stand until their names are called to come into the room. They shall pay *particular attention* to the call of the roll, and move off as quick as their names are called.

8. . . . *All conversation* of any description between convicts whilst *at rest*, or *while marching in line*, or *at the Table* is most *strictly for-*

bidden, and any deviation from this rule will be severely punished.

10. After the Prisoners are all confined *no noise of any description* will be allowed; and all communication between Prisoners is *prohibited*. Prisoners are not *allowed* to have any description of *light burning* in their room over night. . . .

16. Convicts when they have occasion to go aside must not delay, but *return* as *quickly* as possible to their work. . . .

21. Every Convict is required to *demean himself respectfully* towards the Officers of the institution, and to obey *promptly* and *carefully* all orders given.

22. *Any violation* of the above rules will be visited with severe punishment.[45]

As the above rules reveal, the world of the San Quentin inmate was one of regimentation and a silence broken only by the ringing of a bell, a signal to perform an action quickly or suffer punishment. Regulation eight stated that punishment was at the discretion of the prison overseer, who "shall prescribe the kind and extent of punishment to be inflicted on prisoners for any violation of the rules, . . . which punishment in no case shall be cruel or unusual." But it was not deemed cruel or unusual to paddle a prisoner with a wooden slab bored with perforations, "through which the flesh was forced by every blow"; flog him with twenty-four rawhide stripes for talking; confine him to a dungeon cell; or strip him naked, tie him to a ladder, and shoot a stream of water upon his nose, mouth, chest, abdomen, and genitals.[46]

Despite the threat of such punishments, inmates broke rules forbidding talking. Quarrels and brawls occasionally broke out, and in the safety of darkness, old-timers managed to put newcomers through a hazing, such as blanket tossing or some other indignity, to expose cowardice or a deficient sense of humor.[47]

Dismal as his days at San Quentin must have been, Ed was fortunate. Three months prior to his entrance, the state had wrested control of the institution from private parties who had previously leased inmates for their labor. Thus former problems — filth, vermin, a "putty" bread and "green, rotted" meat diet, and a shortage of clothing, shoes, and blankets — were being remedied. In fact, an inspection made a week after Ed's arrival revealed that prisoners were "well fed and clothed."[48]

SAN QUENTIN CONVICTS LINING UP FOR DINNER, 1871. GUARDS CARRY LOADED CANES. *Courtesy California State Library*

During the months their son was making the adjustment to prison life, the Richardsons were not only suffering for him vicariously, but also adjusting to their own lowered status in the community. The justice had the most difficult role, that of passing judgment on citizens who now believed he was not judicious enough to raise his own children properly, let alone arbitrate the problems of others. Needless to say, after the election of the next September, Colonel Richardson was no longer a justice of the peace. In addition, his private law practice had fallen off to such a degree that he could not afford to keep an ad in the paper. Unwise as it seemed to uproot the family at such a critical time, Richardson realized that he must move in order to earn a living. Since the war between the states had erupted in April, returning to his native state in the South was out of the question. Paramount in his mind was doing right by the five children still at home, especially Charles, the second son, who was undergoing typical adolescent problems that had been neglected during the turbulence of past months.[49]

The one bright spot of ex-Justice Richardson's existence was Ed's apparent rehabilitation. Though the enforced silence at the prison was completely contrary to Ed's friendly and communicative nature, officials reported that he was obedient, respectful, and diligent in performing his duties. And despite his confinement as a prisoner on the side of the continent opposite from the raging war, he still had an opportunity to serve the Union. In addition to the brick plant, cooper's shop, and wagon factory, San Quentin officials had recently installed sixty sewing machines for making army uniforms. Ed was among those trustworthy inmates allowed to ferry finished products to San Francisco. Though the assignment provided relief from the oppression of prison walls, it also presented a risk. Prisoners sometimes found it impossible to resist the strong pull of freedom and simply dived over the side in an escape attempt. Such actions proved contagious; convicts who had harbored no conscious desire to escape suddenly found themselves in the water with other escapees. On regular trips to San Francisco, Ed soon had the opportunity to measure the true extent of his rehabilitation.[50]

His first test, however, did not come in connection with the ferry rides. In September 1861, certain prisoners initiated plans for a general insurrection. As he lay on his cot listening to his companions whisper, Ed was faced with a weighty decision. The uprising would be a bloody affair, with unarmed prisoners taking the worst of it, and even the kinder guards being battered, perhaps to death. Yet revealing the plot to authorities would place Ed's own life in jeopardy. The date of the break for liberty had been set for September 12, and as the day neared, the youth wrestled with his conscience. Unsavory as it was to betray his fellow prisoners, he at last decided to report the scheme. Prison officers promptly hatched a counterplot which squelched the riot. Ed's warning, the captain of the guard recorded, had "in all probability" saved "the lives of Officers, Contracters, etc., employed within the walls of the Prison."[51]

Ed's second test followed closely on the heels of the first. During a routine voyage to the port with a load of bricks, other crew members overcame the guards, wrestled weapons from them, and disappeared over the side into the water. There was no time for deliberation; Ed must make a split-second decision. Reacting in accordance with his upbringing, he remained aboard. Back at the prison, he received praise for his moral fortitude while the five scattered escapees holed up in the surrounding farm area waited to be hunted down one by one.[52]

Though his parents were pleased with his progress, they were also troubled over the stigma he would suffer on release. The Colonel wanted to petition the governor for a pardon, but felt it inappropriate for a past officer of the court to make a personal request. Sarah, however, insisted that a clear name would be an incentive for their son. She sat down and penned a letter to Governor John Downey, in words written so neatly and delicately that any reader would formulate a favorable image of their author. The message, as admirable as the graceful penmanship, left little doubt about the character of the woman who had borne and reared Edward Richardson:

Grass Valley Nov 28th/61

To His Excellency
    John G. Downey, Governor of
The State of California —
        Sir:
    I write to petition a pardon for my Son, Edward W. Richardson, now in the Penitentiary for grand larceny serving out a term of eighteen months, which will within a brief period expire. It is not my desire in the slightest, to intrench even had I the power, on the stern and sacred obligations of executive authority, to contravene the course of justice in any manner, however remote; neither to make my Son an exception to those just punishments which are imposed by the Statutes on the transgressors of the law — but to cooperate, virtuously, with you and with Society, in Sustaining the dignity and benignant Spirit of the Law encompassing the highest welfare of the individual and in promoting the best interests of the State.
    It is to this end that I petition you for his pardon, not that his punishment may be lessened, but that he may have that . . . loosening of prison shackles by the Chief Executive of the State, which may have a tendency somewhat, in one so young, to solidify virtue, and prevent the hardening and abandoning recollections of prison rigors untempered by the presence of mercy, and condemnation unmeasured, from which there is no restoration.

Yours Respectfully
and Prayerfully
Sarah M. Richardson[53]

Sarah had hardly gotten her letter in the mail when disaster struck again. To help support the family, her second son had taken work as a laborer in a neighboring county. But following his older brother's example, Charles did not select his companions wisely.

For the parents, it was the nightmare of September 1860 relived. Though Charles maintained his innocence, he was charged as an accomplice to a larceny and bound over for trial. In court, the fair-haired, five-foot-five youth looked even more boyish than his taller, darker brother had. And Charles had a second advantage over Ed. The jury was not at all certain that he was guilty. Still, they wanted to teach him a lesson about the results of keeping bad company. Therefore they declared him guilty, but recommended that he be given "the utmost clemency." They also agreed, while still in the jury room, to "begin a petition for his pardon."[54]

The judge pronounced a sentence of one year in San Quentin. But the sheriff of Sierra County feared the verdict had been unduly influenced by Ed's previous conviction and therefore petitioned Governor John Downey for a pardon. "The boy," Sheriff John Kirkpatrick wrote, is a splendid youth but got in bad company. . . . I was present at the trial and heard all the testimony, . . . doubtful whether the boy is guilty of any participation in the affair." The sheriff urged the governor to act with haste, warning, "I have to take him below soon." The county prosecutor and judge added their signatures to the sheriff's letter, pointing out that Charles was "only of the age of eighteen years — and this is his first offence, he has respectable parents — who are overwhelmed with grief at his disgrace." If the boy were involved, the petition went on, his wayward associates had "acquired a great and overwhelming influence over him" and thus "induced" him to assist in a larceny. Petitioners concluded that should the pardon be granted, the boy would "become a good citizen — and useful member of Society."[55]

When no pardon arrived, Sheriff Kirkpatrick reluctantly delivered the eighteen-year-old convict to the state prison. As of January 3, 1862, Sarah and Colonel Richardson had two sons in San Quentin. Governor Downey spent his final week in office pondering the two petitions and finally decided to grant both. On January 9, Ed and Charles walked through the prison gate, not only free, but with clear names. But the pardon notices in local papers only reminded the community of the family's disgrace.[56]

Foreseeing the problem, the Richardsons had already made preparations to give up their Grass Valley home. Though his physical and mental health had deteriorated seriously under the strain of the two past years, the Colonel attempted to make a fresh start at age fifty-six. He optimistically placed a new ad in a new paper: "S. C.

Richardson. Attorney and Counsel at Law. Especial attention given to all legal business entrusted to his name. Buying and selling Real Estate, mining claims, & etc. Collections promptly attended to. Office on Aurora St. 2nd door west of Esmeralda St. Aurora, Mono Co. California."[57]

The Richardsons' new home, a silver town in the mountains east of Mono Lake, was claimed by two counties. Since a border had not yet been settled upon, California created Mono County, and Nevada Territory created Esmeralda, both with Aurora as county seat. Though the first miners had spent the winter of 1860 huddled in canvas and brush shelters, by the Richardsons' arrival about one year later, brick businesses and a courthouse lined the downtown area, and a school, surrounded by sagebrush, perched atop a nearby hill. The remote setting dictated primitive living conditions, and in addition there was the threat of Mono fever, described as "a distemper prevalent in the regions," supposedly caused by "the poisonous minerals which so largely impregnate the waters." As a further disadvantage, the town of Aurora did not welcome its newest inhabitants with open arms. Harboring suspicions about the Colonel's loyalty, pro-Union residents required that he swear allegiance to the flag before admitting him into their midst.[58]

Since Ed and Charles did not find Aurora to their liking, they went their separate ways, creating a worrisome situation for the parents, who had hoped to monitor their sons' reentry into society. Still, the couple was determined to put the painful past behind them and start a better life for the two daughters and two sons remaining at home. The family might have been able to overcome the stigma of suspect loyalty and the rigors of the mountain environment had not old troubles returned with a vengeance.

Ed had crossed the Sierra to inspect the Carson City area, but early reports of a heinous crime committed there on November 23, 1862, did not make clear his involvement:

A man by the name of Con Mason, formerly of Denver, was shot through the head, in the center of town, by some one who was so close to him that the skin where the ball entered was blackened. It appears that Mason killed a man in Denver and fled the country. His woman . . . has been an inmate of a house of ill fame, and has been keeping him here ever since, supplying him with money and jewelry. About a month ago Mason heard that the brother of the man he killed was coming here. . . . On Sunday his "woman" . . . gave him three hundred dollars that night at twelve o'clock.

He went up to where his woman lived, tapped on the window and was told by her that she had company. He went out, and it seems turned away from town, and when about thirty yards from the house was shot dead, the ball going in at the root of the ear on the left side and coming out in the neck, on the right side. Constable Kelly, who was in company with a man by the name of Richison, stumbled over the body. Upon searching the body it was found that the money and his jewelry were gone. At first it was supposed that he had been killed by the brother of the Denver man, but another view seems to be taken by every one now, and that is that he was murdered for his money. Our officers are hard at work on the case.[59]

Seeing the name "Richison" in the article undoubtedly gave Ed's parents a start. The worst was soon confirmed. A follow-up article stated that county officials had brought in twenty persons for questioning, among them one Edward Richardson. Of all the suspects, only Ed was detained, authorities suspecting he had more knowledge of the murder than he was revealing.[60]

The young man committed to the Carson City jail in November 1862 was far from the idealistic youth committed to San Quentin two years earlier. The honor that had before compelled Ed to prevent an insurrection and to remain on the scow while others escaped no longer governed his actions. On New Year's Eve, he and a fellow inmate broke out, made their way to the St. Nicholas saloon, and there begged for help in escaping. But no one present was willing to provide the two desperate men with money, supplies, or a hiding place. While they pleaded, officers arrived to return them to their cells.[61]

Just as he had done before, Charles followed his brother's example by creating problems of his own. On returning to his hometown of Grass Valley, he happened to meet Ed's old friend Curley Smith. Their alleged escapade made the papers. "FATAL AFFRAY," the *Sacramento Union* entitled its piece. "In a late attack by Daniel Smith and Charles Richardson at Grass Valley, upon a chinaman with sticks and a bowie knife, Smith was fatally stabbed." Though it was later determined that Charles had not participated in the attack, the newspaper did not retract its error. The Richardsons' second son would henceforth be regarded as a cowardly robber who preyed upon a race that was not allowed to testify against white men in court.[62]

Meanwhile, Ed's attempted escape had given credence to the suspicion that he was involved in the Con Mason murder. Ed had no intentions of placing his fate in the hands of a jury. His second escape received even more attention from the press, the Nevada City *Transcript* devoting almost half a column to details of the cunning getaway: "MURDERERS ESCAPED. — Our community has learned, with surprise and mortification, Horace F. Swayze, the murderer of George W. Derrickson, and E. W. Richardson, the supposed murderer of Con. Mason, succeeded in making their escape from the Carson jail." At 2:00 A.M. on February 19, Swayze had called for the guard to come and empty his slop bucket. As the door of the darkened cell swung open, Ed, who had tunneled through from his own cell, joined Swayze in assaulting the jailer,

beating and choking him unmercifully. They then handcuffed and gagged him and locked him in Swayze's cell while they deliberately went to the jailor's room, where they found the necessary instruments by which they relieved themselves of the shackles on their ankles. They also supplied themselves plentifully with loaded pistols and such other weapons as they wanted, and then decamped at their leisure.

It was three hours before the night watchman discovered the wounded man. Despite the apparent beating, authorities suspected the jailer of being a party to the plot.[63]

Ormsby County officials placed a $750 reward on Ed's head, describing him as "five foot eight, black hair, 145 pounds." Though Nevada County editors stated that Ed was too well known in the area to waste space on his description, the reward story made good copy. The shamed parents could do nothing more than await their son's capture, praying he would not be killed by an overzealous bounty hunter. Two weeks later they heard that one of the suspects had been taken alive, but it turned out to be Swayze. He and Ed had spent their first night of freedom in a mining tunnel, Swayze related. When the owners arrived, they took pity on the hungry men, sending them on their way with full stomachs and extra food. The escapees then journeyed to Virginia City, where they parted company. Swayze claimed he had no idea where Ed had headed, thus leaving the parents to agonize over their son's whereabouts and safety.[64]

Succeeding events followed the established pattern. As on the two previous occasions when Ed had gotten into difficulties, his younger brother immediately became suspect. Less than one month after Ed's escape, three highwaymen surprised several Chinese miners on Oregon Creek, tied their pigtails together, and robbed them of their gold dust. A group of citizens—which included B. F. Derrickson, brother of the man Swayze had killed—set out in pursuit. After a long ride, they gave up the chase, dejectedly watching the robbers disappear over a far hill. During the trip home, they happened upon Charles, sleeping at his mining claim, and roused and questioned him. On hearing that his name was Richardson, someone remembered that the youth had been linked to a previous robbery of a Chinese miner in Grass Valley. Derrickson also pointed out that a man named Richardson had recently escaped jail with Swayze, his brother's murderer. The posse was certain they had one of their men. They took him to Marysville and locked him in jail.[65]

Since Charles did not have the Chinese miners' stolen gold dust in his possession, authorities booked him on charges of "attempted" robbery. While he was awaiting trial, the local newspaper informed the citizenry of the suspect's background:

Richardson is the same person who was engaged in a robbery, or burglary, at Forest City some two years ago, for which he was sent to the State Prison, but almost immediately thereafter was pardoned and set at liberty. . . . He is a brother of E. W. Richardson, who escaped from the Carson jail while under a charge of murder, and for whom a reward has been offered. If we mistake not there are three brothers of them, all of whom are leading about the same kind of life. They formerly resided at Grass Valley, Nevada County.[66]

Though a Nevada City paper later corrected the error that "there are three brothers of them, . . . leading about the same kind of life," the correction also included the derogatory article cited above, thus further damaging Charles's reputation. On learning of his second son's plight, the Colonel was inconsolable. The burden of guilt for having brought his family to the frontier and for somehow having failed to pass on his own values to his two older sons was too much for him. He collapsed under the heavy load, leaving Sarah to carry on alone as best she could.[67]

It is impossible to determine whether Charles was actually an accomplice of the Oregon Creek highwaymen, but after the adverse publicity, it is unlikely he could have received a fair trial in Yuba County. On May 28, 1863, at age twenty, he was convicted of "assault with intent to commit robbery" and sentenced to three years in San Quentin.[68]

If Ed heard of his brother's conviction, he may have concluded that by escaping he had taken the wiser course. His involvement in the death of Con Mason is also uncertain. He may have escaped the Carson City jail the first time only because he feared that as a San Quentin convict, the cards were stacked against him. Since the investigation into his knowledge of Mason's murder was never made public, and since he never stood trial, judgment as to his guilt or innocence must be suspended. Nevertheless, he did depart Nevada as a fugitive from justice. It would have been risky to seek help from his parents, and, in addition, they undoubtedly would have insisted he surrender. Thus when Ed separated from Swayze at Virginia City, he had no one to whom he could turn for help. He was completely alone in a hostile world.

Assuming the alias of Charley Forbes—by which he has become known in western history—he headed north. The young desperado arrived at the Salmon River mines in the very month they had become part of the newly created Idaho Territory. But finding Florence in a waning condition, he crossed the Bitterroots to Bannack, now almost a year old and with a population just under 2,000. On his arrival at the camp lining the banks of the Grasshopper, Forbes acquired friends, as well as a reputation. In the lawless territory, the rumor that he had killed a man in Carson City was as much asset as liability, since it proved he could defend himself. Admiring comrades, who like him had traveled the California-Florence-Bannack route and therefore were acquainted with most notables of the mining frontier, boasted that Ed excelled Henry Plummer in

quickness and dexterity at handling his revolver. He had the scabbard sewn to the belt, and wore the buckle always exactly in front, so that his hand might grasp the butt, with the forefinger on the trigger and the thumb on the cock, with perfect certainty, whenever it was needed, which was pretty often.[69]

Several weeks after his arrival in Bannack, Ed had occasion to display his skill with the revolver. The altercation arose over a gold strike he had made in late May. "The richest claim in Idaho Territory was discovered a few weeks since by a young man named E. Richardson," a news correspondent dispatched from Bannack;

it is situate about four miles from here, and is by far the richest claim ever seen. In one day's crushing, with three sluices and four men, there were $2,360 taken out, and on last Saturday they cleaned up in one afternoon's washing, $1,850. The proprietors have refused $25,000 for one half (25 feet) of the claim.[70]

Ed's phenomenal luck was the typical success story that spurred on other miners. The despised prisoner, who in darkness had fumbled to unlock the chains that bound his ankles and then fled to a remote mining claim to beg for food, had in a matter of months become "rich Richardson." But his sudden wealth and the sight of him squandering it in the gambling halls incited envy in some who had been less fortunate. Among them was a desperado named Samuel Turner, a former partner of Bill Bunton at Walla Walla. Like Ed, Turner had run the gold camp circuit, but without the former's success. When Turner asked to buy into the mine, Ed flatly refused. He had already accepted three partners because he needed working capital, but he did not want to reduce his share further. Turner appeared to take the rejection in stride, but in reality he was spoiling for a fight. He spent an entire evening trailing Ed from saloon to saloon, waiting for an opportunity to provoke a quarrel. The method Turner finally chose is noteworthy because it represents a common preliminary to saloon altercations. "Edward Richardson and Charley Reeves were engaged in conversation about some persons in Carson City," the Sacramento reporter recorded,

and the name of Putnam Robinson was mentioned. Turner, who was standing by, exclaimed, "I know the d——d s-n of a b——h." No reply was made, and in a few moments Turner asked Richardson if he was a friend of Robinson. Richardson replied he was and that he thought Robinson a gentleman. Turner said, "you are a d——d liar, and I can whip you or any of your friends." Richardson arose from the table and walked to the bar, where he was again accosted by Turner and asked if he still considered Robinson a gentleman. Upon Richardson replying in the affirmative, Turner pulled his pistol and fired. The ball struck Richardson in the left side, ranging downward toward the right groin. Richardson fell, but arose with his pistol in his hand. Four shots passed between the parties at a distance of three or four feet. Turner received three wounds, the last one through the right eye, causing instant death. The affray caused no feeling, as Turner was a man of bad character and feared by all who knew him. Richardson's wound is now almost well, and before many days he will be out again.[71]

If Richardson was innocent of killing Con Mason, he had only now "got his man." However, according to the correspondent, the killing was self-defense. It is interesting to note that the reporter did not use Ed's alias, perhaps because he had known him in California, or because Ed gave his correct name during the interview in hopes his old acquaintances would read of his exploits.

The prediction that Ed would soon be out and around came true; leaving hired miners to work the claim, he joined the June stampede to Alder Gulch. But there he found no exceptional claims and sought other activities to occupy his time. Evidently the interview at Bannack had stirred memories of his own days in the newspaper business and rekindled a desire to write. Drawing on his experiences in the various camps, he commenced composing a series of articles, some on such serious topics as the "state and prospects of the Territory." Even his severest critics praised the essays that made their way to California and Nevada papers, describing them as "very well written" and "highly interesting."[72]

In addition to mining and writing, Ed also served as a court clerk in Alder Gulch, and while acting in this capacity nearly had a second occasion to exhibit his dexterity with a gun. On June 29, 1863, a Virginia City miners' court met to settle a claim dispute. The courtroom was a conical tent of willows interlaced with brush, which stood on the creek bank at the foot of Wallace Street. Though the tent was barely large enough to hold judge, clerk, plaintiff, defendant, and attorneys, curious spectators followed the proceedings by peeping through gaps in the brush. As Charley Forbes (the former Ed Richardson) sat at Judge William Steele's elbow taking notes, deputies Buck Stinson and Hayes Lyons burst through the doorway and whispered something in Charley's ear. They then hurried outside to confront Deputy D. H. Dillingham. Charley followed a few steps behind. An argument had arisen a few days earlier when Dillingham had stated that Stinson, Lyons, and Forbes intended to rob a miner. Now as the deputies faced off a few steps from the willow tent, Lyons cursed at Dillingham and then demanded, "Take back those lies." As hands moved toward revolver butts, Charley cried, "Don't shoot, don't shoot!" From that point on, events moved too rapidly for observers to determine exactly what happened, but in the end Dillingham lay dead with a shot in the thigh and a second in the chest. Deputy Jack Gallagher disarmed Stinson, Lyons, and Forbes and ordered them bound with logging chains and placed under guard in a cabin on Daylight Creek. But the memory of the Carson City shackles was still strong in Charley's mind, and when his turn to be chained came, he refused, declaring he would rather die first. Six guards drew on him, however, and he was forced to submit to the chains and padlock.[73]

That evening, Lyons stated that he had killed Dillingham and asked that the other two prisoners be freed, but, instead, officers of the miners' court scheduled trial for all three on the following day. Charley wisely insisted that he be tried separately. Court convened early to consider the case against Stinson and Lyons, three judges presiding from a wagon bed and the town blacksmith acting as prosecutor. The audience, serving as jury, voted the two defendants guilty of murder, and the judges sentenced them to immediate hanging.

While a scaffold was being built and graves dug, the second trial got under way. Drawing on the legal training he had received from his father, Charley conducted his own defense. He pointed out that he had shouted to the others not to shoot and, as evidence, produced his unfired pistol. He caught the attention of the assembled body during his final argument when he spoke of his mother and her dependence on him for survival; then he closed with a plea for his life. This speech, Dimsdale declared, was "one of the finest efforts of eloquence ever made in the mountains." Nearly everyone present responded by voting for acquittal. Though a few disappointed onlookers complained that Forbes had been let off only because of his "good looks and education," the majority cheered him, crowding about to shake his hand. After his stunning victory, Charley Forbes immediately rode away from Virginia City and was never again seen in the area.[74]

Claims that Charley later returned and boasted "vauntingly" that he was "the slayer of Dillingham" are incorrect. All accounts agree that he did not come back to Alder Gulch after his trial. Rumors regarding his death are conflicting. Langford assumed that Charley fell "victim to the vengeance of his comrades for . . . securing for himself a separate trial." They supposedly provoked him into a quarrel at the Big Hole River, where Augustus Moore shot him. "Moore killed Forbes's horse at the same time," Langford stated, "and burned to ashes the bodies of horse and rider."[75]

Dimsdale, however, thought that Forbes was killed in Red Rock Canyon, after "being wounded in a scuffle or a robbery. . . . It is believed that Moore and Reeves shot him to prevent him from divulging what he knew of the band; but this is uncertain."[76] As Dimsdale admitted, Charley's death *was* uncertain. Six months after the trial, an event occurred in Placerville, Idaho Territory, which may indicate Forbes was still alive. On Christmas Day, 1863, a shootout occurred between the town butcher and one Colonel Edward Richardson, who claimed to have been an officer in the Confederate army. Information elicited at the examination revealed that

Richardson went into Brown's butcher-shop, passed through into the office, and fired three times at B., who attempted to escape, but struck his foot against the doorsill and fell, R. firing once while he was down. Brown rose to his feet and commenced firing at his assailant, wounding him in both arms, from the effects of which the prisoner had been confined to his room ever since. Brown received one shot in his thigh, a ball passed through his hat and another through his coat collar.[77]

Released under $2,000 bond, Richardson failed to appear for his March 5 court date. The local paper reported that Colonel Richardson "has absconded and left his bondsman to foot the bill." In May, Sheriff Sumner Pinkham captured the fugitive on the Payette River and escorted him back to stand trial. When the jury found him guilty, the judge fined Richardson the sum of $250 and sentenced him to six months in the county jail.[78]

Since no description exists of this Placerville Richardson, it is impossible to determine if it was in reality Charley Forbes, who had survived and assumed a new identity. The Placerville mines would have been the next logical stop for him, and pretending to be an ex-officer of the Confederate army would have allowed him to use his true name without arousing suspicion that he was the man who had evaded justice in Carson City, Nevada. Having observed his father for so many years, Ed Richardson could have played the role of the southern gentleman with ease. And though it seems questionable that Placerville citizens would have believed that a man of twenty-two had already served as a colonel in the Civil War, the accounts of the Butcher Brown incident do reveal a skepticism that his assailant was actually a Confederate officer.

On the negative side of the argument, the Placerville Richardson's middle initial was "H" rather than "W," though an elaborately written "W" might have been mistaken for an "H." The most serious argument against the two men being one and the same is a difference of personality. Ed Richardson, alias Forbes, showed a sense of fair play and a shrewdness not demonstrated by the Placerville assailant.

The riddle is unsolvable. But if Sarah Richardson's son had become the sort of man who would attack an unsuspecting victim, fire at him while down, and then later betray the bondsman, she perhaps would have preferred to believe the rumor circulating in Alder Gulch — that Moore shot her son, burned the bodies of victim and slaughtered horse, and buried their mingled ashes near the Big Hole. As mentioned earlier, Sarah had to assume the full burden of rearing the younger children after her husband's collapse. At first, she and her sister-in-law tried to care for the Colonel at home, but at last it became necessary for them to commit him to a mental institution. Like the news of her sons' numerous troubles, Sarah's commitment of her husband made the papers: "Colonel S. C. Richardson, well known as a pioneer Grass Valleyan, has been taken, as a lunatic, from Aurora, Mono Co., to the Insane Asylum, at Stockton. Colonel Richardson has been crazy for several months past."[79]

Sarah's husband was a declared "lunatic," her second son was in San Quentin, and her firstborn either dead or in a county jail. Though Ed's plea to the Virginia City miners' court suggests that he had been sending money to his mother, his assistance would have been sporadic and undependable. But Sarah proved stronger than the Colonel. With no skills save those associated with being a homemaker and genteel lady, she assumed the task of supporting her sister-in-law and four teenagers.

COMMENTARY ON THE STORY OF ED RICHARDSON

The ordeal of Edward Richardson's conscientious father is not without precedents in American history. Nearly a century and a half earlier — while the opposite side of the continent was still the frontier — another pious, dedicated father had endured a similar agony. "The Evil that I greatly feared, is come upon me," Puritan theologian Cotton Mather confided to his diary in November 1717. "An Harlot big with Bastard, accuses my poor Son Cresy, and layes her Belly to him. . . . What shall I do now for the foolish Youth! what for my afflicted and abased family?"

Four years later, problems with his wayward son still plagued Mather: "Son Increase . . . has brought himself under public Trouble and Infamy by bearing a Part in a Night-Riot, with some detestable Rakes in the Town." But the son's sins did not diminish the father's love for his "poor Cresy." When Mather received word that Increase had perished at sea, he forgot the past humiliation and instead focused his thoughts on "the soul of the Child!" His intense grief he expressed in the line, "My Son Increase! My Son! My Son!"[80] Intense though Mather's pain must have been, ex-Justice Richardson's was probably greater; the Colonel had two errant sons, one accused of the soul-damning sin of murder.

The Richardsons' story illustrates the devastation the desperadoes brought to their families. As youths, Ed and Charles formed bad associations. Ironically, the courts sent them to live among criminals, hoping the young men would be "learnt a lesson." The lesson learned was hardly the one intended. The ex-convicts emerged from behind the walls of San Quentin with altered self-images and with altered sets of criteria for attaining social status. And, as we shall see in the next chapter, it was not only the convicts and their families that suffered from this alteration; the families of their victims suffered more.

TWO

CLEARWATER RIVER MINES

**THE STORY OF HOWARD, ROMAIN,
AND LOWREY**

ELK CITY, IDAHO. *Courtesy Nez Perce County Historical Society*

CLEARWATER RIVER MINES

The summit of Magruder Mountain, apt to be white with snow any month of the year, provides a spectacular view of vast timbered ranges and steep-sided canyons extending from northern Idaho to western Montana. The mountain also overlooks an ancient Indian trail winding through the Bitterroots, a trail chosen by the Nez Perce specifically for the safety it provided from their enemies. Yet along this remote, seemingly peaceful route occurred what newsmen of the day called "one of the most bloody and barbarous homicides known to the records of civilized society."[1]

On a clear October morning in 1863, nine travelers set out from Bannack City, headed toward the Nez Perce Trail. Four members of the party arrived at Lewiston. Of the five missing men, only Lloyd Magruder left a wife and children to agonize for his safety. The story of the Magruder family represents as well as any the combination of violence and personal loss that was part of the frontier experience. The Magruders' story is inextricably entangled with the stories of the other leading characters of the historic drama enacted in the Idaho wilderness.

Caroline Magruder, youngest daughter of a wealthy sugarcane planter, was by 1863 no stranger to the dangers inherent in frontier life. With a small daughter in tow, she had traveled overland to the new state of California to join her husband, and several years later had followed him to newly organized Idaho Territory. During their sixteen years of marriage, she had grown accustomed to caring for the children alone while Lloyd wandered in search of further adventure and new opportunity. Therefore, when he did not return to

Lewiston on schedule, she first thought that he had only changed plans, perhaps detoured to Salt Lake City. Then a family friend, hotel and stage owner Hill Beachey, made an unsettling discovery—part of Lloyd's mule train was already in town. Beachey's anxiety turned to relief when he spotted a long string of mules—piloted by a tall, broad-shouldered man wearing a black slouch hat drooped over his forehead—wending its way into Lewiston. But as the packer dismounted, Beachey could see he was not the missing man.[2]

Since Lloyd's departure from Lewiston, Beachey had been haunted by a nightmare in which he had seen a drifter hack Magruder to pieces with an ax. Thus, as the newly arrived packer signed the hotel register, Beachey questioned him about Lloyd's whereabouts. "Magruder started several days ahead of us," the packer responded. "He ought to have been at home long ago." Beachey was now certain that his dream had been prophetic. "Boys," he cried rushing into his hotel saloon, "they've murdered Mac!"[3]

Hurriedly Beachey obtained an arrest warrant for the four men who had delivered Lloyd's mules to a local rancher, telegraphed the suspects' descriptions to California authorities, and set out in pursuit. On his arrival at Shasta, he was elated to find a telegram from Captain Isaiah Lees of the San Francisco police: "I have arrested Renton and have found six thousand (6,000) dollars. You must get down here as soon as possible or they will be discharged on habeus corpus."[4]

Beachey wasted no time getting to San Francisco. Of the four suspects, only one had resisted arrest. Captain Lees described how old Billy Page "had to be called to three times, with his own gun presented in my hands against his person, before he gave up his arms and surrendered." The other suspects had come along quietly and then retained a lawyer. Beachey immediately hired his own lawyer to fight the writ of habeas corpus. After weeks of court battles, California agreed to extradite the wanted men on condition that Idaho Territory provide them a fair trial. Thus the four shackled prisoners boarded the *Pacific* under Beachey's care. At the mouth of the Columbia, the party transferred to the *Julia*, a smaller steamer manned with an escort of twenty Oregon infantrymen. The capture had generated so much public excitement, the ship's commander reported, that "steam had been kept on the *Julia* for more than thirty hours, awaiting their arrival."[5]

News reporters who had been following each new development in the case now gleefully announced to curious readers throughout the West that the "Idaho murderers" had been apprehended. As the *Julia* got under way, a lucky journalist who had been allowed aboard caught his first glimpse of the alleged culprits. Except for "the guard and the occasional clanking of chains," he would not have "dreamed that they were the bloody murderers who had been tracked for over a thousand miles." Three were good looking and neatly dressed. Their supposed leader, who called himself Dr. Howard, "was talking and chatting with his fellow prisoners, and occasionally would laugh as though greatly amused." The suave gambler named James Romain "appeared perfectly calm, not to say indifferent." The third man, Christopher Lowrey, remained aloof; throughout the entire journey, he stood quietly, his blue eyes pensive and his strong fingers occasionally stroking a short, neatly clipped, blond beard. The fourth man, old Billy Page, who had resisted arrest, was a "striking contrast" to the others. Untidy in appearance and sullen in manner, he sat looking "downcast and stupid" as he sucked at a cheap cigar clamped between tight lips. Now and then, he "cast furtive glances" about him, as though "terrified . . . of danger from a mob."[6]

The press closely monitored the little steamer's progress up the Columbia, considering every toot of its whistle newsworthy. As it approached The Dalles, a reporter wrote, "the boat landing was thronged by an immense assemblage of people eager to get a glimpse of the murderers." The chained prisoners and military guard disembarked, and a cavalry detachment from Fort Dalles grouped themselves about the tight formation and marched them to the fort to pass the night. At dawn, prisoners and entourage departed by wagon for Celilo, where they would catch a boat to Wallula. Those watching the departure thought it highly unlikely that the prisoners would ever see the inside of a courtroom. "The probability is that they will be tried before a 'People's Court,' " one reporter remarked, "and in that event a people's execution is sure to follow."[7]

Meanwhile in Lewiston, a lynch mob bent on sweeping the murderers off to the closest crossbar kept the vigil at Beachey's Luna House Hotel. As the stages transporting the four celebrities and their retinue turned onto the street where the hotel was located, Beachey grew alarmed at the size of the waiting crowd. He had personally promised California authorities that Idaho would provide a courtroom trial. Dismounting, he confronted the angry assemblage, pleading for their cooperation. But had it not been for the military guard and local law officers, he could not have succeeded in depositing his charges inside the Luna House. Following orders of Sheriff James Fisk, the overwrought mob reluctantly disbanded.[8]

The sheriff realized that the enraged citizenry still presented a threat, and newsmen expressed a similar fear, predicting that an attempted trial might well "end in some terrible tragedy."[9] Fisk and Beachey, however, doggedly insisted on following due process of law. Since the little log jail at First and "D" streets was not secure, they decided to retain the prisoners at Beachey's hotel. Though the Luna House was touted as the finest establishment in Lewiston, one early guest described it as "a primitive structure with canvas roof and walls and an earthen floor. At one end were sleeping rooms which were arranged as bunks; . . . in the center was the dining room, where meals were served at one dollar. The other end provided space for an office and a well-stocked bar."[10]

Of course Lewiston was but three years old. Settled by Oregonians in 1860 and named in honor of explorer Meriwether Lewis, the town sat at the confluence of the Snake and Clearwater rivers in Nez Perce Indian country. For two years, a mottled array of wood-and-canvas businesses continued sprouting up to meet the needs of miners in the surrounding area. By mid-1863, however, gold discoveries at Beaverhead and Boise Basin had begun to drain away the population, thus making it necessary for merchants such as Lloyd Magruder to cross the Bitterroots in search of a more promising market. Though there were but five hundred citizens left in Lewiston at the time of Beachey's appearance with his prisoners, these remaining residents, joined by supporters from outlying camps and farms, were sufficient to pose a constant threat to the hope for a trial. As one reporter expressed it, the "unhuman butchery" of the Magruder party had aroused public feeling to an "intensity" seldom equaled.[11]

Apparently it did not occur to either press or public that any of the suspects might be innocent. After all, they had left Bannack with Magruder and later had deposited gold dust at the San Francisco mint. It seemed only natural to refer to the lot as "the Magruder murderers," and any adverse story printed about the infamous criminals was warmly welcomed. A Marysville paper issued an article, part fact and part fiction, detailing the life of Romain, who supposedly had once worked as a runner for a New Orleans gold dust broker, and of Howard, who had chosen a life of crime as a mere boy by helping robbers dig a tunnel to a St. Louis bank. For his part in the plot, the article stated, young Howard received ten years in the Missouri state penitentiary. Though Missouri penitentiary records revealed that the story about the boy bank robber was untrue, it still sold papers. As for the third man, Chris Lowrey, most reporters declared him a mystery.[12]

Only the fourth man, Page, was well known about Lewiston. For several years, gimpy "Old Billy" had lived at the mouth of Washington's Klickitat River on a farm so unprosperous that he was forced to supplement his income by trapping and taking odd jobs, such as mule driving. He was distinctive to the locals for being lame, for "not being troubled with too much sense," and for having what they mistakenly called a "cockney" accent. In labeling him dull witted, his acquaintances failed to consider the fact that the Cornwall immigrant had simply never learned to read or write. A minority did realize that Page's seeming lack of intelligence was due to having been deprived of an education as a child, and they considered him "the craftiest . . . cur in Lewiston." In 1861, he had briefly attained fame by surviving a rattlesnake bite that had brought him right to death's door.[13]

The three lesser-known prisoners excited the most curiosity. Two had, like Ed Richardson, received schooling in San Quentin. But James Romain had no criminal record. Both Beachey and the victim, Lloyd Magruder, had known him as a respectable businessman in Marysville, California. Practicing as a building contractor, Romain had satisfactorily carried out such projects as plastering the Marysville newspaper office. The young contractor seemed to be well educated and to possess "agreeable manners," though on occasion, a deep-seated hostility did erupt. Generally, however, he governed his emotions with all the control of a professional gambler. And in fact, after leaving California, he had followed that line of work. Residents of The Dalles recognized him as the former partner of San Juan Jack, with whom he had operated a "pool game" in a "lager beer cellar" in their town. Though at that time they had not known him to be "guilty of any serious crime," they now considered him "the leading spirit of the party."[14]

On the other hand, Hill Beachey's wife Maggie welcomed Jimmy Romain to the Luna House as a favored guest rather than an accused murderer. She had been a schoolmate of his and insisted he had come from a respectable family. Maggie's kindness and warm hospitality inspired strong hope in Romain. Also in his favor was the trust Magruder himself had previously placed in the former Marysville businessman. Lloyd had not only hired Jimmy to prepare the mule tack for the return trip to Lewiston, but also had allowed him to sleep in his store at Alder Gulch.[15]

The mysterious Chris Lowrey had not slept at Magruder's store, but had joined the party just before its arrival at Bannack.[16] Chris was a native of Pennsylvania, born in 1829 into a family of daring Indian traders. Beginning in the 1750s, Lazarus Lowrey and his sons had spent four decades pushing back the trading boundaries of the Ohio Valley. They accumulated small fortunes by exchanging "Indian truck"—that is silk shirts, beads, brooches, ear bobs, Jew's harps, bridles, saddles, hatchets, pewter basins, and gun flints—for deer hides and beaver and raccoon furs. These traveling traders were described as being "as wild as some of the most savage Indians," since they would "go back into the country" and "live with the Indian hunters" while disposing of goods packed on extensive trains of "ass-horses."[17]

This description of the Indian traders is markedly similar to Francis Parkman's portrayal of the Far West fur traders he encountered on his journey to Oregon: "half-savage men who spend their reckless lives . . . trading for the Fur Company in the Indian villages. . . . Their hard, weather-beaten faces and bushy mustaches looked out from beneath the hoods of their white capotes with a bad and brutish expression, as if their owners might be the willing agents of any villainy."[18]

However, the lucrative business ventures of the "brutish" Lowreys eventually won them classification as "gentlemen" on local tax rolls.[19] Their descendant, George Christopher Lowrey, became a blacksmith, but he retained many of the traits of his semibarbaric ancestors. He was hardy, daring, fearless, and irreverently jocose about serious matters. Though normally reserved, even tight lipped, his impious quips convinced more respectable listeners that he was "wicked and depraved."[20]

But like his ancestors, Chris could also assume the veneer of a gentleman. He stood five foot eight, was well proportioned and sinewy, and had sandy hair, piercing blue eyes, and fair complexion. Two small moles, as symmetrically positioned as beauty marks, dotted the left side of a well-cut chin and a high cheekbone. Though his nose was thin and a bit long, and all of his features sharp, he was not unhandsome.[21]

His father and uncles, the fourth generation of Pennsylvania Lowreys, were rugged outdoorsmen, but also devoted to home and family. Because the 1830 census lists the ages but not the names of the children, it is impossible to determine whether Chris was the son of Samuel Lowrey, a farmer of Lancaster County, or Alexander Lowrey, who cultivated the hilly land on the south side of the Ohio River, just where Raccoon Creek cuts two broad loops into Beaver County.[22]

But whether the son of Samuel or Alexander, young Chris was true to the birthright inherited from great-grandfather Lazarus and his sons of Indian-trading fame. The latest frontier proved an irresistible challenge to Chris, who joined the gold rush to California and found work in Shasta County. But failing to attain quick wealth and driven by a "thriftlessness" that demanded a steady input of money, he eventually got into serious trouble.[23]

On October 24, 1857, he entered San Quentin, sentenced to five years for grand larceny. His sense of humor saw him through the prison hazing, and he earned the respect of other inmates with the warning that he would as soon kill a man as a calf, but beneath his tough, joking facade, he was deeply despondent. The disgrace of being a convict, he later admitted, made him so miserable that he believed he could never again be happy. Feeling that having lost his good name he had nothing left to lose, he escaped prison on August 6, 1860, after having served three years of his sentence. Anxious to be far away from California and eager for wilderness adventure after his long confinement, he headed for Washington Territory. There he signed on as a blacksmith with the Mullan expedition. When the wagon road was completed, he settled down in Elk City and took a wife. The marriage was short lived; after only a few months, his bride deserted him. Depressed over his loss, the blue-eyed blacksmith gave up his job and joined a party passing through Elk City. They were bound for the excitement of the Beaverhead mines, said to be producing some of the purest gold in the world.[24]

Among the party was a small, light-framed, kind-tempered man, using the alias Doc Howard, whom Chris Lowrey would later wish he had not reencountered. Howard's true name was David Renton, and he was the son of a New York City businessman. Born in 1830,

David fell between two older and two younger siblings of a respected, middle-class family. The sudden death of the father proved a traumatic experience for the widow and five Renton children, especially David. His mother's prolonged grieving filled his adolescence with memories that were to haunt him until his own death.[25]

In his early twenties, David married and established a home, but soon became restless. Leaving his wife and two small children with a promise to either send for them or return home himself, he departed for California. On arrival, he was a handsome, fair-haired young man whose only clue to his inner turmoil was a certain hardness to the eyes. He soon acquired a scar on the forehead and blue-ink tattoos on each arm, but other than these two badges of reckless living, he appeared a gentleman.[26]

Renton selected Marysville as a good place to rear a family and there set up what residents called a "horse hospital." As one pioneer recalled, Renton "appeared to attend to his own business" and most people "thought he was endeavoring to do what was right, and allowed him to pursue the even tenor of his way." But having grown up in a cosmopolitan city, Renton later concluded that Marysville lacked excitement. He sold the stable, pocketed the profits, and moved to Sacramento, temporarily taking work as a laborer.[27]

Before he could reinvest in a new business, he was caught up in a disaster which would turn his life around. A Mr. O. F. Rogers, who claimed to have been robbed of a large sum of money, filed a complaint against Renton. When police searched the suspect, they found a considerable amount of money on him and placed him under arrest. Renton remained unperturbed, claiming that a witness could testify that he had been in possession of the funds before the robbery was committed. Then the case took a bizarre turn. A second complainant appeared, charging that Renton had also robbed him, but at the precise time of the first robbery. The doubly accused suspect stood trial, but due to the contradictory charges of the two plaintiffs, the jury could not reach an agreement. For a second time, Renton underwent the ordeal of a trial, but again the result was a hung jury. At this point, the second plaintiff dropped his suit, but Mr. Rogers insisted on a third prosecution. Though the original witness remained firm, swearing for the third time that Renton had his money beforehand, the jury this time found the defendant guilty of grand larceny. The judge pronounced a sentence of five years in San Quentin.[28]

Protesting his innocence, Renton entered the state prison on June 2, 1857, and was assigned work as a steward to the sick ward. When young Mrs. Renton learned of her husband's conviction, she refused to believe him guilty and therefore contacted friends in California, begging them to obtain a pardon. Months of letter writing produced an impressive petition, signed not only by six jurors of the third trial, but also by the robbery victim and plaintiff Rogers. In addition, the prison physician included a statement. Renton, Dr. Alfred Taliaferro wrote, "has served me so faithfully that I do not hesitate to give him my entire confidence. The position he fills under me is one of great trust, and I have never yet had occasion to find the first fault with him."

The prison staff shared the doctor's trust: "David Renton . . . has served during his imprisonment in the capacity of Steward to the Hospital, and has by his fidelity, and honest discharge of duty as such won the entire confidence of the managers here." The judge who had presided at the third trial contributed an explanation of the unusual circumstances surrounding the case:

Renton was convicted upon circumstantial evidence. I thought the circumstances strong enough to justify a jury in finding him guilty. Still for the same offence (for he was charged of stealing money from two men at the same time) two juries hung and the second was dismissed. . . . One man testified that he [Renton] had prior to the larceny the same money that was found on him and claimed to be the stolen money. His testimony was not believed by the jury . . . still I am free to admit it is possible he was wrongfully convicted.[29]

Another court official volunteered the information that at the time of Renton's arrest, "the friends of his boyhood represented to me that he was of a family of high respectability in New York against whom no misbehavior even had ever before been entertained, that he himself both at home and in this City had fully sustained the honorable reputation bequeathed to him until the bringing of this charge."[30]

After perusing the petition, Governor John Weller decided not to wrestle with the thorny issue of Renton's innocence or guilt. Even if the convict were guilty, Weller reasoned, he would soon be free to once again victimize Californians, but by granting a pardon, the governor could impose conditions that might benefit both society and prisoner. Weller decreed that Renton would be pardoned "on condition that he be placed in the custody" of a New York friend and "that he sail on the steamer bound for Panama on the 5th August and that he never return to this state."[31]

Renton gladly accepted the pardon terms, but the homecoming did not work out well. The greatest problem arose from the prejudice the ex-convict encountered, a stigma that his extreme sensitivity to disgrace made unbearable. Years after his release from prison, Renton found the entire experience too painful to discuss, commenting only on "how hard" it was "to struggle against the consequences" of his "great trouble." Convinced that his only hope was to return to the West, he once more parted with his family, again insisting the separation would be temporary. Being barred from California, he chose Washington Territory, where he hoped to amass a fortune and return to New York to support his family with ease. To disassociate himself from the San Quentin shame, he took the name Howard; his new associates tacked on the title "Doc" in appreciation for his willingness to administer to anyone suffering from an ailment or disease.[32]

David Renton had first appeared on the Pacific Coast in the 1850s, a respectable young businessman willing to work hard to accomplish his goals, but Doc Howard, who reached Washington Territory in the 1860s, was hardly recognizable as the same man. A decade had brought a radical difference in life-style. Howard roamed the remote camps, letting off steam at the pleasure halls and keeping a sharp eye for easy money. Though those who traveled with him recognized his bravery, they did not necessarily consider him their leader. On the contrary, a competition existed to test who was most daring and reckless. It was a contest that could quite easily get out of hand. At the saloons, men boasted of their exploits; some boasters only hoped to impress listeners as being men who were too dangerous to provoke, but others reveled in a bad reputation. True, the frontier environment was partially to blame for this antisocial attitude. The Ohio Valley wilderness had turned the Lowrey traders half savage, just as the Far West had brutalized its fur traders. But if the wilds of Washington Territory contributed to the brutalization of Doc Howard and his companions, each of them also brought to the wilderness his own peculiar brand of barbarity.

In late August 1863, Doc Howard's group appeared at Deer Lodge, seeking a guide to conduct them to Bannack. The storekeeper judged them "nice fellows" and recommended that Francis

Thompson (later to become a Massachusetts judge) offer his services. Thompson regarded Howard and Romain as "educated" men of "agreeable manners," but apparently they regarded him as an "easy mark." Had it not been for a chance remark that he made along the trail—that he "did not have any money"—Thompson might have suffered the same fate Lloyd Magruder met in October.[33]

Thus on December 1, Hill Beachey and his four chained prisoners arrived in Lewiston. They could not have selected a more inopportune moment to expect justice. Though the little mining support town had been designated the capital of the new territory of Idaho, a justice system was still in the throes of creation. In offering to house the suspects until the first district court could be called, Beachey was taking on a prolonged period of guardianship. The initial lynch mob had disbanded, but the town was still unsettled by the presence of the detested prisoners thought to have murdered Lloyd Magruder. Newspaper reporters continued dispatching the articles the public craved about Billy Page, the lame, unschooled Cornishman; Jimmy Romain, the smooth-talking builder turned gambler; blue-eyed Chris Lowrey, throwback to his brutish Indian-trading ancestors; and the inscrutable David Renton, whose steely eyes reflected boyhood pain and adulthood dishonor.

But no one was so stirred by the prisoners' presence as the woman who had left her Elk City home to confront her husband's murderers. Caroline Magruder had abandoned her prayers for Lloyd's safe return. Her new agony had become finding his body so she could provide him decent burial. Though boldness was not her nature, she bundled her three children and herself against the cold, left her rented quarters, and determinedly walked to the corner of Third and C streets. There she entered the Luna House and requested to speak to the prisoners.

On being brought face to face with the surprised men, she did not mince words, asking, "What have you done with the body of my husband?"

The prisoners studied the floor, making no attempt to answer. At last Renton raised his hard eyes to hers and broke the silence: "The last I saw of him," he replied, "was about seventy miles from East Bannack."

Caroline refused to acknowledge his answer. Turning to her eldest son, who was but eight years old, she said quietly, "Johnny, beg these gentlemen to tell you what they did with your father."

Tears flooded the boy's eyes and then ran down his cheeks, but he obeyed. "Please give me back my father," he managed.

The guard noted that the four prisoners were "very much affected" by the sight of the weeping boy, but none ventured a reply. Caroline had determined beforehand not to leave without learning the location of Lloyd's body, and she now became frantic. "Tell me," she implored. Then regaining her composure, she added, "I have friends who would bring the body to me." Still the prisoners said nothing. Her courage exhausted, Caroline gathered the children and left.

As soon as she was out of sight, Renton turned on the guard: "For God's sake don't let that woman come again," he pleaded. The scene had resurrected old memories he would have preferred to have left buried. "My father died suddenly," he explained to his companions. "I know how that woman feels. She feels like my mother did."[34]

News of the tense encounter between widow and "murderers" spread through Lewiston like wildfire. In response, the newly assembled Council of Idaho Territory appointed Master John Magruder as its page.[35] The appointment was more than a gesture of sympathy; the boy's wages of a few dollars per day would help support Lloyd Magruder's family. One Idaho paper printed an article providing an example of the many kindnesses that had won Lloyd so many friends. Its editor, while a mere boy, had waded through deep mountain snows to reach the remote mining camp of St. Louis, in Sierra County, California. "There was but one hotel in the camp," the editor recounted, "and it cost $1.00 for the privilege of spreading your own blankets upon the ground floor." But Lloyd Magruder invited the weary lad to sleep at his general store, promising him he would not be "attacked by such a variety of hungry graybacks" as at the overcrowded hotel. The editor called Magruder a "jovial, wholesouled Hercules, who had more friends than any man in town," and other writers expressed their admiration for Lloyd's "intrepidity" as a packer.[36]

Like the Pennsylvania Lowreys, Lloyd hungered for the challenge of the wilderness; in contrast, his gentlemanly qualities were more than a veneer. Born in Montgomery County, Maryland, on July 7, 1825, he was the son of a farmer of Scottish descent. Both parents died during the boy's early years, leaving the rearing of their small children to an older married daughter and her husband,

John Carter. Young Lloyd soon came to think of Carter as a substitute father.[37]

By the time he graduated from the local academy, Lloyd was a tall, genial youth who was eager to follow after older brothers who had already migrated West. In 1845, the same year President James Polk ordered General Zachary Taylor to the Nueces River to protect the Texas border, Lloyd went to live with Charles, an older brother who was developing virgin land in Independence County, Arkansas. Charles had recently married a daughter of Colonel Pelham, a wealthy sugarcane planter from Kentucky, and the newlyweds welcomed Charles's younger brother into their home, found him work as a surveyor, and arranged for him to study law under a judge in nearby Batesville. They also introduced him to Colonel Pelham's youngest daughter, pretty little Caroline, who had just turned fourteen. Though it was love at first sight for Lloyd and Caroline, their meeting occurred just at the time when President Polk's troubles with Mexico were coming to a head. During a skirmish near the Rio Grande, Mexican troops killed and wounded American soldiers. On May 11, 1846, the president sent a war message to Congress, who in turn authorized him to raise volunteers. Egged on by European taunts that untrained American soldiers would soon knuckle under to fierce Mexican warriors, Arkansas rallied to the call for volunteers.[38]

Naively patriotic, Lloyd was among the Arkansans who rushed to enlist. Soon after he departed for the front, leaving his worried sweetheart behind. It was a pattern the couple would follow for nearly two decades. On arrival, the Arkansas volunteers found General Taylor without needed food and supplies, but nevertheless bravely attempting to maintain a front on a barren desert strip. Though Lloyd had hoped desperately to actively defend the honor of his country, he was issued no weapon. Because of his broad shoulders and strong arms, he was well suited to carrying litters for the wounded, a position he held for a year. Still not ready to leave the scene of action when his term expired, he joined the regular army and as a second lieutenant returned to Batesville as a recruiter. Realizing his stay at home would be brief, he proposed to Caroline immediately, and her family hastily arranged a wedding, held August 10, 1847.[39]

Two months later, Lieutenant Magruder deposited his disconsolate, sixteen-year-old bride at her parents' mansion, and at the head of his recruits departed for Mexico. On the Magruders' wedding day, General Winfield Scott had reached the continental divide and caught sight of the Mexican capital lying in the valley below. Thus by Lloyd's arrival, the teenage Mexican cadets defending Chapultepec Hill had fallen, and the stars and stripes fluttered over the palace. But since it was necessary to maintain American troops in the country until the signing of a treaty, Lloyd and his recruits did not return to Arkansas until the spring of 1848. They had not yet heard of James Marshall's amazing discovery in the new land acquired from Mexico.[40]

Lloyd and Caroline, who was several months pregnant, set up housekeeping, and in July their daughter was born. The new parents named her Sarah, after her Grandmother Pelham. The infant had but a short time to become acquainted with her father. An orphan since childhood, Lloyd was poor, and the news of the gold rush to California seemed to him a godsend that could extricate him from poverty. Making the same promise David Renton had made to his family, Lloyd set out overland to the West Coast. Caroline's older brother, Dr. James Pelham, accompanied him, and in San Francisco they met Lloyd's older brother John, who had sailed by way of Cape Horn.[41]

Caroline probably had not realized how lengthy the separation was to be, but it took Lloyd years of experimentation with earning a living on the frontier. He tried mining, then storekeeping in the camp of St. Louis, and finally practicing law in the town David Renton had first selected, Marysville. By the time he had a firm enough foothold to send for his family, it was 1854. With the exception of a few months, Caroline had spent seven years of marriage in her girlhood home, sharing the care of her daughter not with a husband, but with her parents, sisters, and sisters-in-law. Yet when Lloyd summoned her, she felt it her duty to leave behind the security of a lifetime and follow after the stranger with whom she had fallen in love as a teenager.[42]

When she and six-year-old Sallie saw Marysville, they may have been disappointed, but the little river port had made considerable progress since the days when nothing but an adobe ranch house on the bank of the Yuba had welcomed travelers. Though this adobe, described as "venerable and antique," had since burned to the ground, its former plaza now swarmed with restless packtrains waiting to transport supplies being unloaded from steamers over rough mountain trails to the mines. The old ranch had been sectioned into city blocks which propagated brick businesses, frame residences, churches, schools, a hospital, and two daily newspapers. For entertainment, residents no longer had to depend on the scanty fare of early days: the "legerdemain tricks and slack-wire dancing" that had brightened the winter of 1851, nor the "very fair vaudeville company" that in 1852 had greeted its cheering audience in a "spacious canvas theater." Steamers daily cruised the newly deepened Yuba River, connecting Marysville not only with the capital, but also with the international port of San Francisco.

Despite the community's progress, Lloyd had made little headway toward economic security. He welcomed wife and daughter, settled them into a very modest home, and then continued scrabbling for a living. His law practice suffered stiff competition, especially from former associates of Stephen J. Field (later a judge of the United States Circuit Court). As an early pioneer, Field had gotten himself elected alcalde and then added to his law firm such distinguished attorneys as William Walker, a small, towheaded, grayeyed southerner who had bigger plans than Marysville in mind, something along the lines of a Latin American province that he could conquer and govern. Walker would not long be satisfied with defending frontier ruffians accused of stealing gold dust.[43]

A typical case dates back to April 1850, when Alcalde Field sentenced a thief to "receive on his bare back . . . fifty lashes well laid on, and within forty-eight hours from this time fifty additional lashes well laid on; and within three days from this time fifty additional lashes well laid on; and within five days from date fifty additional lashes well laid on." But showing his basic humanity, Field had added the postscript that if the thief returned the bag of stolen gold dust after the first whipping session, remaining punishment would be canceled. After twenty "well laid on" blows, which slashed the skin open and then pulverized the exposed flesh, the convicted man delivered up a bag of gold dust. By Lloyd's time, however, the whipping post had become a remedy for minor crimes only. Grand larceny convicts were shipped off to San Quentin.[44]

Lloyd's law practice and civic duties left him little time to become reacquainted with his family. While her husband competed for cases, Caroline was left alone to cope with homesickness, help Sallie adjust to the strange environment, and attempt to turn their small house into a home. In electing to follow Lloyd to the frontier, she had not only abandoned her gracious life-style, but also become exceptionally vulnerable. She was totally dependent upon a husband who was both daring and trusting, a dangerous combination for one who constantly ventured into the lawless wilderness.

Over the years the small home became even more crowded. The couple's first son, born in 1855, Lloyd named John Carter, after the kindly brother-in-law who had reared the Magruder children back in Maryland. Their second son, born two years later, Caroline named for her brother James. Eliza, the last child, was born in 1859. By that date, Lloyd had attained little wealth but considerable community status. After serving as county clerk from 1856 to 1857, he had made application to take the 1860 United States census for the town. Naturally, his duties included listing members of his own family: Lloyd Magruder, age 34, a lawyer with a home valued at $100 and all other possessions totaling $300; Caroline Elizabeth Magruder, 28; Sallie Pelham Magruder, 11; John Carter Magruder, 5; James Pelham Magruder, 3; and Eliza Lloyd Magruder, 1. At the end of the Marysville enumeration, Lloyd added a paragraph in neat, uniformly slanted letters to explain the omissions. Then he closed with a simple, yet elegantly flowing signature. The 1860 census thus offers an extensive sample of Lloyd's handwriting.[45]

His varied activities, however, were insufficient outlet for his tremendous energy. The town had become so civilized it no longer presented a challenge, and other restless spirits had already succumbed to the urge to search out fresh opportunity. Among these were David Renton, James Romain, and Hill Beachey and his Irish bride, Maggie Early. Though Beachey, Renton, and Romain each headed in his own direction, they were destined to reunite in the tragedy to unfold in the wilds of Idaho. The tragic hero was to be the leading politician of the Lewiston area and the sole support of Caroline Magruder and her four children.

In 1862, Lloyd had won election to the California Assembly, but a budding political career could not restrain his growing curiosity about activities in Oregon. Thus in April 1862, he left Caroline behind while he once more led a band of fellow adventurers, this time in blazing a trail to Canyon Creek. On the John Day River, the party discovered pay dirt, but the laborious routine of mining could not hold Lloyd for long. He was soon off to Lewiston, where he had heard that Hill and Maggie Beachey were operating a hotel and stage line. After looking over the Clearwater area, Lloyd settled in Elk City, where he bought stock in a mining company and set up a general store. Then he sent for his family. Caroline, who had been caring for the children by herself for more than a year, faced a difficult decision regarding her older daughter. Reluctantly, she left Sallie in school at Marysville and departed with the three younger children. Though she could not have known, it would be the last time she would have to pull up stakes to follow Lloyd.[46]

Changes were occurring rapidly on the northern frontier. Though on Lloyd's arrival their new home had been in Washington Territory, when Caroline reached Elk City it was part of Idaho Territory. The overgrown mining camp did not seem a suitable place to rear a family, but Caroline made little objection to her husband's having led them so deeply into the wilderness. From this remote settlement, Lloyd could realize substantial profits by packing supplies to both the Clearwater and Salmon river mines. In addition, Elk City lay on the Nez Perce Trail, which packers could follow over the mountains to the booming Beaverhead mines. There, goods brought even more exorbitant prices. For the first time in their marriage, Lloyd was able to support his wife in the style she had known as a girl, but ironically they found themselves in an area where few luxuries were available. Caroline was not completely denied a social life, however. With Maggie and Hill Beachey to make a foursome, she and Lloyd occasionally attended military balls given by the officers at Fort Lapwai. Such gala events were reminiscent of nostalgic days spent on the plantation.[47]

The newfound prosperity brought Lloyd to the attention of fellow Democrats seeking a candidate for Idaho's delegate to Congress. On August 13, 1863, a group of Nez Perce County residents addressed a letter to Lloyd Magruder, Esq., at Elk City, requesting that he allow his name on the ballot. Lewiston's *Golden Age* provided helpful publicity by carrying the letter on the first page: "Learning that you propose leaving in a few days for the Beaverhead mines, whence in all probability you will be detained from six to eight weeks," the fifty petitioners wrote, "WE, the undersigned . . . ask that you briefly define, to the voters of Idaho Territory, your views on the leading issues of the day."[48]

Lloyd's answer could hardly be described as brief. After a thanks to the petitioners and a few other preliminaries, he stated, "I believe that the 'Union should remain as it was, and the Constitution as it is.' I am opposed to the administration of Mr. Lincoln, because that administration was elevated to power by a party entirely sectional in its organization and character; having no existence in nearly one-half of the United States."

He went on to express regret that slaves had ever "set foot upon American soil," yet insisted on respecting the property rights of those who had purchased them. As a remedy to the war between the states, he advocated a convention, designed to cool passion and restore peace, which would better be found at the ballot box than with bayonet. "The memory and glory of our past history and greatness is as dear and hallowed to the great masses of the south as to the most zealous patriot amongst us," he argued. In concluding, he assured voters, "Should I be so honored as to be selected to represent you, I will . . . endeavor to . . . develop the great mineral, agricultural, and commercial resources of our adopted Territory. I will also endeavor to have established mail and post." Signed "Your most obedient servant and fellow citizen LLOYD MAGRUDER."[49]

In his response, Lloyd not only defined his political views, but also revealed the duality that had made his adult life a series of new beginnings: an attraction to the wilderness, yet a passion for taming it and thus destroying it. He had been drawn to the undeveloped lands of Arkansas, but after having blocked them off with his surveying instruments, he was ready to migrate still farther west. At each new locality, he had repeated the process, throwing himself into civilizing activities, such as providing legal advice and formulating legislation, and then becoming dissatisfied and seeking new challenge. This mobility had also made life a constant challenge for the sheltered teenager who had become his bride back at the first of his adopted homes.

Despite her adversities, Caroline was Lloyd's best supporter, not his critic. The latter position was ably filled by a Republican who launched an attack on the newly declared candidate. Wanting to provide political balance, the *Golden Age* printed an entire column of vicious invective directed at Lloyd. His political enemy declared that Magruder had "fanatical bigotry writhing to the surface through every pore of his skin." Mistaking Lloyd for a southern aristocrat rather than a Maryland-born orphan, the Republican commenced a play on the word "proud": "Of course Mr. Lloyd Magruder would be very proud to represent . . . his fellow citizens in the halls of Congress . . . but thanks to the intelligence of the hardy yeomanry of this Territory . . . you will be 'weighed in the balance and found wanting;' . . . you will not have the 'proud' satisfaction of representing them in the 'abolition Congress,' as one of your kind of secession squirts calls it."[50]

Lloyd would be spared reading the insults. By the time the attack appeared in print, he would already be on the tortuous Nez Perce Trail, armed with a gun borrowed from Hill Beachey. The trip would differ from previous forays. Never before had he faced the danger of returning home over such an expanse of remote trail with bulging cantinas sure to incite the avarice of every drifter on both sides of the mountains.

Only a few days after the Magruders' sixteenth wedding anniversary, Lloyd commenced making preparations to cross the Bitterroots. Six-year-old Jimmy noted his father's excitement at the venture ahead, but also sensed his mother's deep anxiety. For the rest of his days, Jimmy would remember that August day and his own conflicting emotions as he watched his father, black slouch hat pulled low on his forehead, riding a large sorrel horse that led a parade of heavily burdened little mules. The image of his father would have to last him for a lifetime.[51]

During the trip, Lloyd changed his plans. "While on our way from Deer Lodge with Dr. Howard and party we overtook the extensive pack train of Lloyd Magruder, a wealthy trader from Elk City, Idaho, who was taking his goods for sale to Bannack City," Francis Thompson recorded in his diary. "At the crossing of the Big Hole River he heard of the wonderful discoveries at Alder Gulch, and decided to go with the crowd to the new mines." Thompson also jotted down that his companion, Dr. Howard, "only made a short stop in Bannack and went into Virginia City with the Magruder train."[52]

Virginia City, the largest of the camps lining Alder Gulch, consisted of a main street of log buildings, a few with false fronts and rickety boardwalks. There, Lloyd rented a store, worked as the clerk himself, and in a matter of weeks sold out most of his stock. He mailed Caroline a letter, giving her a departure date that was actually two weeks later than he intended to leave. He counted on his wife passing on the news to the Beacheys at Lewiston, who in turn would spread the word.[53] By this precautionary measure, he hoped to deceive any waylayers. His downfall was the failure to consider the possibility of treachery within his own party, to take into account the barbarity men are capable of when faced with the powerful lure of cantinas heavy with gold dust. In short, he was too trusting.

Thus three months after Lloyd's departure from Virginia City, Lewiston authorities were preparing to try four of his traveling companions. But the prosecution faced an apparently insurmountable barrier. They had no body, no date or place for the suspected murder, and not a single witness who could testify that the suspects had even taken the same route as Magruder on their return to the western side of the mountains. Renton, Romain, and Lowrey conceded that they had left Bannack with Magruder, but held fast to the story given Caroline that they had separated from the Magruder packtrain at Big Hole and taken the Mullan road.[54]

Only Billy Page admitted to having traveled the Nez Perce Trail with Lloyd, but he claimed that somewhere along the way, unknown assailants had captured him and killed his five companions. He had encountered Renton, Romain, and Lowrey, he said, upon reaching The Dalles. From there, they had gone to San Francisco to deposit their accumulated earnings at the mint. The four had, according to mint records, deposited only about $7,500, far less than Magruder and the other missing men were thought to have been carrying, and not an excessive amount for Page's party to have earned at the rich Alder Gulch mines.[55]

The prosecution's chances for conviction seemed slim. But Hill Beachey, believing that his dream had been a revelation of fact, hoped to extract a confession from the man most likely to break under pressure — Billy Page. Preparations were elaborate. Across the hall from the prisoners, Beachey equipped a vacant room with four nooses dangling over four dry goods boxes. Then one by one, and with an hour's space between, he escorted Renton, Romain, and Lowrey from confinement to a supposed lynching.

Page's three-hour wait proved adequate. He broke out in "a cold perspiration" and a fit of "trembling," Beachey reported, becoming so weak that he could hardly stand. Beachey then presented him a glimpse of the ropes and boxes and informed him there was "a bare chance remaining" for him. "Your comrades are still living," Beachey said, "they have each made a confession; . . . if you make a clean breast of it, . . . it is possible you may escape by turning State's evidence; but if not, there is no alternative but to hang you all."[56]

Page promptly volunteered to confess. As he spoke, clerks pretended to test each word he uttered against fake documents, which

LEWISTON, IDAHO, EARLY 1860S. *Courtesy Nez Perce County Historical Society*

Page believed to be confessions of the other three. With Page's revelation in hand, the prosecution was ready to go to court. The trial
would be a momentous occasion, the first case tried in a court of
Idaho Territory. Fortunately for posterity, an observant and reliable
witness recorded his impressions of each day's events, a correspondent who wrote under the pen name of "Traveler." As we shall see,
Traveler's articles provide subtle characterization of all involved in
the trial.[57]

January 5, 1864, was a briskly cold day. Before the little, two-
story log courthouse, would-be spectators pushed and jostled in an
attempt to enter. Those lucky enough to crowd onto one of the
crude benches inside found the "densely packed" room overheated
and stuffy. Despite the intense excitement generated by the dra-
matic capture of the suspects, the widow's heartrending appeal for
her husband's body, and the last-minute breakthrough of Page's confession, the correspondent noted that spectators were grimly silent.
Among the audience sat Caroline Magruder, her features taut with
grief, and at her side the three solemn-faced, fatherless children.[58]

With Judge Samuel Parks presiding over the proceedings, the
three defendants were brought up for arraignment. Each pleaded
"not guilty." Next came the selection of the jury, wearisome days of
questioning one hundred fifteen potential jurors. Finally, the attor-

neys agreed on twelve, and on January 19, the trial got under way. Preliminary witnesses provided but little information, only that Magruder had sold his goods in Virginia City and started home with his money.[59]

A defense attorney attempted to point out the vagueness of the prosecution's case by challenging a witness who claimed Magruder had told him that he had a package containing $8,000 in gold dust: "How do you know there was $8,000 in the package?"

Misinterpreting the purpose behind the question, the witness bristled at what he considered to be a suggestion that Lloyd had not told him the truth. "I was told so by a man that never told me a lie," he snapped. The defense attorney, who realized he would alienate the jury if he appeared to be impugning Magruder's character, abruptly abandoned the cross-examination.[60]

At last the day all had been waiting for arrived, the day Page was scheduled to take the stand. As on previous days, court opened at 10:00 A.M. The three shackled defendants, each sandwiched between two guards, shuffled up the aisle, the heavy links of their ankle chains clattering against the rough floorboards. Slowly they worked their way up to the "criminal box," and upon being seated, tried to regain their lost dignity. Traveler observed the three men carefully, the poised Romain, intent Renton, and sharp-nosed, blond-bearded Lowrey. He found all three "good looking, well-educated, well-dressed" and experienced a pang of regret at the thought that all were "young men in the very prime of life." He was certain they would all be leaving soon "for that bourne whence no man returns."[61]

The reporter thought it commendable that two local attorneys, W. W. Thayer and John W. Anderson, had agreed to represent the "friendless criminals" without receiving any fee. The thankless task would not be easy "in the face of a public opinion which had already, perhaps justly, pronounced the guilt of the prisoners."[62]

When called, Billy Page self-consciously limped to the stand and carefully seated himself in the witness chair. A hush fell over the room as the slovenly, rough-garbed immigrant began to speak in his Cornish accent:

I know Magruder; . . . he had a stock of goods; he sold some. . . . I know the defendants were all there some of the time; they stayed a part of the time in Magruder's store; Howard and Romain slept in the store; I stayed in Skinner's house; Lower sometimes slept in there. . . . I came with

Magruder; so did Howard, Romain, Phillips and two brothers whose names are unknown to me. . . . We arrived at a place called Rattlesnake. . . . Here is where we met Lower. . . . We started the next morning early, with 40 head of animals; there were nine of us—myself, Lower, Howard, Romain, Phillips, Allen, Magruder, and the two brothers; after we had traveled . . . Lower told me to stop back—that Howard and Romain wanted to speak to me by myself; Howard stated that Magruder had a great deal of money, and they meant to have it; I had been sleeping by myself; Howard and Romain wanted me to sleep with Phillips; they told me not to be frightened—that they would do the dirty work. . . . They said that night they meant to have the money; Howard said if Phillips should wake up that I must shoot him through the head, but Romain said as I was not a very good shot I must gut shoot him.[63]

As Page was speaking, Traveler continued to observe the three men in the criminal box, who "heard the testimony of Page with as much interest as anyone in the courtroom." When Page, "by his bad English or good 'cockney' accent would give off something to create a smile, the prisoners would also smile."[64]

Page himself remained serious as he went on to explain that the night designated for the murder and robbery passed without incident. The following day, Howard and Romain again told Page that "this night they meant to have the money; they cautioned me several times," he said,

not to be frightened; . . . we came up a very steep trail, about six miles and a half; here we camped, under some big trees; we turned our animals this way, and got supper; it was Magruder and Lower's turn to look after the animals the first watch; . . . Magruder told him . . . that one gun would do them, and that he (Lower) need not take one up; . . . Lower . . . said that he would take an ax up to make a little fence across the trail, build a fire and have a good time the remainder of the night. . . . It was a clear, starlight night. . . . Him and Magruder got ready to go up, Lower walking a little ahead, with an ax in his hand; . . . when they got started up a few steps, Magruder looked back into camp, and then up at Lower, some two or three times, and after went on up; this is the last time I saw Magruder, dead or alive.[65]

Though Page's testimony was long and a little difficult to follow, the star witness had by no means lost his audience. They sat alert, straining after each word as he told how after the departure of Magruder and Lowrey, ax in hand, the other seven members of the party lay down and went to sleep: Page and Phillips together near the fire, Romain and Howard nearby, Allen alone in his tent, and two brothers whom Page could not identify in a tent a little apart from the others. During the night, Page was awakened by the noise of someone walking down the hill:

I looked up and saw it was Howard and Lower; Howard asked me if I was awake; I nodded my head and said yes, and they went and laid down on the blankets with Romain; Howard and Romain then got up and went by me, each with an ax in his hand; they had on no boots, coats nor hats; they went in the direction where the two brothers were sleeping; I soon heard several blows of the axes, and several long, mournful groans; after a few moments they returned and laid down on the blankets with Lower again; in a short time Howard got up with a shotgun in his hands and went to the tent where Allen slept; Romain passed my head with an ax in his hand, stopped about the center of the blankets, and I commenced raising up; he told me twice, in a low voice, to lay still; at the corner of the tent, in the shade, the gun went off; . . . Howard shot Allen while he was asleep in his tent; . . . and Romain hit Phillips at almost the same time a very heavy blow with the ax on the head; Phillips screamed murder, but Romain laid on the heavier two or three times; during this time I was putting on my clothes; Romain called Phillips a s— of a b——, that he had no business to come along, that he told him not to come; Romain said that he wished that Jim Rhodes had come, that he had wanted to kill him for a long time; he then pointed his finger at me and told me that I was frightened, that I was all a tremble; . . . Howard called . . . "Uncle Billy, don't be frightened, all the dirty work is done;" . . . Lower then mended up the fire, and made a big blaze; the light could shine on Allen; Howard took hold of him by the head and rolled it over — so that we could see that all the back part of the head was blown away — and said many a man would have shot him in the shoulder, but he took good aim, put the gun up to the head, and she was a beautiful gun, did her work well.[66]

Howard (Renton) then told Page to pack some equipment and supplies and also to climb the hill to check the livestock. At the upper camp, Page saw no signs of Magruder's body. He returned to find the others standing about the lower fire, complaining that "there was not so much money as they expected." Lowrey informed Page that the upper camp was "where the job was done for Magruder" and that Lowrey had kicked the fire about "in order to burn up the blood." He did not mention Magruder's body.

Page noted that during his absence someone had wrapped the bodies of Phillips and Allen in a tent. "I helped to tie the two brothers up myself," he admitted,

and helped carry them on a stick; . . . we laid them on a big flat rock, on the brow of the hill, ready to roll down the hill. . . . Howard and Lower started up the hill with blankets and picket ropes to tie up Magruder's body, while Romain and myself rolled the other bodies down into the ravine; . . . they then built up a big fire, and we all took a hand in putting pack saddles, blankets, bridles, and everything not wanted, on the fire; after they were burned, we picked out the bugles and rings and put them in a gunny bag, with tin ware and frypans not wanted; I took the pack down the hill and left them over behind a log; . . . they told me to finish packing the kitchen; . . . I was ordered to go ahead on a big sorrel horse that the mules would follow; . . . we came on a short distance, when they began to shoot the animals . . . and killed all of the animals except eight mules and one horse; there was one that I was attached to and did not want him killed, but Howard said that they must kill him — it would be ticklish about the neck if they were not killed; we traveled on. . . . While we were camped on the prairie . . . the money was emptied into five purses; . . . there was . . . eleven or twelve thousand dollars.[67]

At Lewiston, Page gave Lowrey fifty dollars to buy four tickets on the 1:00 A.M. stage while he delivered the gear and livestock to a rancher. "I left them with him just as they were," he testified,

saddles, bridles, blankets, shotgun, leggins, spurs, fry-pan, coffee-pot, tin cups, and a buffalo robe; we mixed up our bread in the mouth of the flour sack; . . . I went to the Hotel de France; when I went in I asked the man if he was sitting up for any one; he said yes, but did not know who it was; I took a drink of brandy; asked him to take some too, which he did; . . . went to bed with Lower; . . . when I got to bed I soon got to sleep; when the stage came they called us up; after we got up and came down stairs we each took a cocktail; . . . we got into the stage and it started for Walla Walla; we got there the same day, in the evening; next morning went over to Wallula and from there to the Dalles; staid one night in the Dalles, then went to Portland, and from there to San Francisco; we were in San Francisco two nights before we were arrested; . . . Lower stopped with me at this private house; . . . we were arrested by Captain Lees, of the Police, at this house.[68]

When Page finished his testimony, it was nearly 4:00 P.M., and Judge Parks adjourned court for the day. "Page has told his tale in court," Traveler dispatched, "and the revelations are awful, and it seems true, at least I think all who heard the confession believe so." Later that evening, the reporter set out for the Luna House. It was a warm night with just a sprinkling of rain, more like April than January, and as he walked, he could not help reflecting on all he had heard that day. He was most haunted by the thought of the two brothers, the quiet men who had kept to themselves and had died unmourned since no one knew their names. Somehow being unknown made their murders seem even more horrible. On the chance that

Page might be able to recall some clue to their identity, Traveler asked guards at the Luna House for permission to interview him.[69]

Page volunteered what he knew, but it was little. "They were light-complected," he recalled, and "about 34 and 36 years old." During the interview, Traveler could see that the prosecution's main witness was "afraid of being turned loose." The reporter concluded that the fear was well grounded. Page did seem remorseful over his role in the atrocity. The confessed accomplice, Traveler later wrote, "wants to go in the spring and show the place and the bodies of the murdered men. After that, he does not care what becomes of him."[70]

The following morning, a Saturday, defense attorney Thayer did his best to shake Page's story. Traveler found the examination "protracted and severe," though it "failed to elicit anything new or directly conflicting." Cross-examinations of minor witnesses turned out equally disappointing for the defense. Thayer and Anderson pointed out the difficulty in positively identifying Page's three companions on the Lewiston stage since all had arrived in town after dark and left before dawn. Hill Beachey, however, insisted that he had recognized all three, and in regard to Chris Lowrey dropped a detail that was particularly persuasive. Chris had appeared at the Luna House bar to buy the stage tickets, Beachey said, "dressed with a soldier's coat, collar up close round his head, and a cap well pulled down over his forehead; I tried to get a look at his face; he seemed to avoid me; I got a good look at his nose—and I thought that I had seen it before and tried to place it." At 1:00 A.M., Beachey had taken a lantern and ridden his stage to the Hotel de France, or the "French Hotel," as he called it. "I recognized Howard and then placed Lower," Beachey testified. Chris's distinctive nose had betrayed him.[71]

Following cross-examination, the prosecution reviewed the testimony, and Anderson countered with a "superior" argument for the accused. His associate, Thayer, then took up the cause, pleading that there had been a complete lack of evidence to place Howard, Romain, and Lowrey at the scene of the crime. Page had testified that on the very day of the murder, the Magruder party had met and chatted with United States Marshal Dalphus S. Payne. Though Payne resided in Lewiston, for unexplained reasons the prosecution had not placed the marshal on the stand to testify that he had seen the three defendants with the Magruder party on the Nez Perce

Trail. Attorney Rheem, of Beaverhead, then closed for the prosecution in a "neat, elegant, and touching speech." As he finished, a light applause rippled through the room, but Sheriff Fisk squelched this one break with court decorum.[72]

The jury retired and, without discussing the case, took a vote. Since it was unanimous, they returned to the courtroom. At 6:00 P.M., Judge Parks read the verdict to the prisoners: "David Howard, James P. Romain, and Christopher Lower are guilty of murder in the first degree, and the punishment shall be death."[73]

Not until Tuesday, January 26, did the judge pronounce sentence. As throughout the trial, the courtroom was packed, and, as usual, Caroline Magruder and the children were present. Hands chained at the wrist and feet fettered, the three convicts stood facing the bench. "Do you have anything to say?" Judge Parks asked.

Romain spoke first: "I have not had time to procure witnesses." "I am innocent," Lowrey said. "You are dyeing your hands in innocent blood. I hope you will ferret out the truth of the affair with the same energy that you have to convict me, not on my account, but for the sake of those far away."

Renton then turned slightly, so as to address the entire assemblage:

I followed this man Page to Bitter Root and went with him to Beaver Head. He is a bad man. He told you a long story, part of which may be true, but the greater part is untrue; I believe you and the jury believe it is true. Since I came to Idaho I have done no man any wrong. I have violated no law unless it be gambling. I have found it hard to struggle against the consequences of a great trouble I got into; I suppose the court and you all know what that was, and know how hard it is to struggle against such trouble; but I have wronged no man, and my hands are innocent of the blood of Magruder; I never murdered Allen; Magruder's widow and poor, fatherless children cannot raise their hands to heaven crying for vengeance against me; I know that God will bring this thing all to light, and that at some future time the true story will be told; I do not ask you to believe me, for I know that God, in his own chosen time, will make all clear; I would rather be as I am, convicted felon and die an ignominious death, than be in the place of Page; I stand before the world innocent of this bloody deed.[74]

"Midst the most perfect silence and the most profound attention," Traveler listened for the judge's response, but Parks ignored the impassioned pleas and proceeded to pronounce sentence, speaking in a low, solemn tone:

The duty which I am now called upon to perform is one of the most painful of my life. I am to pronounce a sentence which will consign to an early
and infamous death three young men, each in the prime of life and strength.
A few years since you left your homes, all respectable, all with useful and
honorable occupations, all with high hopes and all the objects of the love of
relatives and friends. You had more than ordinary energy and intelligence
and might have made useful and influential men in your day and generation. . . . Your history demonstrates clearly the ruinous effects of idleness
and bad company. You abandoned your occupations to hang around saloons,
gambling houses and low haunts of vice. You became the associates of
gamblers and then gamblers yourselves. As there is but one step from
gambling to stealing, you soon became thieves, then robbers and then
murderers, of course. And you have closed your career by one of the most
awful tragedies ever recorded. . . . It is my duty to tell you there is no
hope of pardon or escape. . . . I sentence you three convicted men, G. C.
Lowry, David Renton, alias Howard, and James Romaine, to be hanged
on March 4th, 1864, by the neck until dead.[75]

As the judge spoke the final words, Traveler turned toward the
condemned men. Lowrey and Romain "exhibited neither an embarrassment or feeling," but Renton was "apparently affected."[76] Only
Lowrey spoke out: "I hope that God will forgive you all," he said, "as
I do."[77] Then the three hobbled from the courtroom, the "sound of
their clanking chains" leaving "an ineffaceable impression" upon
Traveler's mind.[78]

During the next thirty-six days, Lewiston law officers hoped to
photograph the convicts, but the latter were adamant in their refusal
to pose. Later they overheard the officers discussing plans to get a
picture of the three hanging from their nooses, and Chris Lowrey
experienced a sudden change of heart. He called to Sheriff Fisk that
he was ready for his picture now. Messengers hastily summoned a
Walla Walla photographer, who set up his equipment in a tent near
the Luna House, and the sheriff escorted Lowrey to the tent. After
Chris had seated himself and struck a pose, the photographer disappeared into his darkroom to fill the plate-holder. In his absence,
Chris sprang to his feet, grabbed the camera, and smashed it against
his chair.

"Why did you do that, Lower?" the sheriff demanded angrily.

Chris grinned. "I thought the thing was loaded," he said. "I was
afraid it might go off and hurt me."[79]

As Chris was taken from the tent, he glanced back to see the
shocked cameraman on his knees, carefully gathering pieces which
he evidently planned to reassemble. The camera still represented a

threat. Back at the Luna House, the prisoners pleaded with Fisk so earnestly that he at last gave them his word that he would allow no picture taking at the execution.[80]

During the final days, jailers allowed the condemned men to visit freely with each other and also permitted newsmen to conduct interviews. "The general deportment of Howard, Romain, and Lower since their sentence," Lewiston's *Golden Age* reported,

betokened much stoicism. They have occupied their time in reading novels, books on spiritualism, and to some extent . . . the Bible. They have at all times, for the most part, been quite cheerful. . . . They have been disposed to inquire, with much solicitude, about events occurring in the outside world. And in some instances they have been shrewd in their comments upon those passing events. . . . They have at no time exhibited any great degree of dread of the important event which was to take them out of this world. . . . Lower remained cheerful . . . and much disposed to speak in a jocose manner of everything connected with the situation.[81]

Like the *Golden Age* reporter, Traveler welcomed the opportunity to interview the prisoners for a final time. He found a "visible change" in their demeanor since the trial, a tendency to "the most ribald jests and sacrilegious allusions." Lowrey especially seemed to enjoy shocking his listeners by announcing to his fellow prisoners "that he would precede them and select the first camping ground," or that he "would like to bribe some s— of a b— to take him up strangler's gulch two days before the time," just to disappoint the crowd. At other times, the condemned men's conversation took a wistful tone, one of them expressing a wish for death so they would be "where they could get a fair trial and where there was no hanging."[82]

In addition to the reporters, Father Brouillet, a Catholic priest from Walla Walla, arrived at the Luna House, offering to administer to the convicts "spiritual wants unceasingly." True to her reputation as an efficient and considerate landlady, Maggie Beachey personally saw to the prisoners' needs. Traveler characterized her treatment of her fallen school chum Jimmy as "tender care." Maggie's sympathy provided Romain with the desperate hope that he alone might escape the gallows, and a rumor arose that in order to better his chances, he had confided to Mrs. Beachey that he and the others had indeed taken the Nez Perce Trail, but that he did not know who had done the killings.[83]

The execution was set for March 4, a Friday. On Wednesday, a guard informed Traveler that on the preceding night both Renton and Romain had fallen asleep as usual. Lowrey, however, "seemed to lay awake most of the time." He "turned frequently in bed, . . . uttering the words, 'D—n the thing!' and 'D—n it!' " In the guard's insensitively understated words, Lowrey "appeared to be much troubled about something."[84]

There were undoubtedly several things on Chris Lowrey's mind as he lay on his cot, wide-open blue eyes peering into the darkness above: bittersweet memories of moments spent with the wife who deserted him, regret for his involvement in the Magruder affair, fear his own death might be slow and agonizing, or worst of all, fear that his courage might desert him on the scaffold. True to his sturdy frontier stock, he had so far proven the strongest of the three, making light of approaching death and playing the camera prank. Even during the sentencing, Renton had begun to weaken, and over the past days it had been obvious to reporters that David was "more depressed in spirits than the others." Romain was also crumbling, surviving only on the slim hope of a last-minute reprieve arranged by the Beacheys. Yet as Chris's two weaker comrades slept on the night of March 1, he had lain awake. In maintaining the mask of bravado, he was paying a dear price. On the night of March 2, the guard again noted that Lowrey was unable to sleep. One of the troubles that had kept him awake for the past two nights he would reveal just before the noose was slipped over his head.[85]

March 3 dawned, their final day of life. The priest arrived early and remained with them throughout the day. As evening approached, Hill Beachey appeared for a final visit, supposedly reporting afterwards that Chris Lowrey "spoke with more apparent candor and sincerity than on any former occasion," claiming that there was a mystery about which "he should have a few words to say on the scaffold." Chris praised Beachey for having brought them to justice, saying "that he himself should have been proud to do the same thing under similar circumstances." Then he came near breaking; he "manifested much emotion even to tears." He said that he had "no desire to live, said that his life had been one of misery for the last seven years [he had entered San Quentin just seven years earlier]; that he could not be happy even if he were turned loose to go out upon the world." At dusk the three prisoners requested a dose of morphine, and, according to the guard, then "slept soundly through the greater part of the night."[86]

The sun rose Friday into a sky of low-hanging clouds, casting a hazy, gray light over the streets of Lewiston. Brisk winds had dried the mud, and each fresh gust sent dust swirling into the air, blinding and choking those who had flocked to town to witness the execution. Elbowing his way through the throng, Traveler entered the Luna House. The priest had arrived before him. They waited for hours. Outside, the crowd continued to grow, swarming about the hotel and clogging the street. It was nearing noon before proceedings finally got under way. "At half past eleven," Traveler recorded,

the infantry from Fort Lapwai entered town and the vehicle that was to convey the prisoners and their guard to the gallows approached. At quarter past 12 the troops . . . formed a hollow square around the vehicle, the doors of the Luna house were thrown open and the prisoners accompanied by their guard emerged from the front (simply hand-cuffed), and took their seats in the wagon, each between two guards, when the order was given and the cavalcade moved for the scene of execution. They looked and acted much the same as upon their trial . . . with the exception of Howard (Renton), who hid his face in his hands for some time as though engaged in prayer.[87]

The wagon moved relentlessly onward, its huge wheels creaking and churning dust clouds. Behind surged the crowd, protecting eyes with uplifted hands and pressing handkerchiefs to nostrils to filter out the dust. The horses quickened the pace, and the crowd, determined not to be left behind, pressed forward against the stiff wind. When the procession passed the house where the Magruders were staying, Caroline hurried to a back room and locked herself inside until the sounds of creaking wagon and trampling feet had died away. She had known Renton in Marysville and realized that there would soon be a new widow and more fatherless children. Taking advantage of his mother's absence, little Jimmy slipped out of the house and joined the masses trailing after the death wagon.[88]

The gallows were in a small valley a mile from town. Nez Perce Indians, who had stationed themselves on a hill that provided a good view, had been waiting since daylight. With the multitude still in its dust wake, the wagon left town and headed up the rutted trail, jolting its passengers unmercifully. At the scaffold, it jerked to a halt, and those inside descended. Renton, Traveler observed,

mounted the steps in a quick, tripping manner, followed by the sheriff. Lower next followed with a slow, steady and firm step, with the appearance of as little concern as though treading the public thoroughfare an unsuspected man. Romaine followed up with an unsteady step like one laboring under an insupportable burden of mental agony. Chairs were placed upon the scaffold and the prisoners were soon seated listening attentively to the exhortations of the Minister and the short prayer.[89]

Traveler and the Lewiston reporter were allowed a seat on the platform so they could better observe the action. They watched Renton rise from his chair and reach up to touch the rope dangling above his head. "As I expect to meet my God," he said, "I am innocent of this murder; my hands were never imbued in human blood." Romain also stood, saying, "I am innocent of this murder. . . . Page is guilty." Then he knelt, and Father Brouillet began to pray aloud. After the prayer, Lowrey approached the reporters. "I could in five minutes clear both the others," he said. Traveler had previously noticed "significant glances and smiles passing between" the men, and he judged that "a new programme had been adopted."

"I am murdered," Lowrey continued, "these two men (pointing to Howard and Romain) are murdered by me. I did not have a hand in this murder. Page told a great story. I could contradict the story but it would implicate seven persons and one who is dearer to me than life."

Ignoring Lowrey's remarks, the sheriff continued preparations. Renton, however, had no intentions of letting the matter drop. He turned on Lowrey, "You ought to have said this before."

"No," Chris answered, "I could not as it would have implicated one dearer to me than life." He glanced at Romain. "Forgive me Jimmy." As the condemned men conversed, the sheriff was adjusting the ropes. Romain watched him and then made an attempt to speak, but as Traveler noted, it "was a difficult matter, as he was laboring under a paroxysm, evidently of fear or anger. He ejaculated these final words: 'I am an innocent man, I want you to distinctly understand that.' "[90] "The ropes were now adjusted," Traveler recounted,

and various suggestions received by the sheriff and his deputy from the two prisoners, Renton and Lower. . . . All now being arranged, the prisoners seemed to "straighten up," and the sheriff asked if they were all ready? Howard said, "All ready." Lower said, "Launch your boat, she is nothing but an old mud scow anyhow." Romaine appeared backward, when Lower turned toward him and Romaine answered, "Yes." The crank was moved, the fatal drop was heard, and the three bodies at the same instant were suspended through the platform.

The fall broke Romain's and Lowrey's necks, but Renton's "was simply disjointed and he struggled for some moments." For thirty minutes the bodies dangled, a doctor occasionally passing among them to grope for a pulse. At last, he pronounced all three dead.[91]

Prior to the execution, Lowrey had informed Sheriff Fisk that he had a letter he wanted the reporters to publish. As soon as the bodies were cut down, Fisk searched Chris's pockets, fished out a folded paper, and handed it to the newsmen. The Lewiston journalist read first, a shocked expression coming on his face. "This note is not fit for publication," he said passing it to his colleague. As Traveler scanned the lines, he agreed that they contained "the most obscene and revolting language that a depraved mind could conjure up."[92] Chris had played his final joke.

The murderers' bodies were placed in separate coffins and buried in a common grave near the scaffold, but it was late spring before the victims' bodies were found. In May, Billy Page led a search party composed of Hill Beachey and six others. They left Elk City on the twenty-ninth and, by starting each day of travel at dawn, reached the scene of the crime on the afternoon of the fourth day. Members of the party prepared a statement of their findings:

The first thing discovered was the gunnysack of tin-cups, coffee-pots, etc. . . . The next discovery was the blankets which wound 'round the bodies of the two brothers; the next discovery was the tent and blankets which Allen and Phillips were lashed up in. . . . We also found pieces of skull bones in this particular spot, and some hair said to be . . . Allen's, also the under jaw of Allen or Phillips; we also found the under jaw of one of the brothers, . . . blue jean coats, . . . the memorandum book, which shows that the two brothers had $1,658.78 on their persons. . . . We found . . . where Page saw Allen shot, a piece of his skull, supposed to have been blown off with the shot-gun. . . . We found the rings, buckles, etc., as described by Page, buried in the ashes. We then repaired to the spot where Magruder received the fatal blow or, we may say, blows, for we found several pieces of his skull which was literally hacked to pieces. . . . He was murdered nearly half a mile from the others; his coat and vest were somewhat torn by the wolves, but enough was left so that they looked quite natural. . . . On our return . . . found the remains of the slaughtered animals. We hope never to witness such a sight again.[93]

Two of the victims, William Phillips and Charles Allen, were "Old Californians," Allen having resided in Sacramento and Phillips in Marysville, where he had known Magruder, Romain, and Renton.[94] Both Phillips and Allen had passed the winter of 1862–63 on the eastern side of the Bitterroots. Allen had attempted ranching in the Deer Lodge Valley, where he had earned the nickname "Old Sport," due to his habitual losses at poker. In July 1862, he had won election as justice of the peace in Missoula County, but he was better known for having once lost a hair-pulling fight to Robert Dempsey's Indian wife. Perhaps it was because he was drunk at the time, but "Old Sport" Allen ended up with a scratched face, two black eyes, and one less tooth. After the death of his ranching partner, Allen had left the area and hired on as Magruder's head packer.[95]

The two victims dubbed the "unknown brothers" were the Chalmers. The elder, Robert, was described as a man "of mild and engaging manners." He was born in Kentucky in 1834 and as a child moved with his parents to Cooper County, Missouri. At age sixteen, he served as an apprentice to a Boonville newspaper editor and a few years after started his own business and assumed the care of his younger brother, Horace. Robert made the mistake of offering his company as surety for a friend who failed on his debt, and thus lost everything he owned. The brothers then moved to Denver and with borrowed funds set up a general store. After selling that business, they went to Provo, purchased fifty head of cattle, and drove them to Virginia City for sale. From Alder Gulch, they headed for Oregon, traveling with the ill-fated Magruder train.[96]

With the June discovery of the victims' remains, the tragedy had nearly run its course. But even the verification uncovered on the mountain did not enhance Page's chances for survival. One early resident expressed the community's attitude toward the witness who had turned state's evidence: "I believe the most guilty was Page, and he got off the easiest."[97] On Christmas Day, 1866, one Albert Igo shot and killed Billy and later escaped jail. Though neighboring authorities recaptured Igo and delivered him to Lewiston, he was never punished. As reporters had predicted, "Owing to the prejudice against Page . . . no jury at Lewiston will find a verdict against [Igo]".[98]

On returning from Magruder Mountain, Hill Beachey presented the fragments of Lloyd's skull to Caroline for burial. As payment of expenses incurred in bringing the criminals to justice, the legislature awarded him more than $6,000.[99] Then in November, Hill and Maggie sold their hotel and stage line and prepared to leave

Lewiston, a sorrowful departure since they must leave behind the grave of an infant child. With their surviving daughter, Gray, they resettled in southern Idaho and there established another stage line and also dabbled in mining. At Ruby City, Maggie gave birth to a son, who lived but nine days. Then shortly after their son's death, Indians stole eighty-six head of livestock from the stage corrals, and the Beacheys decided to relocate to Hunter's Station, Nevada. There, another daughter was born, but Maggie developed childbed fever and, though Hill drove her to a doctor, she died. The baby, also named Maggie, survived but twenty-nine days after her twenty-nine-year-old mother. Hill conveyed the coffins of mother and child across the Sierra and purchased a family plot in Marysville. Then he retraced their path all the way to Lewiston, gathering the remains of their other deceased infants so all could rest together.[100]

Eight years after his wife's death, Hill suffered a paralyzing stroke on the streets of San Francisco and died alone in a rented room on May 23, 1875. Though Gray, his one surviving child, was only twelve at the time, she traveled alone to San Francisco to accompany her father's body back to the Marysville plot. After their varied wilderness experiences, Hill and Maggie had come full circle, back to the little California town where two decades earlier a young man from Ohio had courted and married the daughter of an Irish immigrant.[101]

Strange as it may sound, Caroline and Lloyd Magruder were to enjoy a similar reunion. Though she had twice returned to her parents in the early years of their marriage, upon her husband's death she showed a new independence. She chose to remain in their adopted home, commencing the struggle to support her children with an attempt to regain the money the criminals had deposited at the mint. The director had refused to release the funds since there was no proof that the gold dust belonged to Lloyd, but after a lengthy court battle, Caroline won the case. Her four children lived to adulthood, and all remained in the West. To her grandchildren, she passed down the memory of their grandfather who participated in expanding the nation's borders from coast to coast. At age seventy, Caroline died in Hillsboro, Oregon, and her family honored her request to enclose the pieces of Lloyd's skull within her casket.[102]

The skulls of his murderers found no such easy resting place. Six years after the joint hanging, Dr. F. H. Simmons of Lewiston was still touring the West, presenting "blood-curdling" lectures on the peculiar formation of a criminal's head, and displaying three sample skulls as proof of his theories.[103]

COMMENTARY ON THE STORY OF HOWARD, ROMAIN, AND LOWREY

Though it appears that justice was served by the execution of Renton, Romain, and Lowrey, the case has unanswered questions. For example, Chris Lowrey's claim that someone dear to him was involved in the crime gained a certain amount of plausibility by the later discovery of two unclaimed letters at Idaho City — one addressed to Lloyd Magruder and the other to Samuel Lowrey. (Samuel was the name of one of Chris's two possible fathers.)[104]

Idaho's first courtroom trial was not without its flaws. Page's confession was coerced. Relying on his dream, Hill Beachey believed Chris Lowrey guilty of killing Magruder even before the killing occurred. Though early accounts describe how Lowrey struck Magruder with an ax as the packer bent to light his pipe at the camp fire, the only basis for such a description is Beachey's dream.[105] Page did not witness Magruder's murder and made no assumption as to who swung the skull-shattering ax.[106] Since Chris took no part in killing the other four victims, it is possible that Renton and Romain had obtained his participation by promising him, as well as Page, that they would do the "dirty work."

Neither should the discovery of the remains on Magruder Mountain be construed as proof that all of Page's story was true. It proved only that Page had been there. As a contemporary editor pointed out, "Exactly how deep Page was in the matter will perhaps never be known."[107] Traveler recognized the weakness of the prosecution's case — that it relied solely upon Page, a witness of dubious honesty attempting to save his own life. Page's bad character is verified by his own admission that he made no objection on being asked to "gut shoot" one of the victims. Nor did he have any objection to sharing in the stolen gold dust. Furthermore, it was he alone who resisted arrest in San Francisco.[108] Even more incriminating, portions of his testimony subsequently proved false. On the stand he had claimed that all of the treasure but $1,000 was given as a bribe to police captain Lees, yet mint director D. B. Cheeseman notified Caroline that he had the money. As for Captain Lees, he angrily denied having accepted a bribe, pointing out that he had held the prisoners until Beachey's arrival. To settle the questions brought up by Page's charge, San Francisco commissioners conducted an investigation, calling as witnesses the attorneys of both Hill Beachey and the prisoners, as well as Cheeseman. Investigators reported that Lees had "acted as an efficient and faithful officer," and that William Page's charge against Lees was "wholly untrue."[109]

Thus the commissioners concluded that Page had perjured himself on the stand. And Beachey's testimony that Renton, Romain, and Lowrey caught the Lewiston stage with Page, condemning though it is, still does not place the three on Magruder Mountain. Only Page's testimony places them there. Neither prosecution nor defense called to the stand U.S. Marshall Payne, the one man who could have answered the crucial question of whether Renton, Romain, and Lowrey were on the Nez Perce Trail, as Page testified, or whether they took the Mullan road, as they claimed. Though the Lewiston newspaper stated that Romain and Lowrey made partial confessions to the Beacheys, neither man corroborated such a confession at the gallows. It is doubtful that ex-convicts of San Quentin could have received impartial judgment in a small town where the victim was so popular. And they were denied the right of appeal.

Despite the foregoing considerations, Page's testimony seems to recreate precisely what took place on that "clear, starlight night." His simple story holds together quite well. Even the characterization is exact: Renton and Romain lay the plans; Lowrey jovially sets off the action, carrying an ax to build a fence so he and Magruder can "have a good time" on night watch; in the act of killing Phillips, Romain's latent rage explodes, wishing that "Jim Rhodes had come, that he wanted to kill him for a long time"; and lastly, Page's fright provokes differing reactions from Renton and Romain, the latter shaking his finger threateningly at Page while Renton says comfortingly, "Uncle Billy, don't be frightened." Because of Traveler's keen powers of observation, his opinions deserve serious attention in any evaluation of the trial of Idaho's ax murderers. He had the advantage of hearing Page's words spoken and at the same time observing body language, and the correspondent concluded that in spite of minor errors, the star witness's testimony seemed to be true.[110]

Though Renton, Romain, and Lowrey appear to have been guilty, their sentencing and execution was, of course, not legal. As defense attorney Thayer had pointed out, at the time Idaho Territory had no criminal code. Though Judge Parks overruled Thayer's objection, Idaho's supreme court later reversed Parks's decision. Thus the execution of the ax murderers was illegal. Still, the execution itself was not a criminal offense due to the lack of criminal law! Idaho's strange predicament had arisen because it consisted of former parts of the territories of Washington, Dakota, Nebraska, and Utah. Its creation act had failed to continue preexisting laws of the parent territories until Idaho Territory could enact its own. Thus the Lewiston court did not have authority to try or execute the Magruder murderers; yet, court officials can hardly be faulted for carrying out what they supposed was their legal duty.[111]

In retrospect, it seems fitting that a mountain in Idaho's wilderness area bears the name Magruder, honoring a pioneer trader whose packtrains represented a literal lifeline to the miners. It also seems fitting that the death of a frontier lawyer should result in the first trial held before the first court of Idaho Territory; that trial, despite its illegality, showed a *respect* for due process of law.

THREE

SALMON RIVER MINES

THE STORY OF CHEROKEE BOB AND BILL MAYFIELD

GHOST TOWN OF FLORENCE, IDAHO. *Courtesy Slate Creek Ranger Station*

SALMON RIVER MINES

TWO REBEL GAMBLERS

The Magruder case had set Idaho Territory's legal machinery in motion, but the great failing of the justice system would be its inability to rehabilitate convicted criminals. In this regard, the more established courts of California had already proven ineffective. Edward Richardson, Chris Lowrey, and David Renton had all entered San Quentin for nonviolent crimes, yet as ex-convicts all had engaged in violence. Their prison experiences, combined with the attached stigma, had fostered careers of criminality.

In sentencing the Magruder murderers, Judge Parks had traced their inexorable progress to the gallows. They had frequented saloons, gambling houses, and bagnios. From these bad associations, they became gamblers, then thieves, next robbers, and finally murderers. But the factors involved in a desperado's criminality are numerous, complex, and interacting. Judge Parks failed to mention, for example, the impact of a term in San Quentin. The story of Cherokee Bob and Bill Mayfield will introduce still another factor — the regional and racial prejudices brought to the West by easterners.

Cherokee Bob and the two people closest to him — Mayfield and redheaded Cynthia — formed one of the best-known romantic triangles of the Old West. But what is not so commonly known is that there were apparently three love triangles and three tragic endings. Perhaps no other gold camp desperado has been so inaccurately portrayed as Henry J. Talbot, alias Cherokee Bob. He was not an ignorant ruffian, as Nathaniel Langford claimed, but came from a highly respected family.[1] And though Bob became a professional gambler in the West, he was apparently a square dealer. Yet on the supposedly tolerant and democratic frontier, his secessionist lean-ings and mixed blood brought him continual grief. Few residents of the primitive camp called Florence cared that Talbot was an "hon-orable name" in distant Wilkes County, Georgia.[2]

Wilkes County had originally belonged to Cherokee Indians, who in 1773 had given up their ancestral lands in payment of debts owed to white traders. The first surveyor sent to this wilderness area west of the Savannah River described it as vast cane swamps, shaded by forests of huge black oaks. Here and there a deserted lean-to pole dwelling jutted out of foliage, and from green savannas rose ancient terraces and majestic grass-covered mounds.[3]

To this idyllic setting, the first Talbot migrated in 1782. He left behind in his native Virginia an impressive plantation and an equally impressive record in the House of Burgesses, where he had served with George Washington, Patrick Henry, and Thomas Jefferson.[4] Of the early settlers of Wilkes County, John Talbot was known as one of the "most substantial and richest." On his 50,000-acre estate, which he named Mount Pleasant, he erected a modest home. The ground floor had two panelled rooms separated by a narrow stair-case leading to two upstairs rooms. The exterior was weatherboard — with upper story walls and roof shingled after the English fashion — and a full veranda had brick floor and plaster ceiling.[5]

In Wilkes County's second decade, Eli Whitney came to Mount Pleasant to tutor the Talbot children. Talbot donated a building where the inventor could continue the perfection of his cotton gin,[6] and he also donated two acres for the first church in the area. The church — built on "the pattern of the old English churches with a high, boxed-in pulpit in a front corner from which the preacher looked down upon his congregation" — sat amidst Talbot's vast cot-ton fields, worked by one hundred slaves. John and his younger brother, Mathew, were not only elders of the Presbyterian church, but also leaders in the development of Washington, the county seat.[7]

The second-generation Talbots carried the tradition of commu-nity service as high as the state governorship, and built homes much larger and grander than those of their parents. The subject of this chapter, Henry J. Talbot, belonged to the third generation. He was a younger child in a family of three brothers and three sisters whose father had made their plantation nearly self-sufficient. Besides the thousands of acres seeded to cotton, there were fields of wheat, corn, oats, and peas, which fed family, slaves, and livestock, flocks of chickens and turkeys, and herds of pigs, sheep, cattle, mules, horses, and oxen. A garden provided sweet potatoes and greens for the table, and a bee palace supplied honey. Storage sheds held vats of butter and as much as 2,500 pounds of bacon at a time, and the Talbots' stills produced some of the finest whiskey in the county.

Upon the death of John and Mathew Talbot, they bequeathed to their descendants such cherished possessions as the family Bible, other instructive books, a churn, a fiddle, a sideboard mounted with looking glass, and a fine set of blue china. The name of Henry J. Talbot appeared as a beneficiary in two wills.[8] Also passed down was the claim of noble ancestors—a Norman knight who had come to England with William the Conqueror, a gallant warrior who had fought for Henry IV, an earl who had assumed custody of Mary, Queen of Scots, and several Talbots who had belonged to the Order of the Knights of the Garter. The Georgia Talbots considered themselves deserving heirs of their ancestral coat of arms bearing a silver shield adorned with three green lions, a black talbot (mastiff dog), and a silver and green wreath. Their more immediate ancestors had fought in the American Revolution. The maternal lines also presented a notable heritage. Henry's mother was a Cherokee Indian, who instilled in her children a deep pride in the intelligence, honor, and bravery of her people. Thus the Talbot children believed that the blood of proud warriors—both white and red—flowed in their veins, and their comfortable life on the plantation and high standing in the community seemed to validate family traditions.[9]

When word of the gold rush reached Wilkes County, Henry was but a teenager. Too immature to appreciate the security and completeness of his existence, he was consumed by a desire to see the goldfields. His father, now in his early eighties, firmly forbade the boy to consider abandoning his home, but Henry's longing was uncontrollable. At age fifteen, he ran away. Unaware that he had less than fifteen years of life ahead of him, he optimistically headed West, traveling overland and ending up in Mariposa County, California. Though he had disobeyed his father, the boy felt great love for his elderly parent and dutifully wrote home about his adventures in the new land.

His muscular torso and strong arms provided the required strength for placer mining, but the rigorous labor convinced him it was not the life for him. In attempting to find other work, he encountered the prejudice that was to plague him throughout his stay in the West. Though it was his father's gentlemanly Southern manners that the homesick youth attempted to emulate, he had inherited the physical characteristics of his Cherokee mother—swarthy skin, dark eyes, and raven-black hair. Not recognizing him as the son of a wealthy planter, other forty-niners relegated him to the status of half-breed. In advising the boy to remain at home, his sagacious father had probably foreseen the discrimination his dark-skinned son would suffer if he attempted to live where the Talbot name was unknown. But having his share of Talbot pride, Henry was determined to stick it out on the frontier. First, he needed to find a profession.[10]

Where "there was a great deal of money," one gold seeker observed, there was also a "great deal of gambling."[11] Even respectable miners with wives and children admitted to being addicted to the "seductive enchantments" of the vice, relating how the "passion" had grown on them until they spent every moment available reveling "in the excitement of gaming." Resolutions to stay away from the gambling halls were fruitless. "It is the most fascinating of all the pleasures I ever indulged in, and dangerous," one devotee wrote, "because it is almost impossible to resist its allurement after once enjoying its excitement."[12] Drawn by this excitement, young Henry Talbot aspired to earn a living by servicing the gaming addicts. He commenced his education at the tables, quickly acquiring the skills the dealers so aptly displayed.

In setting himself up as the professional who defended the bank against all comers, he lived with risk and even came to relish it. His background enabled him to play his role well. Wearing glossy boots, black suit, stiff-collared white shirt, brocade vest, and tie pierced with diamond stickpin, he sat with shoulders erect and black eyes flashing as he deftly flipped cards. Then in low-voiced drawl, he proclaimed the fate of those gathered at his table. Because of his youth, it was essential he prepare for the inevitable testing by arming himself with revolvers and knife.[13] Though he had not chosen a profession of which his respectable father would have approved, the gambler's code of ethics—such as being fair, charitable, and fearless—incorporated Henry's childhood teachings.

Professional gamblers were legitimate businessmen. They "occupied the same level in society," Mark Twain wrote, as "the lawyer, the editor, the banker." Artist J. D. Borthwick expressed admiration for the gamblers' "very gentlemanly" appearance and their stoicism in accepting loss with total indifference. But other early writers placed the profession in the same category as robbers and prostitutes. Dimsdale condemned gamblers for their sin of Sabbath breaking, though he acknowledged their generosity: "When a case of real destitution is made public . . . it is a fact that gamblers and saloon keepers are the very men who subscribe the most liberally." Likewise, Langford begrudgingly admitted that gamblers paid their bills and otherwise maintained "a standard of honor . . . which it was considered disgraceful to violate."[14] These quotations form the composite image Henry Talbot chose to uphold — that of a sharp-dressing businessman who displayed stoicism, generosity, and coolness under pressure.

Gamblers incited more than a little jealousy; one mining camp resident reported the considerable "ill-will" existing between "the roughly-dressed miners and the usually flashy-dressed gamblers."[15] In Talbot's case, he suffered such hostility, plus the prejudice excited by his Cherokee blood. In addition, his intense pride in his southern heritage was almost universally perceived as arrogance.

Thus when trouble with the law came, his chances of acquittal were slim. Those were times, Henry Talbot wrote, when "the law, in California, was striking indifferently the innocent, as well as the guilty." In describing frontier courts, one editor wrote that "the best and most intelligent citizens are driven . . . from the jury box, while the ignorant who never read anything and never know much, are allowed to fill their places." Historian H. H. Bancroft agreed, describing early jurors as immoral loafers who lounged about the courthouse awaiting the opportunity to earn a few dollars without putting in an honest day's work. And Mark Twain characterized mining camp jurors as those "who will swear to their own ignorance and stupidity." He suggested changing the jury system so "as to put a premium on intelligence and character, and close the jury box against idiots, blacklegs, and people who do not read newspapers."[16]

Henry Talbot may well have had the sort of jury described above. When one of his acquaintances stole a horse, authorities accused him as an accomplice. Talbot insisted he was innocent, but the prosecution had no difficulty finding witnesses willing to testify against him. The jury declared him guilty, and though the usual sentence would have been from one to four years, the judge imposed the full ten years allowable by law.

On March 21, 1854, Mariposa officials delivered the twenty-year-old Talbot to San Quentin. Two months prior, the three hundred inmates had transferred from the prison ship to the Stones' forty-eight cells; thus, from the first day, the new facility was overcrowded. The diet was abominable, and personal cleanliness impossible. Under such conditions, Talbot became San Quentin's 354th prisoner, and not a very cooperative one. He was not only embittered by the injustice, but also fearful that his ninety-year-old father could not survive the shock of learning of his son's imprisonment. Therefore, Henry chose the alias of Cherokee Bob.[17]

He found himself living among three hundred of what a visiting reporter considered "the most hardened and reckless desperados on earth." Bob's natural obstinacy and inherited pride caused him to balk at "demeaning himself respectfully" before prison officials. The "sufferings" which he endured at the hands of guard and inmate alike, he claimed, were too numerous to relate. He also suffered constant fear that his father would become alarmed at receiving no letters and contact California authorities for help in locating his son. This fear was aggravated by the presence of prison physician Alfred Taliaferro, also from a prominent family of Wilkes County, Georgia. At any moment, the doctor might recognize Cherokee Bob as the missing Talbot son. These numerous problems caused prisoner number 354 to view escape as his only salvation. He joined those plotting to confiscate the prison sloop as a getaway vessel.[18]

On December 27, 1854, the insurrection erupted near the site of the sloop. Inmates succeeded in wounding the captain of the guard in his hand and arms, the *Alta* reported, but as a prisoner was in the act of climbing the mast to adjust the rigging, he took a ball through the body. Guards continued a spray of fire which prevented other prisoners from boarding the sloop, and desperate inmates broke for the Contra Costa hills behind the prison. As they spread in all directions before firing guards mounted on horses, twenty-six men were shot. Of the seventeen who achieved freedom, all but one were carrying musket balls or buckshot.

Guards found Cherokee Bob lying unconscious in the woods and carried him to the prison sick ward, which was already "filled with the wounded and dying." The doctor pronounced Bob "mortally wounded." Bloodied and feverish, he lay on a cot, rambling deliriously about the slaughter he had just witnessed: "Watkins was shot in the arm and another ball had passed through his lungs. He was spitting blood. . . . William Powers was badly wounded in the leg. . . . Richard Berry had a few buckshot in his shoulder. James Adkins was badly wounded by a musket ball, but by mounting him on a horse he was able to proceed." In the evening, the prison overseer informed reporters that "Cherokee Bob was sinking rapidly."[19]

Despite the dismal prognosis, Bob survived his wounds, and, fortunately, the prison doctor did not recognize him as a Talbot. But the close call with death had not diminished his desire for freedom; he began an impatient wait for a better opportunity. Four months after the insurrection, the overseer assigned Bob to a small woodcutting detail monitored by one mounted guard. While felling a tree, Bob and two other convicts suddenly dropped to the ground and on all fours scrambled into the undergrowth. When a fourth inmate noted their absence, he signaled the guard, who commenced firing. One concealed man took a ball and immediately fell dead, and Bob and his companion sprang to their feet and ran. Though the guard continued firing at the two fleeing men, both disappeared into the woods.[20]

Bob was free of the prison walls, but the life of a fugitive presented new hardships and dangers. Since his participation in the sloop debacle, he had been forced to bear the mark of a troublemaker—a half-shaven head. Thus anyone he encountered would recognize him as an escaped convict. After seven months of living in hiding, he was recaptured. Defeated, repentant, and ready to serve out his long term, Cherokee Bob reentered prison on January 11, 1856. Several months later, the Mariposa postmaster reported another unclaimed letter addressed to H. Talbot.[21]

Bob was now determined to become a model prisoner. His "uniformly good behavior," as he described it, "succeeded in enlisting . . . the sympathies" of some of the guards, thus relieving a portion of his stress. Still, the letters accumulating at the post office weighed upon his mind, especially since he had many years to serve and his father was of an advanced age. Finding himself "friendless," and therefore having no one else to turn to, Bob composed a letter to the governor:

I have been far from home since 1849, leaving my old father, when I was only fifteen years old; I was twenty years old when I was convicted and ever since, shameful of my situation, I never wrote to my father. I could not be the bearer of such tidings; for my proud father could not have survived the disgrace, the shame of his unfortunate son. I could not and would not be the murderer of my genitor. For this principal motive, I have kept silent and, by so doing, refused, denied me the only help I could hope for. I have even concealed my name, for fear, that my inquisitive and anxious father should, through his own exertions, be made cognizant of my condition. A confinement of ten years is the dear price of my silence, and I have undergone four years of my long sentence.

Clemency is, and has always been the most beautiful prerogative of men at power. I implore your mercy, Excellency, in the name of my old father, longing for his unfortunate son. . . . I am desirous to enjoy again my long-lost liberty, to enter again in the path of life, with renewed energies, and prove by my exertions that I am worthy of the Clemency bestowed on me.

I am most respectfully, of your Excellency the most obedient and humble servant.

Cherokee Bob[22]

Bob sent his letter to Governor Weller on March 3, 1858. A petition signed by influential citizens usually received speedy attention from a governor, but this lone plea of a friendless prisoner demanded less promptness. Still, Weller was moved by the letter, and though he took no action, neither did he reject the request. Instead, he kept Bob in suspense for nineteen agonizing months. Then on October 14, 1859, the governor at last signed a pardon, but it was another seven months before prison authorities complied with the order. Finally, on May 15, 1860, Bob walked out of San Quentin. The exact date of his father's death is unknown, but it is doubtful that the aged parent survived long enough to ever again hear from his son.[23]

Though free, Bob discovered that his reputation was permanently marred in California's gold country. In early 1859, while he had been waiting for Governor Weller to respond to his pardon request, a rumor circulated that Bob was already free. Therefore, he was falsely accused of committing robberies. On March 1, 1859, the Mariposa *Star* printed an item about a stage holdup in Calaveras County. Not realizing that Bob was behind San Quentin walls, an eyewitness identified him as one of the robbers. "It is thought," the *Star* stated, "that Cherokee Bob was the robber who was killed." No retraction of the error was ever printed.[24] A similar rumor that spread through Placer County found its way into a local history:

CHEROKEE BOB'S REQUEST FOR PARDON. *Courtesy California State Archives*

Two highwaymen concealed themselves in a ditch above the road, and when the stage came within proper distance they leaped upon the "boot," and before the bewildered driver knew that he had two unwelcome passengers on board, Wells & Fargo's treasure box, containing $6,000, was in their possession. They buried the money and separated, Cherokee Bob crossing the mountains to Carson, and Driscoll, making his way . . . to Vernon. . . . Both Driscoll and Bob were comparatively unknown in a country where so many similar characters committed their depradations. . . . Driscoll . . . admitted his guilt; was sent to State Prison for a long term . . . and Cherokee Bob took the treasure as a sort of legacy.[25]

The portion concerning Jim Driscoll was true. On September 14, 1859, Driscoll entered San Quentin, sentenced to ten years for a Placer County robbery. But Cherokee Bob was not the partner who inherited the treasure. As San Quentin records confirm, Bob was not outside the prison between January 11, 1856, and May 15, 1860.[26]

Realizing his tarnished name would only bring him new problems, he headed for Washington Territory. A few months before
Bob's release from prison, a former Californian named E. D. Pierce
had left Walla Walla on a prospecting trip into the Clearwater River
country. Since this was Nez Perce land, he made the trip under
guise of trading with the Indians. Pierce turned up just enough gold
to whet his appetite for a second expedition, which resulted in a rich
strike on Oro Fino Creek. Though Walla Walla residents feared
that gold seekers would set off an Indian uprising, by the spring of
1861 the rush to the Clearwater mines was in full swing. Walla
Walla was suddenly flooded with goods arriving overland from Wallula, and its streets swarmed with miners and packtrains bound for
the Clearwater diggings. The ten saloons that opened to serve the
transient population provided an opportunity for Bob to return to
his former trade.[27]

Besides the Clearwater gold rush, the spring of 1861 brought a
second historic event which would affect Bob's life: the firing on Fort
Sumter and the ensuing Civil War. When seasoned troops stationed
at Fort Walla Walla departed for combat, California Volunteers arrived
to replace them. From the day of their arrival at the fort, the California soldiers received a poor welcome. "Captain Magruder would
not come out to receive us as we marched towards the fort," one
volunteer wrote home; "the rumor here is, that the officers at this
place are Secessionists."[28]

Neither did the California Volunteers prove popular with Walla
Walla citizens. "Either the soldiers down at the post are the wildest
boys that ever did soldier," the local editor quipped, "or else the
whiskey they get about town here is the meanest stuff that ever did
whiskey." The annoyed editor described the "crazy drunk" Volunteers as "a perfect nuisance," adding that it was "horribly disgusting
to see goodlooking soldiers make such beasts of themselves."[29]

The enmity between Walla Walla's residents and the soldiers
was matched only by the enmity the latter felt for the Indians they
had been sent to control and for all Secessionists in general. Contemporary newspapers reflect the Volunteers' prejudice against the
natives; one article, for example, describes a meeting of Californians bent on destroying "any and all Indians" who dared to set
foot in their area.[30] Another item discloses the Volunteers' attitude
towards Secessionists residing in the West:

Whenever you find a snob or flunky . . . you find a Secessionist. . . . Brain-less creatures, unable to feel what there is noble and dignified in sharing the identity of a great nation, drivel out their feeble and idiotic sneers, and think it a fine aristocratic thing to be a Secessionist. These miserable toad-ies are infinitely more offensive than out and out traitors. It sometimes becomes a duty to squelch an insect of this kind: do it though the opera-tion disgusts you.[31]

Thus gambler Cherokee Bob Talbot not only incited the soldiers' jealousy with his elegant manner and dress, but also invited their derision by being both Indian and ardent Secessionist. The troops garrisoned outside town regarded Bob as one of those snobs who thought it a "fine aristocratic thing" to be a Southerner. They quoted him as boasting that "he could take a negro along with him, carry-ing two baskets loaded with pistols, and put to flight the bravest regiment of the Federal army."[32]

Anxious to put Bob's boast to the test, the California Volunteers found their opportunity in April 1862. A news correspondent described the "cabin fever" conditions that engendered the confron-tation:

The winter here has been an arctic one. . . . Communication with the coast was closed for so long a time that all kinds of supplies were very scarce. After the whiskey and brandy froze up, the boys run a while on burning fluid and coal oil but finally they gave out and we had dry times of it until navigation opened. Since the fighting whiskey has got in this spring, times have livened up. . . . They are a nice crowd these California Volunteers. . . . All the winter they have had an anger. . . . They are such a pest in the country that the citizens petitioned General Wright to remove them, preferring to have no troops rather than such a lawless, undisciplined mob.[33]

As the correspondent reported, the spring shipment of whiskey served to refuel the hostility already existing between community and military, and when an affray broke out at the theater, Cherokee Bob was at the center of the action. Sheriff James Buckley and Dep-uty George Porter, both Secessionists, were attempting to keep order during a performance of the famed Susie Robinson. When a certain lieutenant became rowdy, pioneer Herman Reinhart recalled, Dep-uty Porter announced, "in his bulldog way of speaking," that if the young officer did not sit down, he would make him. "I guess not," the lieutenant replied. At the challenge to his authority, Porter drew his pistol, saying, "Hush up! you son of a —!" When the lieutenant knocked the pistol from Porter's hand, Cherokee Bob, who had been deputized for the event, rushed to the deputy's assistance, and at the same moment soldiers sprang from their seats to support their officer. Suddenly fifty pistols rang into action while screaming women and children scattered in all directions in search of exits. During the confusion, Sheriff Buckley shot the lieutenant in the mouth, killing him instantly, and, at the sight, one soldier burst out the front door only to fall dead upon the boardwalk. Before the shooting ceased, two more soldiers received slight wounds, and two peace officers lay sprawled upon the stage, one bleeding from thigh and arm, and the other with one leg shattered from knee to thigh.

Angry over their two losses, the soldiers rushed back to the post for weapons and ammunition and were in the process of towing away two cannons when superiors halted them. Though their intent of shelling the town had been foiled, several Volunteers returned to Walla Walla and surrounded Sheriff Buckley's house. Upon learning that the sheriff had fled the area, the twice-frustrated soldiers turned their attention to finding Cherokee Bob. A thorough search of the town, however, disclosed that Bob too was gone.[34]

After his sudden departure from Walla Walla, Bob settled in Lewiston and worked as a dealer in the Nicaragua, a saloon that advertised that its doors had no keys because they were always open. An early resident has left a vivid picture of Bob's place of employment. "The Nicaragua," Judge Robert Leeper recalled, "was filled with shouting, swearing, fighting miners, cowboys, gamblers and the other gentry that filled Lewiston to overflowing. In it every evening danced Anita, most famous of all Spanish dancing ladies. . . . Here, too, trod the elegant Plummer. . . . Here Harry Gale gambled, he who feared neither man nor devil, who once cut the heart out of a man for speaking to his girl."[35] That Bob was able to hold his own in such an atmosphere is a tribute to his adeptness as a dealer and to his skill with a weapon.

While in Lewiston, he befriended a fellow gambler named William Mayfield, who was at the time a fugitive from justice in Nevada Territory. The two men shared not only their calling, but also an intense loyalty to the South. Though Mayfield could not boast a family so illustrious as the Talbots, his forebears were honorable. The first had come to America in 1653 as a servant indentured to a wealthy landowner, but by the next century, the Mayfields were themselves landowners, and like the Talbots, fought in the American Revolution. In the 1800s, one branch of the family migrated from Virginia to Missouri, where William H. Mayfield was born in 1838. As a youth, Bill joined the gold rush, ending up as a laborer in a Sacramento brick factory. When silver stampeders crossed the Sierra, he followed, taking up residence in Carson City and there learning the gambling trade.[36]

Then in November 1861, the twenty-three-year-old Missourian got into trouble with a Unionist law officer by welcoming to his home Henry Plummer (later to be hanged by Montana vigilantes). Since ex-Marshal Plummer had left California as a wanted man. Sheriff Blackburn tried to arrest him, but Mayfield transferred his wounded guest to another hiding place. The sheriff, known as a most unpredictable man, became infuriated at being outwitted by a Secessionist.[37]

John S. Blackburn had become a deputy United States marshal in 1859 while Carson was still part of Utah Territory. The well-to-do native Ohioan, then twenty-seven, was described as tall, full bearded, imposing, and popular. However, not long after assuming office, he earned the reputation of a dangerous man who had little respect for the law. Even his marriage to a nineteen-year-old beauty newly arrived from Illinois did little to mellow him. A November 1859 incident illustrates the "dissipation" and "unbridled license given to his temper"[38] for which the marshal was famous:

Mr. Blackburn, U.S. Marshall of the Carson Valley District shot a man dead, in a drinking Saloon at Carson City, on Saturday last. The ball took effect between the eyes, and the man died instantly. His name was Stevenson. They came up from the Humboldt together, quarreled, Stevenson called Blackburn a son of a b——h, upon which Blackburn shot him over the left eye, killing him instantly. No arrest has been made up to the time of our informant leaving.[39]

Nor was any arrest ever made. One resident declared that Blackburn inspired such fear that he could with impunity assault "the most prominent and esteemed citizens." Thus "a feeling of insecurity and terror pervaded the community; . . . a large and influential number of citizens felt that the man who should kill Blackburn would be doing a great public service."[40] Bill Mayfield would be that man.

With the organization of Nevada Territory in 1861, Blackburn had become sheriff of Ormsby County, and it was in that capacity that he came to Mayfield's home to arrest Henry Plummer. After the fruitless search, Blackburn attempted to douse his fury at the nearest saloon, but the whiskey only aroused his anger further. He tracked down Mayfield and accused him of hiding a criminal, but Bill managed to avoid a confrontation. Later that evening, the two men met at the St. Nicholas saloon.

"I'll arrest Plummer," Blackburn announced. "I can arrest anybody. I can arrest you."

"You can arrest me if you have a warrant," Mayfield answered.

"D—n you, I'll arrest you anyhow," Blackburn insisted.

Onlookers quickly surrounded the drunken lawman, trying to force him outside, but he broke free and lunged at Mayfield. Bill drew his knife, sinking it into his advancing assailant, but Blackburn continued forward with the weapon lodged in his chest. Snatching the handle and withdrawing the blade, Bill stabbed his opponent again and again. Then, as Blackburn at last collapsed to the floor, Bill ran from the saloon. Within a matter of minutes, twenty-one-year-old Sarah Blackburn was a widow.[41]

The $4,000 reward offered for a sheriff-killer was Mayfield's undoing. Three bounty hunters found him hiding in a Carson City stable and delivered him to the police. "A guard of soldiers has been placed over his prison, so that he may neither escape nor be rescued," the paper reported; "of course if the law be enforced, the supposition is that he will hang."[42]

Mayfield was aware that the fate that awaited him was not so much for killing Blackburn as for being a Southerner. Despite the heavy guard, he was determined to escape. Madam Hall, a sympathetic friend, agreed to smuggle him the required tools, and on her next visit tucked a small knife in her stocking. Alone in his cell, Mayfield sawed through the rivets of his leg-irons, but just as he was removing them, a guard peeped through the "Judas hole" and discovered him. Suspecting that the confederate had been Madam Hall, the prison overseer allowed her to make a second visit and then arrested her. A body search revealed "two very fine files, hid in her stockings." After such a close call, the overseer increased security by placing Mayfield under an even heavier guard.[43]

Governor James Nye recognized that the Mayfield case was becoming a political issue that might explode into a local war; therefore, he obtained a fifty-man military guard from Fort Churchill and ordered an immediate trial. Two able attorneys—John McConnell and Jonas Seely—volunteered to represent the defendant, but despite their efforts, a jury found Mayfield guilty and the judge sentenced him to hang. His counsel charged that the trial had been unfair "inasmuch as not a single Democrat was upon the jury." But the strong anti-Secessionist feeling in the county extinguished all hope for a new trial or for a pardon. As a last resort, McConnell obtained a brief stay of execution and the withdrawal of the military guard from the prison.[44]

Residents who hailed Mayfield as their liberator from a tyrannical sheriff now had one final chance to save him. On the night of March 15, they slipped a file into his cell and then hovered outside in the darkness with a thousand dollars cash and a horse. "The guard was walking back and forth in the wardroom," Mayfield later recalled,

while old man Curry was sitting playing poker with some of his work hands about ten feet from my cell. I got down on my knees, and, watching the old man's eyes, started for the door. As I got to it I saw the old man raising the hand that had been dealt to him, and, as his eyes were directed toward me, I thought I would wait until he got a big hand, for, being an old gambler myself, I knew it would always excite an unsophisticated gambler to have a big hand dealt to him. A few minutes afterward a big Irishman who was playing in the game got a big hand—queens and sevens before the draw. He bet twenty beans; the old man saw it, and they took one card each. The old man drew a king, making him a king full; the Irishman drew a queen, making him a queen full. They bet and bet until they had about 200 beans in the pot. All this time I was fixing to go, and I came to the conclusion that if I could not go out on that hand I never could, and so I went.[45]

Outside, Mayfield gratefully accepted the cash, hopped onto "the fleetest horse in the Territory," and rode to the far side of the Truckee River. He could have made an easy getaway, but his heart was still in Carson City. Turning back, he rode to Huffaker's ranch, twenty miles out of town, and asked if he could stay for a few days so he could visit his lady. Days stretched into weeks. At last the new sheriff sent a warning to the Huffakers that he would search their ranch for the fugitive. In spite of the notice, Mayfield lingered until the posse arrived, and Mrs. Huffaker had to hustle him off to her clothes closet and conceal him behind her dresses. Though the sheriff saw a pair of boots protruding below a dress hem, he went back to town and reported no success. Nevertheless, Mayfield's supporters were growing weary of protecting him and advised him that he would be left to his fate. Realizing he must give up his love, the heartsick fugitive once again mounted the fleet horse and headed north.[46]

In Lewiston, he resumed the gambling profession and formed a warm friendship with Cherokee Bob Talbot. Evidently, Bill was the sort of man who was always in love, because when he met Cynthia, a charming, redheaded divorcee working as the Luna House hostess, he forgot about his Carson City sweetheart. Now he and Cherokee Bob had one more thing in common: they were in love with the same woman. At first, they chose to ignore the problem, hoping it might somehow resolve itself.

Though no immediate solution to the love triangle presented itself, the month of June did provide a powerful distraction. Ecstatic reports were arriving daily from Florence, a remote gold camp near the Salmon River. Three-fingered Smith had in one day taken $1,600 from his claim, and two mining partners using a single sluice had recovered twenty pounds of gold in twenty-four hours. "I could name hundreds," one Florence visitor wrote, who "are making from five hundred to a thousand dollars per day."[47] The rush to fabulous Florence was on.

Since gamblers were obliged by the nature of their profession to pack up and follow wherever the money was flowing most loosely, Mayfield and Cherokee Bob merged into the parade of gold-crazed humanity headed for the Salmon River mines. They took Cynthia with them. The 100-mile route between Lewiston and Florence was described as "one solid, moving mass of human beings and animals — a perfect column moving forward . . . as many as 600 to 1,000 daily."[48]

A popular stop on the Lewiston-Florence roadway was the Hotel de Cayuse, whose menu revealed not only an enterprising owner, but one who had a good sense of humor:

Dinner bill of fare at the Hotel de Cayuse, near Florence, for Sunday, June 22nd,

                    SOUP
    Oyster

                    FISH
    Salmon . . . . Gulch Sauce
            GRAND ENTRE
    "Collard" and Bacon
    Roast and Fried (principally the latter) Lamb, Ram,
        Sheepmeat, and Mutton
    Liver, Bacon, etc.

VEGETABLES

Beans . . . . Salmon River Greens
Potatoes au Lewiston
Corn and Peas growing in Yamhill

DESERT

Dead Horse Mince Pies — (very fine)
Coffee and Tea
Nuts
Liquors — at Adams & Andrews Saloon, about half a mile.[49]

Refreshed by a stop at the Hotel de Cayuse — and probably at Adams & Andrews Saloon as well — stampeders were ready to tackle the 6,000-foot range east of the Salmon River. The trail swirled around the base of a sparsely forested mountain and then spiraled upwards for circular mile after mile. Travelers clung to the steep, dusty path girding the mountain and nervously watched the canyon below them deepen. Near the top, the timber — tall, scaly-barked pines, silvery-blue firs, and spreading, lacy-branched cedars — became thicker. Then at the very top, the small basin that held the camp opened. Florence was encircled by a ring of towering pines that stretched to meet an inverted bowl of mild blue sky, and two uneven rows of narrow log buildings lined its single crooked street. The entire clearing swarmed like a stirred-up ant colony: braying mules — cinched with packs of shovels, gum boots, tin kettles, whiskey, and flour — clogged the main thoroughfare, and in the outlying meadow, miners sliced the grass carpeting with sharp spades and peeled back a foot-thick layer of turf. First, they attacked the exposed clay, next, a layer of sand, and lastly, the bed of gravel holding the precious metal. Over the babble of multilingual voices rose the thin, screeching wail of a fiddle, luring new arrivals to the saloon.[50]

Liquor was flowing freely, as if to make up for the whiskey famine suffered in early spring. Two "whiskey mills" had been able to meet the all-male inhabitants' needs only through the harsh winter months, when men had shared a bottle as they huddled tightly about fires inside the camp's five log residences and three stores. At night temperatures had fallen to 27° below, and during the day drifted snow covering all windows kept rooms in complete darkness. The only light came from fireplaces. Despite five-foot drifts, Walla Walla expressman Cincinnatus (Joaquin) Miller regularly led his packtrain up the slippery trail. When animals could go no farther, men took over, demanding the wage of forty cents a pound. These "Boston jackasses," as the human beasts of burden were called, strapped snowshoes to their feet and as much as seventy-five pounds of flour, bacon, coffee, beans, sugar, onions, potatoes, and butter to their backs. Then with the late-breaking spring, the world had flooded in making the camp the most populous city in Washington Territory. Ten thousand gold seekers were attempting to squeeze out a claim in an area large enough to accommodate about one third of them.[51]

Mayfield and Talbot arrived just as the rush was peaking. Instead of looking for work at one of the existing gaming houses, they set up their own in a large log building at the end of the main street, providing Cynthia with a smaller cabin for her private residence. As in most mining towns, those who did not actually "exercise their muscles in the mines" began early in the day to "assemble in the streets and drinking houses."[52] Thus the two Rebels' saloon flourished.

Things might have run smoothly had the friends not been in love with the same woman, but the situation was gradually growing more tense. By autumn, matters had become intolerable, and Mayfield at last confronted Talbot. Since both men valued the friendship, they avoided gunplay, agreeing instead to ask Cynthia to choose between them. To the surprise of nearly everyone acquainted with the dilemma, she selected Bob, causing some to remark snidely that her decision must have been based on Talbot's recent acquisition of a second saloon in Oro Fino. Though Mayfield may have been most surprised of all, he kept his disappointment under tight wraps, as any good gambler would have done, wishing the couple luck and presenting them his share of the business. Bob was elated over having won the woman he loved, but not wanting to be bested by his ex-partner, he insisted that Mayfield accept full payment for his saloon shares. Thus they parted as friends. However, there may have been some truth to the gossip that Cynthia loved Mayfield more, because as he left, she commenced to cry.[53] If Bob took his lover's tears as a sign that their relationship was doomed, he was correct; Jacob D. Williams would see to that.

While Mayfield was making preparations to leave Florence, an exodus was already in progress. Streams of miners and merchants were departing in search of a new camp or simply returning home. A story told of one group of disappointed gold seekers illustrates how unprepared some immigrants had been for their stint at the mines. One party of easterners had come to Florence as a hired crew of placer (pronounced "plasher" by old-timers) miners, but instead of pitching in with pick and spade, they only strolled along the riverbanks, gazing up at the magnificent canyon walls and leisurely kicking at rocks as though they expected to uncover an egg-sized nugget. When their employer reprimanded them, the greenhorns petulantly replied that they had made the long trip with the understanding that they were to be "pleasure miners." After their boss explained the manual labor involved in "plasher" mining, his crew mysteriously disappeared. Search parties wasted hours combing the banks of the Salmon for drowned bodies before they learned that the missing men had unceremoniously headed back East.[54]

Unlike the novice placer miners, Bill Mayfield orchestrated a conspicuous farewell, undoubtedly intended to relieve his inner turmoil. He was tormented not only by the painful loss to his best friend, but also by harassment he had endured from local Unionists during his stay. In retaliation, he planned an unusual going-away party, inviting as guests any Rebel bummer who could borrow a horse and designating the Union merchants left in the waning camp as unwilling hosts. The party was set for October 6, 1862, and at precisely 9:00 P.M., Colonel Mayfield and his motley cavalry swept into the Florence clearing, announcing their entrance with raucous hurrahs for Jeff Davis and the Confederacy. After a few passes through town, they dismounted, dashed into the enemies' saloons, restaurants, stores, and hotels, and grabbed whatever was closest at hand. Then with their plunder, they galloped off into the night.

An indignant reporter who wrote up the "Rebel raid," concluded with the rhetorical question of "whether some authority can not be established in that quarter whereby such robbers and traitors can be brought to punishment." But Mayfield did not stay to test the authorities' reaction; he set out immediately for Boise Basin, where diggings were supposed to be rich enough to support a whole host of gamblers.[55]

Bill's October fling spread his fame as a daring desperado, and a series of unfounded stories continued to augment his reputation. A Sacramento paper falsely proclaimed that Mayfield and Plummer had spent November terrorizing Florence: "They go outside of town once or twice a week, stop the stage, take the treasure, and then return. They are said to pursue this course . . . unmolested."[56] Though in reality Plummer had left Florence in August and Mayfield in early October, the news stories continued even after a correspondent submitted a correction, declaring the reports of Mayfield's and Plummer's exploits to be mere "lies."[57]

As late as January of the following year, some California papers had not received word that the two fugitives from justice had left the Lewiston area. One article is notable for its abundance of convincing detail in a completely imaginary account:

MURDERERS AND ROBBERS UNDER SENTENCE OF DEATH. . . . Mayfield . . . and Henry Plummer . . . under sentence of death by a peoples' Court . . . for robbing and killing one Murky. . . . Murky was jerked off his horse by the murderers with a lariat, and his head was found separated from his body about twenty-five paces distant. The purse of the murdered man, containing over $600, was found in the possession of Mayfield, and his boots were worn by Plummer. . . . Mayfield wounded three men before he was captured, and was finally brought to bay by a big Missourian, who suddenly leveled a rifle at him and brought him to a stand, when he was seized from behind and pinioned. By this time the . . . murderers have probably been brought to suffer the penalty of their crimes.[58]

Lewiston's *Golden Age* felt obligated to set the record straight by labeling the Mayfield and Plummer article not only "untrue," but "without the slightest foundation." And though the *Sacramento Union* also carried the correction, it had little effect on Mayfield's unduly magnified reputation.[59]

Even with his rival safely off to the Boise mines, Cherokee Bob's romantic problems were not resolved. Apparently a second triangle had developed. Though Florence was nearly drained of population, a saloonkeeper named Jacob Williams still operated as Bob's competitor. According to Judge Robert Leeper, "Jakey" Williams was the husband Cynthia had divorced back in Lewiston. If correct, it is understandable why Jakey harbored resentment for Cherokee Bob, referring to his former wife's lover as a degenerate Rebel "breed." Though Jakey and his fellow Unionists were not impressed by the gambler's honorable family ties in Wilkes County, Georgia, they did respect his skill with a weapon. Thus it was with judicious caution that Jakey scoffed at the Southern gentleman and his "lady."[60]

The fated conflict between Cynthia's former and current loves commenced on the final day of 1862. With Jakey and his friend Orlando Robbins serving as committee chairmen, residents had planned a gala New Year's Eve ball. Cynthia, of course, was anxious to attend, but Bob was expecting heavy betting at the tables that night and insisted he must remain at the saloon. Not wanting to disappoint Cynthia, however, he requested his associate Willoby, known as Red Face Bill or Poker Bill, to escort her to the dance. Being a fellow Georgian, as well as a brother gambler, Willoby could not refuse.[61]

On the night of the celebration, Bob sent the couple off with the admonition that his redheaded sweetheart — dressed in an alluring ball gown and glittering with jewelry — was "to be respected as a decent woman ought to be." "If things don't go right," Bob told them, "just report to me." Cynthia and her escort made a fashionably late arrival. As they stepped into the long, narrow log cabin which had been transformed into a "festooned ballroom," fiddlers were gaily sawing at their instruments and couples were whirling across the floor. But Jakey had been watching for his ex-wife's arrival, and before she could even remove her wrap, he hurried to intercept the couple. "You'll have to take Cynthia home," Jakey informed Willoby. Since he was in a minority at the mainly Unionist gathering, Willoby quietly complied. Cynthia had not only missed out on the festivities, she had also been singled out as a social outcast. When she told Bob about the incident, he was outraged. He swore he would avenge the insult.[62]

For one day Jakey managed to avoid any contact with his foe, but on January 2, 1863, Bob issued a direct challenge. In response, Jakey grabbed the loaded shotgun he kept behind the bar and strode down the snow-packed street toward Bob's saloon. Friends quickly armed themselves and joined him, forming a small posse. The shootout lasted but a few moments. When it was over, Willoby lay dead, blood from fourteen wounds staining the snow. Bob, who had taken five balls, also lay in the snow, but he was still alive. Bystanders carried him inside his saloon, and Cynthia stopped up his wounds. For three days, Bob clung to life, alternately praising the courage and shooting skill of Williams and Robbins, and pleading with Cynthia to follow Mayfield to Boise Basin and reunite with him. Bob mistakenly believed that he had killed Jakey, and Cynthia did not wound his pride by informing him otherwise. As Mark Twain observed, "In a new mining district the rough element predominates, and a person is not respected until he has 'killed his man.' That was the very expression used." Bob's last words reveal his pride in his newly attained status, and as well indicate that his Indian heritage was on his mind: "Tell my brother I have killed my man," he said, "and gone on a long hunt."[63]

At the examination, Justice Rand acquitted both Williams and Robbins, declaring that Bob and Willoby had assaulted them "with intent to kill."[64] When the ground had thawed sufficiently, residents buried the Rebels on cemetery hill, about half a mile north of town. Though not a single log building remains in the meadow that once held the mountaintop mining camp, a restored marker designates the grave of Henry J. Talbot, the young Southerner who died so far from home, thinking he had killed his man.

After Bob's death, the third love triangle fell into shape. The first had positioned Mayfield, Cynthia, and Talbot at each angle; the second, Talbot, Cynthia, and Jakey; and now it became Mayfield, Cynthia, and Jakey. But instead of reconciling with her ex-husband, Cynthia kept her vow to Bob and went to find Mayfield. Again, Jakey followed her. But it was impossible for him to compete with his rival. The Missouri gambler was enjoying a phenomenal run of luck in the latest boomtowns. Mayfield, one news correspondent claimed, was now "worth some fifty thousand dollars." Jakey relinquished the field to his wealthy adversary and found himself a new wife. After settling his bride into a house in Idaho City, he took work as the city watchman, but the couple's life together was brief. During the few months spent on the job, Jakey made a dangerous enemy. At 4:00 P.M. on November 10, 1863, he happened to encounter his antagonist, George Owens, in the City Bakery. "You're a d——d liar," Owens taunted. Jakey doubled his fist and swung at Owens, knocking him to the floor, but in the process, he tripped and tumbled on top of the fallen man. As the bakery owner rushed to break up the fight, Jakey repulsed him. "Let me alone," he demanded. "I'll manage him." Spectators clustered about the clinched pair could see nothing but Jakey's flowing cape, shrouding the combatants like a tent. Suddenly a knife clattered to the floor, and Jakey grabbed it, slashing at the air in feeble attempts to cut his opponent. Then his hand relaxed, fell to the floor, and lay still. The baker lifted the cape, revealing Jakey's limp form. Though still alive, Jakey's entire right side was stained red. An examination revealed that Owens's knife had completely severed two ribs. Within a few moments, the wounded man expired. The following afternoon his widow held the funeral, which was largely attended, and on Christmas Day citizens presented a benefit vaudeville show at the Idaho Theater for the second Mrs. Williams.[65]

CHEROKEE BOB'S GRAVE, FLORENCE, IDAHO. *Photo by Boswell*

Cherokee Bob's other slayer, Orlando Robbins, made a second appearance in frontier annals by attempting to kill another Rebel gambler. In Boise County, where he was serving as deputy to Sheriff Sumner Pinkham, Robbins led the posse which arrested Pinkham's killer, gambler Ferdinand Patterson. The deputy then helped to found the Idaho City Vigilance Committee and launched an attack on the jail, unsuccessfully attempting to lynch the gambler. Later, Robbins made a name for himself as one of Idaho's most prominent law enforcement officers, outliving his friend Jacob Williams by many years.[66]

Cynthia's reunion with Bill Mayfield had been even briefer than Jakey's second marriage. While the flush gambler was dealing a card game in the spring of 1863, a customer known only as Evans challenged him. As customary in such an instance, Mayfield drew on his accuser. Since Evans was unarmed, Mayfield sportingly allowed him to leave the premises, advising him to "go and heel himself." "The next time we meet," the gambler warned, "one of us must die." Though Mayfield was adhering to gamblers' unwritten rules, Evans subscribed to no code of ethics. The following day, he peered out his cabin window and spotted Mayfield treading a narrow plank slung over a mud puddle. While Mayfield was minding his step, Evans fired with a double-barreled shotgun. Mayfield jerked his hand toward his revolver, but fell before he could draw it. Within two hours he was dead. Though authorities arrested Evans, he broke jail. For some time Cynthia mourned her lover, swearing that someday she would find the escaped murderer and kill him herself. Later she became a prostitute, and the charms that had attracted Jakey, Bill, and Bob continued to win admirers. According to one pioneer, she was "the cause of more separations, more quarrels, more deaths, than any other woman that had ever lived in the Rocky Mountains."[67]

COMMENTARY ON THE STORY OF CHEROKEE BOB AND BILL MAYFIELD

Cynthia Williams does not deserve full blame for Talbot's and Mayfield's numerous problems. Sectional hostilities transplanted to the West played a role in Mayfield's Carson City troubles, both Blackburn's attack and the pro-Union jury's verdict, and Bill's resentment of Unionist heckling — such as fining a Rebel for being "too loud-mouthed" in his cheers for Jeff Davis — motivated his Florence raid.[68] Likewise, the Walla Walla theater shootout was an example of an outbreak of violence that had originated from the war in progress in the East. In addition, the sectional bias of early writers has done further damage to the two Rebel gamblers' reputations. "The gamblers and roughs at Walla Walla and all the mining camps were Rebels," Reinhart wrote, and "these gamblers and desperadoes were the terror of the Union people."[69] The writer seemed to regard Rebels, gamblers, and desperadoes as synonymous.

Despite the North-South overtones to their story, the two Southerners died while adhering to Western codes. In the next chapter, we examine the life of a desperado who died not for the honor of his lady or his profession, but for the honor of becoming a gold camp "chief."

FOUR

GRASSHOPPER CREEK MINES

THE STORY OF JACK CLEVELAND

BANNACK, MONTANA, WITH GRASSHOPPER CREEK IN BACKGROUND. *Photo by Boswell*

GRASSHOPPER CREEK MINES

GUNFIGHT AT THE GOODRICH HOTEL SALOON

It was December 1862 when Jack Cleveland and Henry Plummer rode into Bannack, the new mining camp located on Grasshopper Creek. Barren hills crowding the narrow valley were dusted a powdery white, and a persistent, biting wind gusted down canyon. The latest El Dorado, they discovered, was no more than two short rows of log cabins somberly facing off across a main street. Though the four hundred restless miners wintering around saloon hearths may have noted the two newcomers' practice of sticking together and concluded that they were intimate friends, nothing could have been further from the truth.[1]

The two old Californians were about the same age and were both from the East coast, but similarities stopped there. Plummer was coolheaded and polite, Cleveland blustery and unpolished. Cleveland was not his true name, but an alias he used to disassociate himself from an unsavory past, which he went to great pains to conceal. Born in New York state in 1828, John Farnsworth had moved with his family to Jo Daviess County, Illinois, where he had grown to young manhood. As a youth, he migrated to California and unsuccessfully tried his hand at mining in Sacramento County. After his initial failure, he drifted to gold-rich Nevada County and there became involved in his mysterious trouble. Refusing to accept responsibility for his own actions, he blamed his disgrace on the Nevada City law officer who had exposed him, Marshal Henry Plummer. The young marshal's star was on the ascent: he was a leading political figure, his mining claims produced well, his businesses flourished, and his combination of toughness and gentleness attracted women. But just as dramatically as Plummer had risen, he plummeted to the same depths of shame as Jack Farnsworth. Plummer's downfall, however, did not lessen Jack's feelings of vindictiveness; once fastened on an object of revenge, he was tenacious. To his chagrin, county officials persuaded the governor to grant Plummer a pardon, and within a matter of months, the ex-marshal was back in Nevada City, sauntering down Broad Street and displaying the same behavior that had inspired Jack's hatred in the first place. In his pockets, Plummer jingled a collection of ore samples from his latest claims and readily displayed them during saloon conversations. When the *Democrat* editor examined the pocketful of gold-flecked quartz, he was so impressed that he returned to his tiny office and wrote a piece about them for his next issue.[2]

But with plenty of money and free time on his hands, the ex-marshal gradually slipped to the level of those he had formerly arrested. He became a heavy drinker, a regular gambler, and the lover of a woman who worked for Mr. Ashmore, the owner of a theater and house of ill fame.[3] Despite his decline in social status, Plummer continued to behave like a law officer. When he dropped in at Ross's restaurant for a supper of fried clams — presumably the meal the New Englander had most craved while subsisting on the prison diet of stale codfish and putty-bread — he recognized another customer as an escaped convict. After arresting "Ten Year Smith," Plummer escorted him around the corner and up the hill to jail. The former lawman's skill with a weapon still earned him respect, even if only from San Quentin escapees. It was Plummer's reputation as a gunman that Jack coveted most of all, and he was determined to someday catch his quick-drawing enemy off guard.[4]

Month after month, Jack trailed his intended victim. It was a full-time job because Plummer was as addicted to incessant action as any other gold camp follower. Then in October 1861, Plummer had an enigmatic conflict with William Riley, and Jack temporarily lost track of his prey. It was the summer of 1862 before he was able to pick up the trail again. Now known as a desperado, Plummer had joined the rush to Florence, where another former Californian had recognized him and sent word to the Nevada City newspaper. Jack, who had assumed the surname Cleveland to shrug off the unsavory past about which he was so secretive, hastened to Florence. His desire to kill Plummer and thus assume the title of "chief" had

NEVADA CITY, CALIFORNIA, 1852. *Courtesy California State Library*

become an obsession. It was not difficult to locate his man, but at the Washington Territory camps, Jack faced the same problem as in California. To become "top gun" at the mines he would have to best his opponent in public. This required more waiting for the rare moment when Plummer might drop his guard. Though Jack carefully concealed his past disgrace, he made no secret of his continuing manhunt. Pioneers recalled how he "frequently uttered threats against the life of Plummer, and never lost an opportunity publicly to denounce him."[5]

Throughout a summer so oppressively hot that men and horses were "nearly melting," Jack Cleveland trailed his quarry over dusty lanes at the Salmon and Clearwater mines. As he made the rounds of the pleasure halls, his bravado swelled in direct proportion to his intake of alcohol. After gulping a few mouthfuls of sweet rotgut, he would proclaim himself "chief" and then brag that he was out for big game. "Plummer," he would inform his saloon audience, "was his meat!" A threat against a man of Plummer's reputation always produced a moment of respectful awe for its utterer, a moment Jack evidently treasured, judging from the frequency with which he reenacted the scene.[6]

As Jack stuck to his man like a burr, a strange intimacy gradually developed between the two easterners who had both suffered a painful loss in the West. If Jack drank too much and became disorderly, Plummer kept him out of trouble, disciplining him as though he were a child: "Behave yourself now, Jack, or I'll take you in hand." Though the older of the two, Jack would shamefacedly obey. Still, Plummer realized that Jack was a constant threat, as well as a nuisance, and evaded him when possible. Thus when Plummer, Reeves, and Ridgley rode to Oro Fino to visit Patrick Ford's six-girl Spanish dance hall, they did not invite Jack. By the time he caught up, the excitement was over. The corral shootout had left Ford dead, Ridgley wounded, and Plummer's horse crippled. On hearing that the able-bodied had headed in the direction of Elk City, Jack set out in pursuit.[7]

At the time of his arrival — early September 1862 — the little town spread along each side of a trail winding through a creek basin had already fallen victim to stampedes for more promising diggings. Since every arrival and departure attracted attention, Jack was able to ascertain that he was only a short distance behind his prey. Plummer and Reeves had stocked up on provisions and started across the Nez Perces' ancient route to buffalo range. In the 1850s, this 113-mile passage through the Bitterroots had been scouted as a wagon road, but rejected as too treacherous and too short on game and water. Leaving the lush meadow and rolling, timbered hills surrounding Elk Basin, the trail passed through some of the roughest of wilderness areas: dense timber, narrow, steep-sided canyons, craggy ridges barren of vegetation, and lofty peaks glistening with snow. Since Indians rarely used the trail by then, a rider could travel through miles of undisturbed beauty in comparative safety. The main problem was finding game and water. There were some rushing streams and placid lakes which provided succulent trout, and though deer, elk, moose, and mountain goat were not as plentiful as on the longer LoLo Trail, a limited amount of game was available.[8]

By riding from dawn to dark, Jack could reach Red River Meadows the first day, Mountain Meadows the second, and on the third night camp along the Little Salmon River. Then on the fourth day, he would climb to the timbered site where Magruder was to die the following year. From that point, it would be a difficult day's journey up a steep, rocky trail to the summit and a few more days (depending on how many times he lost his way on the net of crossing paths) to the Bitterroot Valley.[9] Calmed by the sound of a fast-moving, rippling stream and awed by rugged ranges that dwarfed him to a mere ant inching his way across their vastness, Jack might have emerged from the ancient Indian passage a new man, purged of hostility and reborn in tranquility. His actions, however, show that no such transformation occurred.

When he reached American Fork, the community that had grown up around the Stuart brothers' sluices on Gold Creek, it was nearing the end of September. A few day's before Jack's arrival, James and Granville Stuart had jotted down in their diary that travelers named Plummer and Reeves had spent a few days with them and then departed. Jack lingered only long enough to get a fresh mount and to determine Plummer's route. By riding hard, he managed to overtake his enemy, who was mounted on a fine horse and leading a second animal packed with blankets and supplies. Though Plummer was notorious for keeping his thoughts to himself, he must have realized that all of his overtures of friendliness had been rejected and that Jack was still determined to kill him. The two men rode on together, tension between them thick enough to slice with the bowie knives they wore slung at the hip. The long wilderness stretch ahead would provide Jack ample opportunity to surprise Plummer, but he was still set on a public display that would win him the mantle of chief.[10]

Their path was Captain John Mullan's wagon trail, described as a "parched road of red and gravelly clay," that crossed the winding Little Blackfoot River three times. After descending the pass, they entered Little Prickly Pear Canyon, an eight-mile gorge where wind and water had carved nearly perpendicular walls into rough turrets soaring a thousand feet into the sky. The course of the swiftly flowing, willow-bordered river was so circuitous that their horses must splash through its icy water eighteen times. The pair made odd traveling companions, Jack sullenly tailing the ex-lawman like a shadow, and Plummer wary, yet outwardly calm.[11]

After winding their way through the narrow canyon, they arrived at the point where Wolf Creek flows into the river. Then a mile and a half farther, the merged streams plunged, in the words of one admiring beholder, "with a thousand sparkles and a deep breast of water" into the mighty Missouri. The route paralleled the huge arc formed by the Missouri as it gradually swerves from a northerly to an easterly direction. The next stream to contribute its waters was the Dearborn, and several miles past its mouth arose a welcome landmark, the curiously shaped rock called Bird Tail, which signaled the nearness of the government's Indian farm.[12]

To reach the farm, they had to cross the Sun River, whose northern bank lay in Blackfoot country. At the time, Agent Reed was acquainting the new farm manager, James Vail, with his duties. Though Vail had attempted to raise a crop, he was beset with problems. As one visitor reported, the Sun had flooded the fields, the Indians were "drunk," mosquitoes were "intolerable," rattlesnakes were "plenty," and Vail's log house was "not fit to live in."[13]

On exiting the troubled farm, their trail wound alongside the sandy-bottomed river for a few miles and then climbed a bluff. Since many emigrants were using the route, grass was scarce, and the only game left was antelope. The two adversaries were now less than sixty miles from Fort Benton, where Plummer planned to catch a boat down the Missouri and return to his native state, Maine. In September, the vast, butte-dotted plain they were traversing is met by a dome of pale blue sky, often spread with billowy cumuli, so that when the roadway follows a long, gradual ascent, it seems to lead directly into the clouds. But it is doubtful that Jack appreciated nature's spectacle; time was running out, and the trek had not yet presented the proper moment when he could assert himself as chief. If he had hopes that Benton (the last of the chain of forts the American Fur Company had erected along the river route from St. Louis) would provide a gambling hall setting, he would be disappointed.

Leaving the plains north of the Missouri, the road descended to intercept the river. From the high bluff they could see the little fort below, squatting at the very edge of the broad waterway. The river's banks and islands were covered with frothy green weeds, but beyond, shrubs glowed a bright yellow, and grasses had already dulled to a drab brown. On the bank opposite them, a charcoal-gray bluff decorated with a narrow rim of chalky minarets rose even higher than the two corner bastions of the fort's adobe walls. A lone canvas store stood outside the fort, but inside they found a trading post stocked with furs, robes, boots, cotton and wool fabric, ready-made clothing, tinware, food staples, and the best selling item of all, whiskey.[14]

Alexander Culbertson and his Blackfoot wife ran an orderly post, at least as orderly as could be expected under the circumstances. There was a neat row of shops — blacksmith, tailor, tinmaker, and carpenter — and above them were the tradesmen's sleeping rooms. The fort's three acres were overrun with keelboat crews, packers, gold seekers, and Indians — all slapping at the hordes of voracious mosquitoes that swarmed up from the river, and at the same time jostling one another to shy away from the snout of a snappish wolf dog or to step over a fresh "pony pie."

Both Cleveland and Plummer experienced disappointment at Benton; not only was there no saloon, but the current Indian crisis was preventing boatmen from making river runs. Like the others inside the fourteen-foot walls, they were literally trapped until Blackfoot hostility subsided. Monotony was relieved only by mealtime, when all gathered around long wooden tables in the two-story kitchen. Here, three times daily, a black cook served a fare of meat, beans, corn, rice, bread, butter, mustard, and coffee. The Culbertsons provided place settings of tin plate, tin cup, and spoon, but each guest supplied his own knife.[15]

The wait at the fort was far from pleasant, especially for men with a low tolerance for inactivity. On the plains beyond the fort hovered the restless Blackfeet, tribes of wanderers dressed in bead-ornamented buckskin and trailed by packs of wretched dogs, described as "ill-shaped" and "of a dingy color" because their masters allowed them no diet save "offal of fish and game." The stench within the fort was comparable to that of a long neglected stable, which must have been especially offensive to a stickler for cleanliness such as Plummer. Though the ex-lawman usually made an effort to be courteous, he could also be moody and irritable, and having a man as boisterous as Jack Cleveland constantly at his elbow would have worn on the strongest nerves.[16]

Jack probably toyed with the idea of killing his antagonist at the fort rather than taking the chance that Plummer might escape, and then there was the constant worry that the strain of their confinement might *accidentally* set off the long-delayed confrontation. The pair might have shattered the inactivity at Fort Benton at any moment had James Vail not ridden in early one morning. He was begging for help in defending the two women and two children stranded at the government farm. Jack was no coward, and when Plummer volunteered to accompany Vail back to the farm, he went along also.

To avoid Indian trouble, they rode at night. Throughout the journey, all were undoubtedly haunted by visions of a massacre during Vail's absence: ashes, embers, and mutilated bodies pierced with arrows. Horror stories were always in circulation, such as the grisly incident involving a girl of five years (Vail's daughter was four). After attacking a wagon train bound for Walla Walla, vengeful Indians had chopped off the little girl's legs at the knee and then forced her to hobble about on the bleeding stumps, or so the newspapers had reported.[17]

But they reached the Sun River, proceeded up its broad valley, and found the farm intact: a cluster of log buildings surrounded by a stake palisade. At their approach, the watchman swung open the gate, revealing the single small cannon that stood between them and extinction. James Vail had but two employees, an Indian hunter and a teenage city boy who had come West to work as the farm's hired hand. If Cleveland and Plummer had entertained fears about their own safety, they were now confirmed. It was obvious that the few men gathered inside the fortified farm could not long resist a seige by a large war party. Still, attempting to move the women and children to Benton would have been even more risky. The newcomers immediately began reinforcing the wall, and the wait for attack began.[18]

Vail provided his protectors with their own cabin, and because of Plummer's penchant for cleanliness and neatness, he took charge of household duties. Jack was responsible for gathering firewood. The forced companionship during a time of mutual peril might have done for Jack what his journey through the Bitterroot wilderness had not. Plummer's considerate ways might have eventually dissolved resentment had Vail's sister-in-law not been at the farm.

Electa Bryan was slender and had a pretty face, pale hair, and large, dark eyes. She was shy, yet artlessly frank. As soon as Jack saw her, he fell hopelessly in love. But fate had played a cruel trick; Electa had stirred the same emotion in Plummer.[19] The lady had a choice to make, and while she deliberated, the rivals quarreled bitterly, hurling accusations and threats. Evidently, Jack believed himself as handsome and magnetic as Plummer, and therefore equally capable of winning Electa. But she soon made it clear that she was in love with Plummer. Bitter over the rejection, Jack hurried to the Vails' cabin and informed his host of Plummer's troubles in California and Oro Fino. Though James and Martha Vail were upset at the news, Electa did not waver. She insisted that Plummer had never killed anyone except in self-defense, that he was a "pure, good man," and that anybody who said otherwise was lying.[20]

Even nature seemed to be on Plummer's side, providing the lovers with long days of gentle sunlight brightening the endless expanse of blue sky and reflecting a hazed image of yellow-leaved cottonwoods on the surface of the meandering Sun River. More than fifty years after that Indian summer, a pioneer named Francis Goss claimed that its details were still clear in his mind. He had also been at the farm, he stated, and had helped to fortify the walls during the feared uprising. Goss recalled the courtship that took place that autumn of 1862 between the "handsome, striking-appearing man with the manner of a gentleman" and the "tall, slender and beautiful girl" with "an abundance of auburn hair." In his old age, Goss also spoke of the Plummer's brief marriage, describing the husband as "kind and affectionate." When Electa left Bannack for Salt Lake City, Goss went on, Plummer provided her "plentifully with money," telling her "he would join her there soon." Then, after vigilantes hanged Plummer, Martha Vail showed Goss a letter from Electa: "I have a son who has been named for his father, but if he was the man they say he was I can never shed a tear for him." Goss believed that Henry Plummer, Jr., grew to manhood in Iowa. If Goss's memories were accurate, they would resolve one of the mysteries surrounding Jack Cleveland's enemy, but Electa's stepdaughters contradict Goss's claim, insisting that the Plummers had no children. That Goss had confused actual events with the myth of the Plummer gang is apparent: he also remembered Bill Bunton and George Ives being at the Sun River farm that fall and planning to steal Vail's herd of Indian ponies and oxen.[21] In reality, Ives was, at the time, at the Salmon River mines, and Bunton was busy getting into trouble in the Walla Walla area.[22]

Yet Goss's recollection of Jack Cleveland was lucid. While the two were replacing stakes in the wall around the farm, they discovered that both had resided in Jo Daviess County, Illinois. "Do you know George Tyler, who used to keep the Galena Hotel?" Jack asked.

"Yes," Goss replied, "he was my uncle."

"You ought to know me, then," Jack said. "I worked for him. I also drove stage for Fink at Galena. My right name is Farnsworth, but if you ever write one word back to them that you have seen me, I'll kill you—your life won't be worth ten cents." Goss resolved to remain silent about having encountered his former townsman.[23]

Weeks passed, and the Indians launched no attack. By snowfall, Vail concluded that hostilities had subsided, and Plummer prepared to leave the farm, promising, however, to return in the spring to marry Electa. As he headed for the Bannack diggings, Jack was riding alongside. Exactly what transpired after their departure will never be known, but one account has kept treasure seekers busy. Supposedly, Plummer believed that Jack intended to rob him somewhere along the trail ahead. Therefore, when they passed the next farm, he stopped and privately asked the owner if he could hide his money there and return for it later. The farmer consented, and Plummer buried his gold dust in a cache near the creek. As the farmer's story leaked out, treasure hunters periodically arrived to dig for the buried treasure. The farmer's son was certain that Electa herself had twice appeared, and while she and a relative spaded up the creek bank, he had played with little Henry Plummer! "It would be difficult to convince some people," a Montana editor commented in 1882, "that there is not a treasure box hidden somewhere near . . . the Sun River."[24]

Like the existence of the gold cache, the date of Cleveland's arrival at Bannack is a matter of dispute.[25] But on whatever day, he and his partner made lasting impressions on the miners huddled about mud-and-stone fireplaces. "Plummer," one of them recalled, "speedily became a general favorite" for his "counsel and advice," and Cleveland just as speedily earned the reputation of "a desperado of the vilest character." Jack continued his habit of swaggering into a saloon and announcing his intentions of killing Plummer. When Bannackites tried to pry into the source of the trouble between the men, Jack suddenly became uncharacteristically taciturn. On the subject of his California past, his lips were sealed. But his reticence only whetted the appetites of the curious. His listeners concluded that the Cleveland-Plummer feud was not only "irreconcilable," but also nearing a head. Though Plummer sat around the saloons stony faced, making him nearly impossible to read, his patience did seem to be wearing thin. Still, Jack persisted in his attempts to provoke a quarrel, recognizing the latest boomtown as an ideal setting for outgunning "the quickest hand with his revolver of any man in the mountains."[26]

As the cold, unvarying days dragged on, cabin fever reached such epidemic proportions that the most innocuous remark could set off gunplay. No one felt the strain more than Jack. In addition to the tension created by his constant need for watchfulness, he was short of money, and unlike one immigrant resident, Conrad Kohrs, Jack was unwilling to work for the town butcher for twenty-five dollars a month plus free board.[27] Jack did fancy horse trading, however, and when Billy Terwilliger displayed his two long-legged mounts, Jack scraped up sufficient funds to buy a half share. As part of the deal, he had to give Terwilliger half ownership of his own horse. But their transaction took place at an inopportune moment. About the same time Jack rode to Red Rock Creek, where one horse was boarded, George Evans disappeared. No amount of scouring the snowy countryside could produce a body, but searchers did discover some bloody clothing stuffed in a badger hole. It was enough to convince them that someone had robbed and killed Evans. Though some blamed Charley Reeves and Whiskey Bill Graves for the supposed murder, Jack was also a suspect. Receiving the cold shoulder from suspicious citizens only increased the resentment that had been festering in him since his California troubles.[28]

January 14, 1863 — the last day of Jack's life — dawned no different than previous mornings: "Some six inches snow on ground," miner James Morley entered in his diary, "and wind strong and keen." As usual, Jack made the saloon rounds, somewhat defensive because other customers noted that he now had money to pay for his drinks. Then in the afternoon, Plummer entered the Goodrich Hotel saloon and squeezed a place for himself on a low bench before the fire. As he conversed with Jeff Perkins, seated beside him, the door banged open and in stalked Jack, already inebriated. His belligerent demeanor suggested that the crucial moment might be at hand.[29]

"I'm the chief!" Jack blurted out. For emphasis, he followed with a few curses. "I knew all the d——d scoundrels from the other side," he continued, glancing meaningfully at Plummer, "and I intend to get even on them." Whirling toward the bench, he addressed Perkins, rather than Plummer as everyone had expected. "Pay me that money you borrowed in California!" he demanded. When Perkins nervously insisted that the money had already been repaid, Jack only leered at him. "If it has," he came back sarcastically, "it's all right," but at the same moment he rested his fingers on his holster and commenced fondling the pistol butt. Then he made a second complaint about the unpaid money.

While Perkins squirmed under the pressure, Plummer shot Jack a warning glare. "Behave yourself," he said evenly. "Perkins paid the debt and you ought to be satisfied."

Jack gave the appearance that he would obey Plummer, as on previous occasions, and the barber in the corner took a firmer grip on his razor and made another swipe at his customer's beard. Taking advantage of the lull in the action, Perkins slipped out to obtain a gun. He intended, he said afterwards, to come back and shoot Cleveland.[30]

Apparently, things were proceeding exactly as Jack had planned. Sensing success, he unleashed a string of profanities. "I'm not afraid of any of you," he raged, grasping his pistol again.

But his intended victim had not been fooled by the charade. As Jack touched his gun, Plummer sprang to his feet like a loosed tiger. "I'm tired of this," he said. Before Jack could finish raising his pistol, Plummer fired a warning shot into the ceiling above Cleveland's head. But Jack would not be cowed. Whiskey had bolstered his courage, and he continued the motion of lifting his hand. Plummer fired two more quick shots; the final one struck Jack's leg, and he crumpled to his knees, scrabbling for the gun he had dropped. "You won't shoot me when I'm down, will you, Plummer?" he pleaded.

"No," Plummer replied.

Gun in hand, Jack hefted himself to his feet, trying to appear submissive. Then he jerked up his hand, but before it was halfway raised, a shot whizzed into his ribcage, ricocheting away from his body. A second shot entered his cheek, and he collapsed onto the saloon floor, bleeding from the face. Plummer sheathed his pistol, turned away from the sight, and walked out the front door. Not a single man stirred to assist Jack.[31]

Minutes later, Conrad Kohrs opened the front door of the butcher shop, which was located down the street from the Goodrich Hotel, and discovered Cleveland sprawled outside. "I carried him in and tried to learn from him why Plummer had shot him," Kohrs reported, "but could get nothing out of him." Spectators gathered around the wounded man, who lay on the butcher shop table covered with a blanket, and continued to question him. But to all their inquiries about his problems with Plummer, he responded, "It makes no difference to you." For one moment, he wavered from his resolve to die

game: "Poor Jack has got no friends," he said feebly. Then he sto-
ically added, "He has got it, and I guess he can stand it." Shortly
after, he drew a final breath.[32]

COMMENTARY ON THE STORY OF JACK CLEVELAND

After Jack's demise, Hank Crawford — the owner of the butcher shop —
took up the feud with Plummer, eventually uttering the very words
by which Jack had lived and died: "Either him or me!"[33] On the
other hand, Crawford's employee and Jack's rescuer, Conrad Kohrs,
represents the antithesis to the Mountain Code adherent. Recalling
a time when a rough stepped up to him in a saloon, called him vile
names, and spit in his face, Kohrs remarked, "I was obliged to
stand all this abuse and at the first sign of resistance I would have
been shot." Choosing a temporary loss of dignity rather than a
shootout, Kohrs survived the perilous mining camp environment to
become a wealthy rancher.[34]

But Jack Cleveland was willing to risk death to become a "long-
tailed hero of the revolver." At Plummer's subsequent murder trial,
the defense attorney exposed the secret past Jack had so determinedly
guarded. "Plummer tried today before a jury and 'honorably
acquitted,'" James Morley recorded in his diary on January 22,
1863, "the man shot having been proved a desperado and outlaw,
said to have belonged to Watkins' band in California." Morley, in
turn, revealed Jack's secret to posterity.[35]

The account of the Cleveland-Plummer gunfight differs with
the teller. Two early residents, who claimed they witnessed the fight,
avowed that it took place in Skinner's saloon and that Plummer
used a Derringer; others maintained that Cleveland got off the first
shot. But the disagreements do not detract from the importance of
the event. Prior to January 22, 1863, the miners' courts at Grasshopper Creek had dealt only with mining claim disputes. Beginning
with the Plummer trial, the miners assumed responsibility for criminal cases, an important step toward bringing law and order to the
area.[36]

The trial provides insight into the code of justice operating on
the mining frontier. Assuming Plummer fired first, which is possible considering his skill with a weapon, the verdict of self-defense
presents a marked departure from the modern interpretation of the
term. The code followed in Bannack — "Never draw your pistol unless

you intend to use it"—was called the California Rule. "If a man made even a motion towards drawing a weapon," one gold rush participant explained, "it was considered perfectly justifiable to shoot him first."[37]

The two combatants at the Bannack saloon were Old Californians, well versed in the rule. Both knew that a weapon was never drawn out of bravado. From the moment Cleveland first touched his gun while threatening Perkins, those present understood the rules, and all acted accordingly. Perkins rushed home for his own gun, planning to return to kill Cleveland. Jack was fair game for his intended victim. But Jack's "meat," as he put it, was not Perkins, but the man known as the quickest shot in the mountains. Plummer, the jury concluded in a matter of minutes, was justified in defending himself against an intended shot, whether fired or not. The shootout not only instigated the first criminal trial at the Beaverhead mines, but also left a vivid example of the mining frontier code in action.

FIVE

ALDER GULCH MINES

THE STORY OF GEORGE IVES

VIRGINIA CITY, MONTANA. *Photo by Boswell*

ALDER GULCH MINES

In December 1863, an Alder Gulch miners' court tried handsome, affable George Ives for the murder of an orphan boy. The proceedings had many of the same weaknesses of the trial that would be given Renton, Romain, and Lowrey the following month. In the Idaho ax-murder case, however, Billy Page's story was so compelling that the verdict probably would have been the same under more favorable circumstances. But at the Ives trial, an impartial jury might have acquitted the defendant. Even as it was, controversial testimony produced a hung jury. The murky events surrounding the final months of the defendant's life present a marked contrast to his earlier days. Like Henry Talbot, George came from a prominent family.

"Ives" derives from a Gaelic word meaning chief or leader, and the Ives family has produced its share of leaders. Among the many who might be mentioned are Guillbert Ives, who crossed the English Channel with William the Conqueror; Corporal Amos Ives, who distinguished himself as a minuteman during the American Revolution; Mathew Ives, who served in the Massachusetts senate; James Merritt Ives, who joined lithographer Nathaniel Currier in 1850 to form the print-making firm of Currier & Ives; the subject of this chapter, who reigned as chief of Alder Gulch; and moving to more recent times, Burl Ives, who achieved fame as a folksinger.[1]

George Ives's fifth-great-grandfather, William, was the first to come to America, arriving at Boston Harbor in 1635 as one of the sixty-seven passengers aboard the *Truelove*. Later, William joined a company of well-to-do Puritans—led by Reverend John Davenport—

who set out in 1638 to found a trade center that could compete with Boston. After cruising southward for two weeks, the group disembarked at a "fair haven" just where the Quinnipiac River joins Long Island Sound. On the first Sabbath in the wilderness, the Puritans gathered under a huge oak tree to listen to Reverend Davenport preach an apt sermon entitled "The Temptations of the Wilderness." Then in preparation for entering into the New Haven Civil Compact — a covenant which declared the Scriptures to be the foundation of their government — they engaged in a day of fasting and prayer.[2]

From local Indians, the New Haven settlers purchased land, giving in payment two dozen knives, four cases of scissors, and a dozen each of coats, hatchets, hoes, spoons, and porrigers. They laid out the town in a half-mile square: a central green surrounded by house lots, which were in turn surrounded by farmland granted to each free planter. George's ancestor received a total of nineteen acres.[3] Succeeding generations of Iveses gradually penetrated farther into the virgin land, moving up the streams emptying into the sound. George's great-grandfather, David, traveled as far north as the present boundary of Connecticut and Massachusetts to cofound the village of Southwick in the hills west of the Connecticut River. After tilling the fields and planting tobacco, the Southwick settlers constructed a meetinghouse, school, tavern, store, and Congregational church, which David and his wife Dolly attended regularly. David also served as a village selectman and as captain of the militia.[4] On his death, his children laid him to rest in the village cemetery and erected a tombstone with the following inscription:

Capt. David Ives who died Dec. 11, 1815, aged 66
In grateful memory of a parent dear the mourning children place this
    marble here. . . .
Now cold in death beneath the dust he lies —
The immortal part has on swift pinions flown, to take its sentence in the
    world unknown.[5]

Here at Southwick, Massachusetts, David's son Roland married and began a family. But on the birth of a seventh child, both infant and mother died, leaving the widower with six surviving offspring. Four years later, the oldest son, Roland, Jr., brought a bride to preside over his father's household. Thus in 1834, George Homer Ives — first child of Roland, Jr., and Almira — was born under his grandfather's prosperous roof in a village cofounded by his distinguished great-grandfather.[6]

But like David, the two Rolands grew restless in the staid little community where they had been born and reared. In the spring of 1837, Roland, Sr., and his son Stephen set out to explore Wisconsin Territory, recently formed from Northwest Territory. A short distance from the southwest shore of Lake Michigan, they purchased a large farm. The original owner, Joseph Call, had purchased the land from the government for $1.25 an acre. George Homer was three when his father uprooted the family and took them to join the grandfather and uncle in the new home. There were ten of them: George's grandfather; his three uncles, Stephen, Homer, and Gideon; his two aunts, Maria and Charlotte; his parents, Roland and Almira; himself; and his baby brother, Albert.[7]

Though the Iveses had bought the land for raising livestock, they had also inherited a lively business. Joseph Call had cleared a small area of trees, and with the rolled logs constructed buildings in which he could service passing travelers. A two-story log house and a log barn sat in the midst of the small but dense forest of oak, walnut, and elm, which was bounded by extensive plains of low, rolling hills. When the Iveses assumed the role of innkeepers, customers changed the name of the stopover from Call's Grove to Ives Grove.[8]

Almira and Roland, Jr., earned a reputation as generous, gracious hosts. One early traveler long remembered the warm reception he enjoyed at the Grove. Too poor to own a horse, he had set out on foot for Racine in the spring of 1839. "A heavy rain came on and he was wet to the skin when he got to the tavern," his daughter later recorded. "He never told the story without expressing gratitude to the tavern keepers, man and wife, for the hospitality shown, for the loan of clothing while his own was being dried, and excellent food, and a comfortable bed."[9]

Though the guest expressed satisfaction with the food and lodging, living conditions at Ives Grove in 1839 were primitive — a table set with pewter and a diet of venison acquired from the surrounding forest. Only a year prior, Potawatomi Indians had abandoned the area and moved West, thus eliminating one danger, but just beyond the clearing lurked bear, wolves, and lynx. The Iveses had no neighbors, no church, and no school. Yet despite such "privations and dangers," a local history stated, "the settlers were contented, happy . . . and submitted cheerfully to the inconveniences. . . . Religious services on Sunday were held . . . when a passing missionary came."[10]

One persisting danger was prairie fire. The Grove was described as a verdant island in the midst of a vast, drab, treeless prairie. When fire broke out, flames raced to the very edge of the Grove, encircling it and leaving the Ives family virtual prisoners, uncertain whether the conflagration would burn itself out or make the leap to the forest. But the Grove proved immune to prairie fires, allowing its owners to proceed with their challenge to the wilderness: cutting timber; rolling and burning logs; plowing; planting wheat, oats, barley, and potatoes; and stocking herds of cattle, horses, sheep, and pigs. All of Roland, Sr.'s, six children took up residence at the Grove except for Stephen, who settled in the lake port of Racine and cofounded the first newspaper in the area. The opening issue of the *Racine Weekly Argus* appeared on Valentine's Day, 1838, but due to high costs and low profits ceased publication the same year.[11]

With the gradual settlement of the southeastern corner of Wisconsin Territory, activity at Ives Grove daily increased. Farmers came from as far west as the Rock River, hauling wagonloads of produce to Racine harbor and returning home with supplies. The five roads passing the Grove were busy much of the year. During dry weather, the cumbersome wagons bounced in and out of deep ruts, and with the rains, bogged down in mire. To improve the transportation essential to continuing development, the government allowed a private company to construct a toll road from Janesville, on the Rock River, to Racine. This "plank road," built on an elevated bed bordered by long timbers spread with oak planks, soon became the most popular route for both farmers and stages, and since it passed directly in front of the Ives inn, business flourished.

To meet the increasing traffic, Roland, Jr., built an elegant new tavern. With oak and walnut timbers cut from the grove, he erected a long, three-story building, roofed with white-oak shingles and topped with a brick chimney at each end. Five separate doorways opened from the ground floor, five glass-paned windows lit the second, and full verandas graced both. A store, post office, restaurant, and saloon were located on the first floor, bedrooms on the second, and on the third, a "spring floor," used for dances, roller skating, and other socials. In their improved facility, Roland charged a dollar for a night's lodging, which included barn space and feed for a six-animal team, and for the driver, a bed, supper, breakfast, and "short" of whiskey. Additional orders of whiskey, a guest recalled, were "drawn from a barrel and sold at three cents a glass." At such a high price, he added, "there was very little drunkenness among the settlers in the neighborhood."[12]

For children of the wilderness, such as George and Albert Ives, the advent of the plank road provided a glorious spectacle. They marveled at the sight of long lines of travelers stretching from the inn in both directions over "level farm lands and up and down the low hills" for as far as the eye could see. There were trains of fifty to a hundred vehicles passing at one time: "wagons pulled by three pairs of oxen," straining against the weight of wheat and other produce, "herds of cattle and sheep being driven to market, occasionally a lone horseman or a dashing stagecoach drawn by a four horse team." At the peak season, the Grove barns accommodated fifty teams a night. When every bedroom on the second story was full, Roland spread the dance hall with cots, considerately surrounding each with a small booth to afford privacy.[13]

Though the continual activity created by daily stages and the harvest rush presented a stimulating environment for George and Albert, they were nevertheless children inhabiting a basically adult world. In the early years at the Grove, when the two boys were still too small to be of much help at the inn, they had little company other than each other and their pets. When it became necessary to shoot a mother bear who strayed too near the inn, the settlers remembered that the little tow-headed Ives brothers "took the bear cubs and tamed them and had them for pets for a long time."[14]

Not until the 1840s did the three generations of Iveses residing at the inn begin to acquire neighbors. Among them was the Bush family, who carved out a farm and racehorse stable west of the Grove. George's oldest aunt, Charlotte, soon fell in love with and married young John Bush. When she left home, she took with her the younger sister, Maria. The new couple bought land between their parents' farms and devoted much time to breeding fast horses. John Bush raced his stock at a half-mile track on his father's farm and at a second course east of the Grove, and George spent as much time as his parents would permit at the Bush stable and racetracks, developing a love of the sport and a riding skill he would later display during a desperate effort to escape from an unauthorized posse at Alder Gulch.[15]

About the same time Charlotte and Maria left home, their brothers, Homer and Gideon, acquired land of their own in a county to the north. During this period when his younger children were leaving home, Roland, Sr., who had gradually been losing his sight, became totally blind. The year 1845 also brought the birth of Almira and Roland's only daughter, Mary. With his wife occupied in the care of the infant, his brothers and sisters gone, and his father adjusting to his handicap, Roland had to assume most of the responsibility for managing farm and inn. His grain and potato fields were extensive, and he ran more than thirty head of cattle and horses, a hundred sheep, and a pig herd large enough to provide the inn with twelve hundred pounds of pork yearly. For help, he turned to his two young sons. Though George was only eleven, the handsome, blond, blue-eyed boy was tall and strong for his age; he could manage most farm chores as well as lend a hand at the inn — anything from unhitching the horse teams to flipping griddle cakes while Almira nursed the baby. George would be well prepared to some day manage his own ranch and business.[16]

In 1848, Ives Grove became part of a state, rather than a territory, and by 1850 boasted a small frame schoolhouse. The school had no desks; the few scholars who reported for the first sessions shared a long bench and rested books in their laps. The three Ives children of course attended: George Homer, age sixteen, Albert, thirteen, and Mary, five. During the summer term, the teacher was a young lady, but in the better attended winter term — when older boys were freed from field work — a firm-handed schoolmaster officiated. Many of the high-spirited youth, such as George Ives, had never before suffered the confinement of a schoolroom.[17]

George would have preferred not to be in school at all. Like the adventuresome young men of preceding chapters, he was anxious to join the rush to California, and like many parents, his were insistent he remain at home. Thus the 1850 census taker reported that the oldest son of Almira and Roland Ives was attending school, however unwillingly. But on turning eighteen, George was off to the mines, taking the overland route and selecting California's Sierra County as the most likely place to earn a fortune. Shortly after his arrival, the state's 1852 enumeration took place, but George was not at camp when the census official made his appearance. The slightly inaccurate information provided by his new acquaintances presents the impression he had made on his fellow miners. They knew only that he had been born somewhere in New England and reared somewhere near Lake Michigan; as for his age, they guessed he was about twenty-five, the extra seven years being a tribute to the teenager's maturity.[18]

Proving more stable than Ed Richardson, David Renton, Chris Lowrey, Henry Talbot, Bill Mayfield, and Jack Cleveland, George Ives made a satisfactory adjustment to the new environment. Though he undoubtedly participated in camp revelry, the other miners found that George did not have "much of the braggart about him" and was ordinarily "peaceable." He worked hard at his employer's mine and got into no scrapes with the law. Perhaps his prepossessing appearance (all six feet of him) made it unnecessary for him to prove himself. He had a splendid physique, an acquaintance recalled, and "light complexion, neatly shaven face, and lively blue eyes." And in addition to being handsome, he earned the reputation of "an accomplished marksman" and a "bold rider." Thus "lesser" men "gathered about him as to a magnet."[19]

Having come through seven years of California turbulence unscathed, he headed north, arriving in 1859 at the military post in Clark County, Washington Territory. Here, the commanding officer hired George to take charge of the military packtrains, a service he performed so well that, according to one account, he became "a favorite among the officers and men." Miners passing through the area also had reason to praise him. When a group of highwaymen laid plans to rob a party headed for Portland, George warned the intended victims, allowing them to keep their gold dust. As in California, George left the Washington garrison with a good reputation and an admirable work record.[20]

After the 1860 discovery of gold at Oro Fino Creek, he visited that area, and in late spring of 1861, Pierce City. That summer he followed a stampede to Elk Creek Basin, where the first of a series of anecdotes about him and his fine horse arose. As George rode his dapple-gray, roached-maned mare — the envy of every man in camp — into an Elk City saloon, the proprietor rushed over and grabbed the mare by the bridle. Annoyed at the interference, George pulled his pistol, cocked it, and aimed at the owner's head. But on doing so, he recognized his former employer in California. Flushing with embarrassment, the horseman offered the saloonkeeper the prized mare as a gift. Fortunately for George, his former employer declined.[21]

With the June 1862 rush to Florence, bold rider and gray steed were off to that camp, and at its waning, off to Warren's. But even at the lively Clearwater and Salmon diggings, George became involved in no brawls or gunfights. In November, he investigated the mines on the other side of the mountains, accepting the invitation of a former Nevada statesman named George Carrhart, and his partner, Charles "Old Sport" Allen, to spend the winter on their ranch in Deer Lodge Valley. It was February 1863 when Ives and Carrhart appeared in Bannack.[22]

Preferring home-cooked food, George made arrangements to take meals at the cabin of Mrs. Wadams, who claimed the distinction of having been the first white woman in Bannack. In her declining years, Mrs. Wadam's daughter, Sarah, still remembered their tall, handsome boarder. He was "pleasant and well mannered," liked to attend the town dances, and showed the courtesy of remaining sober in the presence of ladies and children.[23] His behavior in the presence of his peers was quite another matter; despite his previous good record, George could not withstand the temptations offered by the Grasshopper Creek camp. One afternoon while he and Carrhart were walking down Main Street, a quarrel broke out between them, and each hurried back to retrieve a weapon checked earlier in the day. George returned seconds before his former companion and was standing with his back turned when Carrhart reappeared in a doorway. Rather than shooting his opponent in the back, Carrhart waited until George turned to face him and then both drew at the same moment. Carrhart's shot misfired, and George's missed by a mere inch; a second shot by each also failed to score a hit. Carrhart then ducked back inside the doorway, extended his hand, and fired several times without striking his target. Though George returned the shots, his opponent was protected by the building. When his pistol was empty, George also headed for safety, but Carrhart, who still had one shot left, fired at the retreating figure, striking George in the side. Though the ball passed completely through his body, ripping into the path before him, George continued running.[24]

While he was recuperating from the wound, his dueling partner came for a talk, and the two men patched up their differences. Nevertheless, George's eleven-year record for being friendly and peaceable was somewhat tarnished. Like his British forefather, George had migrated to a distant, unsettled land. But his New Haven grandfather had suffered no spiritual dulling from his contact with the wilds. George's associates, however, were far from puritanical. They did not preface the stay at Bannack with a period of fasting and prayer, nor was there any counterpart of the Reverend Davenport to enlighten the Grasshopper Creek miners on the temptations of the wilderness. At the mountain diggings, Dimsdale wrote, "sin" was quite "general," and religion was "played out." Though George may have inherited many of his colonizing ancestor's admirable traits, the two centuries that separated them had brought a marked decrease in the spirituality accompanying the frontier experience.[25]

Not long after his recovery from Carrhart's ball, George joined a daring venture to explore the Yellowstone River country; the ill-fated journey would sorely test the amount of courage and endurance the seventeenth-century Ives had passed down to his nineteenth-century descendant. Little was known of the Yellowstone Basin other than the report John Colter had given on his arrival at Lisa's Fort in 1807. After listening to the former member of the Lewis and Clark expedition relate his harrowing escape from Indians and ensuing experiences among the stinking, steaming waters, his amazed listeners dubbed the enchanted land "Colter's Hell."[26]

Members of the Yellowstone expedition left Bannack on April 9, 1863, and George caught up to them two days later. They traveled east, following maps made during the more celebrated expedition of Lewis and Clark. On the sixth day out, they camped with Chief Winnemucca, giving him some tobacco, which cost fifteen dollars a pound back in Bannack, and receiving from the Paiute some much-needed elk meat. In the evening, they gathered about the camp fire, smoking and, as Captain James Stuart wrote in his journal, "exchanging lies," reminiscent of saloon boasting. "They spun long yarns about what they had done during their buffalo hunt," Stuart recorded, and "I built some marvelous castles in the air about what we were going to do, how we would build towns, kill Indians, buffaloes, etc. etc."[27]

Despite his boasts, three days after the Indian meeting, Stuart began confiding to his journal his concern about the horses. Not only were the mounts weak, they were also developing saddlesores. "I am afraid some of us will have to walk," Stuart worried. The changeable weather did not make the going any easier: "Cold and windy . . . snow squalls . . . snow drifts . . . the horses sunk into the mud three or four inches every step and occasionally almost mired down." Still there were breathtaking views from atop mountain divides and constant encounters with wildlife: "great big fat" prairie dogs, huge wolves, hundreds of elk, and herds of antelope and bighorn sheep. And the night guard would be entertained by "the meadow-larks singing at all hours" or the hair-raising serenade of a wolf or coyote band. George Ives—known as a man who loved being a "free rider" through mountain and plain—was in his element throughout the journey. In fact, George was so enthusiastic that each morning he rose before the others to gather firewood and hunt game. Captain Stuart soon came to rely on Ives as "the most accommodating man in the party."[28]

By May 1, they were nearing the mouth of the Big Horn River and enjoying themselves by stampeding massive herds of buffalo. When a hunting detail killed two cows, cut out the tongues and tenderloins, and headed back to camp, three orphaned buffalo calves followed after them, vainly trying to suckle their horses. Finally, one calf gave out, another strayed off, and the third "got his thigh broken by a kick." Though there was abundant meat for the men, the horses were in "pitiable condition" and "very tenderfooted." Then on May 5, after having come four hundred miles, they reached the junction of the Yellowstone and Big Horn rivers. "Great was the excitement in our little party," Stuart wrote. In celebration, they carved their names in a sandstone cliff between the two rivers. George made two inscriptions: "G. H. Ives 1863" and, next to an Indian pictograph of a bonneted warrior counting coup, "G. Ives."[29]

Since the purpose of the expedition was to discover gold mines and secure town sites, they had been prospecting all along their route, but Big Horn City represented their first projected settlement. Much as George loved the wilderness, he was also a cultivator; like the other fourteen members of the party, he selected one hundred sixty acres adjoining the future town of Big Horn. But as they headed south, their elation at becoming colonizers faded: "Very disagreeable traveling to-day," Stuart commented, "strong northwest wind that raised clouds of dust." When they noted fresh Indian tracks on the following day, their mood became even more somber; the concerned captain placed all "on the lookout." Then a grisly, and ominous, sight appeared in view: "the remains of an Indian *buried up a tree!*" To cheer themselves, they succumbed to the lure of the "most exciting sport"—chasing a buffalo herd. Though it was "death" on the spent horses, and seemed a shame to slaughter the magnificent beasts, the men were too caught up in the excitement to resist. Whooping, they whipped their horses to full speed in pursuit of the herd, firing over one hundred shots, killing two buffalo outright, and leaving "plenty" more mortally wounded. "And such another time as we had!" Stuart rhapsodized. His men agreed that "it was great fun."[30]

But the somber mood soon returned. Shortly before the city plotting, there had been one unsettling encounter with a Crow party, and now the Indians seemed to be trailing them again. As they rode, Cyrus Watkins suddenly experienced a premonition of coming tragedy. The "mournful cooing of a dove," he said, made him "think of his boyhood days and of his mother's home," and he was powerless to shake the sad feeling. By nightfall, Stuart was so anxious over the Crow threat that he insisted on standing guard himself. Though he may have kept his thoughts to himself, he was also struggling with his emotions: "It is eleven years to-day since I left the home of my boyhood," he noted in the journal. "Who knows how many more it will be before I see it again." Then he added, "if ever?"[31]

Though they may have had difficulty in falling asleep, Stuart's men turned in early. George shared a tent with Ephraim Bostwick, Henry Geery, and the melancholy Watkins, whose mood had proven contagious. George may well have lain awake contemplating his days at the Grove and wondering if he would ever again see Almira Ives. Though he would not, he would at least survive the fated ordeal with the Crow. His three bedfellows would not.

At 11:00 P.M., a volley of shotgun fire shredded their tent and a shower of arrows followed. Bostwick was "shot all to pieces, but still alive"; Watkins had taken a ball in the temple, George a ball in the hip, and Geery an arrow in the shoulder. From nearby tents came the cries of other injured men, and, beyond, the wounded and dying horses squealed their fright. Stuart commanded the party to lie still and make no further sounds; through the long hours they lay in pitch darkness, awaiting the next onslaught. The only sounds were the moans of the wounded, the whisperings of the enemy, and the occasional whiz of an arrow passing overhead. At dawn they discovered Watkins "crawling around on his elbows and knees," though nearly insensible, while the Indians observed him from the mountainside. By 3:00 P.M. there still had been no second attack, and Stuart decided they should try to escape. Watkins appeared to be dead, and Bostwick, who did not want to delay his companions,

shot himself. Abandoning several hundred pounds of flour, the thirteen survivors mounted up and headed southwest. They noted the
Crow dogging them on a parallel course. To accommodate the
wounded, Stuart traveled the mountain trail slowly, but not until
10:00 P.M. did he order the men to make camp in the Big Horns.[32]

The following day they continued their flight on a rugged, snow-
choked trail, ever aware of the trailing war party which outnum-
bered them ten to one. At supper that night, Geery accidentally
shot himself with his own rifle and, not wanting to hold back the
rest, "blew out his brains" with the same weapon. At the sound of
the firing, the other twelve came running and discovered Geery's
"dying form." Though they had never yet allowed themselves to
become "disheartened," they now gathered about Geery's corpse and
"all wept like children."[33]

They arose at dawn. Though they had no food save a bit of
bread, they could not retrace the four-hundred-mile trail that had
brought them to the Big Horn junction. They were forced to follow
a circuitous twelve-hundred-mile route. As they climbed higher into
the snow-covered mountains, they dismounted, walking ahead of
their horses to tread a path. In "getting through the snow and fir-
timber," Stuart wrote, Ives "broke his gun clear off at the breech."
Still they proceeded, riding when possible, but fearing they might
soon be afoot permanently, since even beneath the snow there was
little grass for the horses. Despite their continued flight over the
rugged pass, Stuart realized they could not evade the Indians: "Those
devils seem to be eternally after us."

One night, a mare gave birth to a colt, but because it hindered
its mother's progress, they had to kill the newborn. As they reached
lower ground and warmer climes, thousands of crickets descended
upon them, chewing at their clothing and blankets and swarming
over the meager bread supply. Then, after a fifteen-day exodus
through Crow country, they at last sighted the telegraph poles along
the emigrant road to Oregon. "The boys couldn't stand it any longer,"
Stuart recorded, "but gave vent to their feelings in all kinds of motions
and noises. We were equal to a Chinese camp on a drunk for noise."
It was another twenty-five days before they arrived at Bannack,
with hair and beards so long, and clothing so tattered, that acquaintances could not recognize them. If, prior to the expedition, twenty-
nine-year-old George Ives had secretly entertained any doubts about
his manhood, they were now laid to rest. He commented that after

the "many narrow escapes," he "had confidence in his own resources." A second remark provides an interesting clue to his personality. Despite the hostilities between the two races, he said, he did not hold the Indians "in disdain."[34]

On their arrival at Bannack, a stampede to Alder Gulch was in progress, and being the gold camp veteran that he was, George joined. But he had been a farmer before a miner, and perhaps the loss of his Big Horn spread had stirred a longing in him. Beyond the mounds of rock and earth lining the bustling gulch stretched lush valleys of tall, waving grass. Teamsters pouring into the area needed to board their livestock, and George had the experience to operate such a business. He established two ranches, one on an island in the Madison River and another ten miles west of the cluster of mining camps strung along the gulch. At the booming town of Virginia City, he opened an office.

He seemed to experience no difficulty in settling into the life of a respectable businessman. Like his father, he was generous with his profits, frequently making loans to friends. One note, made in Virginia City on July 4, 1863, promised that Lester Hending would within ten days pay George Ives the sum of fifty dollars. This document—preserved in historical archives—is a reminder that George Ives once walked the earth; a second reminder, he had preserved himself on the cliff at the Yellowstone-Big Horn junction. Though some of the other names were soon rubbed smooth by wind and water, two decades later travelers could still make out the letters "G. Ives." Yet it was not for being a member of the Yellowstone expedition or for his generosity that the carver of those five letters would be remembered in the pages of Western history.[35]

In September 1863, George made another prospecting excursion, this time through the Snake River Valley. It was less lengthy and more profitable than the Stuart expedition. On his return trip, George happened to encounter the newly appointed chief justice of Idaho Territory and his secretary, Wilbur Sanders, and provided the newcomers their first glimpse of a gold nugget. "Ives . . . sat his saddle like a swan on a billowy lake," Sanders recalled. "He had plenty of money. . . . Having been so long in the vicinity of the frontier, he was well posted as to those enterprises and industries which insured profit." True, the livestock-boarding business at Alder Gulch was thriving. George had hired employees to man the office and ranches and had erected brush wickiups to house his herders, leaving himself free to supervise the three sites and take occasional excursions.[36]

By this time, news of the sorrowful events at home had reached him. Roland, Jr., had died, and due to thirteen uncollectable loans her husband had made, Almira had lost the Grove. As of March 30, 1861, the date of foreclosure, the widow had been left without inn or farm on which she could support herself, her teenage daughter, and her blind father-in-law, age seventy-four. The court had granted Almira only $254.63 from the estate, deducting from that sum twenty dollars she had already spent for her husband's coffin and another six dollars for "Horses & Hearse for funeral." For sustenance, the three proud Iveses were forced to rely upon Albert, and whatever help George could send.[37]

Throughout his sojourn of the West, George had kept in contact with his family, always notifying them of his latest address. And as a tribute to his home state, he had named a stream flowing through one of his ranches "Wisconsin Creek." Consciously or not, he seemed to be recreating his childhood environment, inviting passing travelers to spend the night at his ranch and, the following morning, cooking breakfast for both crew and guests. Just as during the harvest season at the Grove — when customers filled all beds and spilled out into the clearing — on any autumn morning of 1863, a ring of shaggy heads might be seen emerging from a ring of blankets that encircled the Ives ranch wickiups.[38]

Though George may have enjoyed showing off his cooking expertise at breakfast, he took dinner and supper at boardinghouses. When overseeing the Virginia City office, he ate with a family who resided in a large log cabin on Wallace Street. "Because my father was a freighter," Molly Sheehan wrote, we "were well provisioned and always set as good a table as was possible in a remote mining town. My stepmother's and Ellen's dried apple pies and dried peach pies were rare delicacies, much in demand." Opposite her at the table, Molly was accustomed to seeing such notables as the "discovery men," Bill Fairweather and Henry Edgar, but the guest she remembered most distinctly was George Ives. "Childlike," Molly admitted, "my attention was directed to him because of the long blue soldier's overcoat which he wore. From admiring that I went on to notice that he stood head and shoulders above most of the men who gathered around our table, that unlike the others he was smooth-shaven, and that he was blonde and handsome."[39]

PETE DALEY'S RANCH HOUSE. *Photo by Boswell*

When at the Wisconsin Creek ranch, George frequently ate at Mrs. Daley's table. Though Pete Daley's log residence and stage stop was smaller and cruder than the Ives Grove inn, it bore a strong resemblance to George's former home. It was a long, two-story building with verandas on both floors. The Daleys also kept a saloon below and held dances above. As pioneer George Bruffey's memoirs make clear, George Ives came to feel at home with the owners:

We had a short, pleasant, never-to-be-forgotten visit with Pete Daylies. Our meal, the first at a table in the new land, consisted of beef and cabbage from the Bitter Root Valley, some two hundred miles to the northwest. George Ives was at the table with us. The conversation centered on vegetables, and Mrs. Daylies thought it possible to raise potatoes there, as those she had brought from Salt Lake were doing well, while George Ives thought one a fool to think of raising vegetables in a country where it frosted every month in the year.

Though George was only exhibiting his habit of "taking an interest in what was happening around him" as well as the ease he felt with the family, his comment exasperated the Daleys' other guest. "We gave up," Bruffey wrote, probably not realizing that George had spent years cultivating potatoes and qualified as an expert on the subject.[40]

George had a mixed reputation in the Gulch. Wilbur Sanders heard talk that the tall blond dressed in the long-tailed, blue military coat was "drunk in the towns with increasing frequency," and some merchants complained that George led his horse into their stores, selected the items he wanted, and then left, casually requesting that his purchases be put on the bill. They were afraid to deny him credit. There were also more serious charges against him — that he enjoyed firing at saloon lamps just to hear the crash and that he once demonstrated his horse's training by backing her into the window of a store.[41]

Yet other residents regarded the young businessman as a "perfect gentleman." Molly Sheehan claimed that George had pleaded with John Wagner not to rob her father of his heavy buckskin purses during his freighting trip to Salt Lake, for the sake of "Jim Sheehan's nice wife and two little girls." And attorney William Pemberton stated that "Ives was a young man of fine native ability, decidedly prepossessing in appearance, who never touched whiskey. He had an office in the same building as I and tended well to his business."[42]

Despite George's many friends and supporters, the stories of his revelry persisted, and they did him no good when his trouble arose. In December 1863, a Nevada City businessman who was hunting near Robert Dempsey's ranch stumbled upon the frozen body of young Nicholas Tiebolt. The victim lay on his face with his right arm under him and his left arm reaching above him, as if to clasp a willow branch. A shot had passed just above the left eye, and the wrists and neck seemed to bear rope markings. The hunter left the corpse displayed in a wagon on Nevada City's main street for some time, and few citizens missed seeing it. Miner John Grannis, who had come down from Summit to board his oxen, wrote in his diary on December 16: "Saw a Dead man that was found Dead on Stink water."[43]

Outraged citizens refused to wait for officials to investigate the crime, but instead formed a posse and rode to the Wisconsin Creek ranch, located six miles from where the body had been found. In the gray light of dawn, they arrested George's herder, "Long John" Franck, as he lay sleeping amidst comrades inside the wickiup. The herder had become suspect by refusing to help the hunter load Nick's body in the wagon. "I did not do it, boys," Long John stated. One posse member pulled a pistol, handling the weapon and saying,

"You had better look out for another world." According to one report, they then "took him secretly to a convenient place, and putting a rope around his neck, with one end over the limb of a tree, slightly elevated him, which was repeated the fifth time, when he was nearly strangled to death. This . . . brought him to his senses." Whatever the means of intimidation, Long John Franck eventually volunteered the information that his employer, George Ives, had done the killing.[44]

Some posse members were in favor of immediately arresting George, while others lay down their shotguns, stating that they did not believe Ives would commit a murder and therefore would not participate in his arrest. But the rest of the posse turned their weapons upon the dissenters, forcing them to acquiesce. Seeing himself surrounded by a circle of heavily armed men, George agreed to accompany them to Virginia City, even though they had no arrest warrant. First, however, he insisted on preparing breakfast for all present. After his guests and the posse had eaten, he saddled a spotted, bobtailed pony and with the others crossed the icy creek and took the seven-mile stretch that led to the main roadway. At Dempsey's ranch, the party arrested an additional suspect named George Hilderman and then proceeded east through the Stinking Water Valley. It was impossible, Dimsdale claimed, for horsemen "mounted on fleet cayuses, on the magnificent natural roads" to resist the temptation to race. At the end of one contest, the bobtailed pony suddenly spurted ahead of the pack, continuing on at top speed. The arresters spurred their mounts into pursuit and finally overtook the jaded bobtail in a rocky ravine. They discovered their unarmed prisoner crouching behind a boulder, but when they drew on him and ordered him to come out, one reported later, George obeyed with "a light and careless laugh." Though some of the guard wished to hang him on the spot, others insisted on holding a trial first. For the rest of the trip into town, the prisoner "rode with his hands tied behind him and his feet tied one to the other beneath the horse's belly . . . the halter . . . suggestive of the hanging to come."[45]

A hanging was precisely what many citizens were eager to witness. They had spent half a day viewing the scavenger-exposed flesh of the young orphan's corpse. "I remember well," one viewer wrote, "the angry crowd that gathered around the pathetic sight, and the excitement it caused through the gulch." Then the twenty-six armed

riders, forming a hollow square around their prisoners, arrived, raising the already existing excitement to a feverish pitch. On seeing
the "angry crowd," George expressed the fear that he could not get
a fair trial in Nevada City, but his captors refused to take him on to
Virginia City.[46]

The trial commenced on December 19, 1863, a Saturday. Since
dawn, residents of the Gulch towns had been streaming into Nevada
City. Though many were hoping to witness an execution, others
were George's friends, who had arrived to express their outrage at
the charge against him. By ten o'clock, more than a thousand over-
coated men stomped about in the half-frozen mud of a sunless main
street. It was afternoon before proceedings got under way. By then
the sun had broken through the clouds hovering over the surrounding snow-covered mountains, but the feeble rays did little to relieve
the bitter cold. Court reporter Pemberton had to slip on a pair of
gloves to keep his fingers limber enough to write. Two massive freight
wagons drawn up before a two-story log building on the east side of
the street served as witness box and a bench for Judge Don Byam
and Associate Judge Wilson. Near the wagons, court officers built a
large bonfire from cord wood confiscated from an absent owner.
Twenty-four jurors sat on benches arranged in a semicircle about
the fire, and the two court reporters occupied a small bench and
table next to them. Surrounding the open-air court, one hundred
guards, armed with shotguns and rifles, restlessly paced.[47]

Prosecuting attorney Wilbur Sanders called the hunter who had
discovered the body as his first witness, and William Palmer, a
hurdy-gurdy house owner, scrambled onto the tall wagon. The rough-
garbed young Englishman perched upon the high box-seat presented
a rather bizarre picture. Despite the cold, he was bareheaded, and
his hair was so long that it dangled upon his shoulders. He spoke in
a loud, clear voice, relating that he had shot a prairie chicken which
fell to earth near the frozen remains of Nick Tiebolt. George Ives —
bound in logging chains secured with padlocks — sat calmly listening to the testimony.[48]

Since the prosecution wished to link the defendant to the two
stage robberies that had occurred the past fall, Sanders next called
several witnesses who claimed "that Ives had spent weeks along the
line of exit out of the country where treasure was carried." However, George's *presence* along the stage route was all Sanders could
substantiate, so dropping that tactic, he summoned his star witness.

George Bruffey had not heard about the trial, but happened to wander into town just at that precise moment, finding Nevada City "in a great commotion" over the appearance of Long John Franck. Spectators who had grown bored with lackluster minor witnesses and retreated to stores and saloons for some refreshment were pouring out of main street businesses and craning their necks to catch a glimpse of the mysterious witness who had been kept in hiding. Long John did not disappoint them. As Bruffey watched the tall, unkempt, "cadaverous-looking" man climb to the box, he concluded that the star witness was "one of the worst-looking men he had ever seen." Another observer, close enough to get a good view because he was acting as guard, noted that "Long John was looking particularly uncomfortable in his exalted position of an Informer."[49]

Sanders instructed Franck to describe "the circumstances of the killing," and, though Long John had not been present at Tiebolt's murder, he proceeded with his narrative. In early December young Nick had come to the wickiup Long John shared with his Indian wife and asked for his livestock. On the boy's arrival, George Ives, Alex Carter, and Tew Crow were also present at the ranch. After examining the written order, Long John rounded up the two large, silky-coated mules and delivered them to their owner. Ives then calculated the boarding bill, and Nick opened a buckskin purse, containing about four hundred dollars, and shook out the appropriate amount of gold dust. Then he mounted one mule and rode down the valley, heading toward the Alder Gulch road. As he watched Nick depart, Ives commented to the others that "it was a pity to let all that money go and the mules also." Then he tossed a gold coin in the air, said the lot fell to him, and rode after Nick. Ives trailed his victim for six miles, Franck claimed, and then holloed. As Nick turned around, Ives shot him in the head, collected the buckskin purse and the mules, and "in a short time" was back at the ranch. Long John was the only person who had seen Ives return with his plunder, since Carter and Crow had "disappeared in a jiffy" after the coin toss.[50]

With Franck's testimony, the prosecution rested its case. The defense now faced the difficult task of establishing an alibi for a murder committed on an unknown date. Nevertheless, Honest Whiskey Joe did testify that George Ives was elsewhere on the estimated date of the murder, and George Brown, a bartender and rancher, attested that it had been Alex Carter, not George Ives, who had delivered Tiebolt's mules to the Big Hole ranch some time after Nick's disappearance. Throughout the defense's presentation, an unruly audience interrupted with "cat-calls and other signs of disapproval." And though defense attorneys, who had themselves been drinking, protested the lack of court decorum, the judges overruled their objections. In closing, the defense reminded the court that they had not had sufficient time to summon needed witnesses, and that the plea for more time had been dismissed as a mere technicality. Though George Ives must have realized that things were looking rather grim for him, he remained, as he had throughout the proceedings, quiet, mannerly, and "without apparent anxiety."[51]

On the third day, the lawyers presented their arguments, and at 5:00 P.M. the judges dismissed the twenty-four jurors for deliberation. The two scribes, Pemberton recalled, "were carried along by the jury so that in the event of any dispute as to the testimony, we could refer to our notes. We were placed in the corner of the large jury room of a log cabin, and the jury proceeded to ballot." But the services of the court reporters were not needed; there was only one ballot.[52]

To the hundreds waiting in the street, the twenty-minute deliberation may have seemed much longer. Darkness was settling into the narrow valley, bringing with it an added chill. Guards continued their ceaseless marching, and behind them the crowd shifted about restlessly. George, wearing his blue soldier coat, sat gazing into the fire, quietly waiting to hear the words that would either restore his freedom or take his life. Only he appeared "unmoved." At last the jurors appeared at the door of the cabin and filed back to their benches, the orange flames of the bonfire tinting their stern, tight-lipped features. Then the foreman passed a signed report to Judge Byam, who read aloud: "Guilty."[53]

But the voting, Byam noted, had not been unanimous. One juror, known as "a thoroughly honest and conscientious man," had stated that he "could not vote against his conscience," and he was "not satisfied that the evidence showed Ives to be guilty of the murder of Tiebalt." But prosecutor Sanders was determined not to let victory slip through his fingers; he hopped onto the wagon and addressed the crowd: "The dissenting juror is one of the road agents, beyond all reasonable doubt. I advise hanging the prisoner immediately. There are many lawless people assembling to free him." The judges deemed that the responding ayes were louder than the nays and sent Sheriffs Robert Hereford and Adriel Davis to prepare the gallows.[54]

Ives rose from his bench and, though hampered by his leg chains, began working his way through the throng. When he reached Sanders, he clasped him by the hand. "Colonel, I am a gentleman," George said, "and I believe you are, and I want to ask a favor which you alone can grant."

"If there was any tremor in his voice," Sanders recalled, "I did not detect it, and the great crowd . . . was hushed into profound silence."

"If our places were changed, I know I would grant it to you," George went on, "and I believe you will to me. I have been pretty wild away from home, but I have a mother and sister in the States, and I want you to get this execution put off till tomorrow morning. I will give you my word and honor as a gentleman that I will not undertake to escape, nor permit my friends to try to change this matter."[55]

Sanders refused the request. Slowly, George returned to his seat and commenced composing a letter to Almira, but he was constantly interrupted by friends, many in tears, who wished to bid him goodbye. He was able to write but one sentence: "I am surrounded by a mob who are going to hang me, and I am seizing the few moments which remain of my life to write you." Then the sheriffs returned to perform the execution. Since to die with boots on would have suggested that he was guilty of murder, George asked the guards for a pair of moccasins. But when they placed them upon his chained feet, he became chilled and asked that they restore the boots. "Do you have any final requests?" Sheriff Hereford asked.

"I'd like to speak to Long John," George responded.[56]

But the sheriffs refused. They pinioned the condemned man's hands behind him and signaled guards to draw closer, "A rope," one guard later wrote, "was placed about Ives' neck and thus decorated he was marched in the center of a solid body of men bristling with guns in slow procession to a large log house in course of construction." As spectators clambered atop nearby buildings for a better view, the sheriffs ordered George to walk onto a plank balanced on dry goods boxes. When he reached the end of the plank, Sheriff Hereford looped the rope over a beam and then asked for final words. "By this time," a guard recounted, "the moon had risen and shed a bright light upon the weird scene below. The crowd now hushed about him, with upturned faces, awaited what he had to say."

"Alex Carter killed the Dutchman," George said.

"As he stood there well up in the sight of everyone," the guard went on, "he was for all a pathetic figure. A fine handsome young fellow in his military cloak, wonderfully cool and brave in danger, a born leader of men, . . . he had the making of a hero in him. . . . There was no cringing . . . but at the last dread moment his thoughts wandered away to his home . . . where his widowed mother waited news." George's last words made a deep impression upon the guard; he spoke them clearly and without a tremor in his voice: "Tell my mother I died an innocent man."[57]

Above him, every roof was covered with observers, and, from the crowd standing below, a chant arose: "Hang him! Hang him!" In response, sympathizers shouted back, "Hang Long John! Hang Long John!" Those who opposed the sentence surged forward, and guards surrounding the gallows leveled shotguns and stood ready to fire. Overwhelmed by the confusion, Sheriff Hereford stepped back to the safety of the building and shouted to the guards, "What do you say, boys, shall we hang him?" Receiving no response, the sheriff continued to hesitate. But two of the guards standing near a dry goods box gave it a quick yank.[58] George fell, hitting the end of the rope and twisting slowly, his face turned upwards, unseeing blue eyes staring at the bright moon. "His neck is broken," Judge Byam said. "He is dead."[59]

The guards, who had become so excited that the slightest movement or noise might have drawn their fire, clicked their locks, and the crowd went wild, screaming and knocking each other to the ground as they fled. But no shooting occurred, and the turmoil gradually subsided, a strained silence taking its place. For one hour, George's body swung in the cold night air. Then a doctor pronounced him dead, and officials cut the body down, carried it to a wheelbarrow shop, and placed it upon a bench. The following morning, friends held a burial service on cemetery hill, just above the main street. Ironically, it was Forefathers' Day. Thus while the Ives families who had remained in the security of Massachusetts and Connecticut were celebrating the day the Pilgrims first set foot on the wilderness soil, the native New Englander who had come West was laid beneath the ground in the wilds of Idaho Territory.[60]

COMMENTARY ON THE STORY OF GEORGE IVES

The Nevada City trial held in December 1863 was not sufficiently impartial to render a just verdict regarding Ives's guilt. The public display of Nick's scavenger-torn body had aroused the community to an unthinking vengeance. All accounts reflect the atmosphere of predetermined guilt: "Ives . . . was universally recognized as the principal culprit" even before the trial, Sanders wrote, and Dimsdale alluded to "an instinctive and unerring conviction that the worst man in the community was on trial." In addition, William Clark, who organized the arrest posse, had previously engaged in a violent quarrel with George.[61]

Not only was the mood inappropriate for a fair hearing, but in the open-air court, the defendant received unfair treatment from start to finish. Certain members of the defense team were intoxicated, but even had they been sober, they did not have time to prepare a case. The judges denied the motion to "delay the matter until the sense of offended justice had somewhat died out of the community; till opportunity had been afforded to ascertain who were the witnesses." And the practice of overruling the defense's objections continued throughout the trial.[62] Also, the pro-hanging faction of the audience harassed defense witnesses and attorneys and hurried the proceedings along simply because standing in the street was cold and tiresome. The existing hostility between North and South worked its way into the trial, resulting in the Unionists siding against the defendant. To Ives's disadvantage, guard Reginald Stanley wrote, the Union men were in the majority.[63]

As for the single witness who gave information about the murder, he admitted to having been six miles from the scene of the crime. He offered his testimony to save his own life. In regards to the jury's verdict, ignoring the dissenting juror's vote violated the safeguard built into the justice system specifically to protect the accused in such instances of potential injustice. While the dissenting juror had listened to all testimony, the street crowd who voted for an immediate hanging had spent the three days of the trial shifting about town and imbibing. In consequence, they were not qualified to vote on a man's life. Bruffey's statement that Long John "swore positively that Ives killed the Dutchman" suggests that some of the audience may not have been aware that Long John made no claim to having witnessed the murder.[64]

The lone juror appeared justified in concluding that the prosecution had not proven its case. Certain questions were left unanswered: who first suggested that Ives was Tiebolt's murderer, Long John Franck or William Clark? and how did Alex Carter obtain the two mules he delivered to the Big Hole ranch after Nick's death? Ives's request to speak with Long John after the trial suggests a desire on his part to clarify in his own mind his employee's testimony. George's statement on the gallows convinced many that Alex Carter was indeed the murderer. Yet when one of the defense attorneys denounced the hanging, authorities promptly locked him in jail. The Vigilantes, who formed soon after, accepted Ives's accusation of Carter as truth. An Oregon correspondent who reported Alex Carter's lynching claimed that Alex did confess to killing Tiebolt. Even Nelson Story, Sr., one of the guards who pulled the box out from under George Ives, wrote that it was "Alexander Carter, who killed the Dutchman."[65]

Reportedly, Henry Spivey, the juror who voted not guilty, stated that "if Ives had been tried as a road agent, he would have voted for his conviction." The comment is puzzling since prosecutor Sanders wrote that he did not put any stage drivers on the stand.[66] Though George was never charged with a stage robbery during his life, after the hanging Dimsdale prepared a list of crimes attributed to Ives. His first robbery, Dimsdale charged, was stealing mules while employed at Fort Walla Walla. Reinhart also mentioned this alleged crime in his memoirs: "George Ives . . . was government herder the hard winter and stole over 150 mules and horses and run them off and reported them dead; . . . he and a man named Stubbs run them to British Columbia." Stubbs was a rancher from the Touchet River, near Walla Walla, and he and a companion were killed while attempting to spirit a government herd across the Canadian border. But the problem in linking Ives and Stubbs is that George was not employed at Fort Walla Walla, as Dimsdale and Reinhart believed, but at a garrison four counties distant. Reinhart's memoirs incorporate both reliable and unreliable information, and it is impossible to determine into which of the two categories the passage quoted above falls.[67]

Second, Dimsdale claimed, Ives committed robberies in the Snake River Valley under the alias of Lewis. Yet Sanders, who at the trial introduced evidence of George's travels, wrote that the Snake River robberies could not "be traced to any particular person," and that "there was no definite proof . . . of Ives' complicity."[68]

Next on Dimsdale's list was the October 1863 stage holdup, in which two men wearing hoods and blankets intercepted the coach shortly after it left Rattlesnake Station. Dimsdale maintained that the two robbers were Ives and Frank Parish, but the stage driver disagreed. And Langford's informants agreed with the driver rather than Dimsdale. They identified the Rattlesnake robbers as Parish and Bob Zachary. Since the culprits not only wore disguises, but also spoke with "a feigned voice and dialect," it is understandable that their identity was uncertain.[69]

In regards to the fourth incident, Dimsdale and Langford agreed that Ives was one of the disguised party that robbed young Henry Tilden on Horse Prairie on the night of November 14, 1863. In reality, no robbery occurred on that occasion. All who heard Tilden's story reported that the boy was carrying no money at the time.[70]

The next of Ives's reputed exploits was the second holdup of the Virginia City-Bannack stage. Again, robbers wore blankets and masks, but this time they also covered their horses with blankets "from the ears to the tail." A pistol taken from a stage passenger, Dimsdale stated, was found in the possession of one of the men in the wickiup at the time of George's arrest at Wisconsin Creek. Langford reported that Ives once boasted to a stage driver, "I am the Bamboo chief that committed that robbery," but Langford did not name the driver who reported the conversation.[71]

Dimsdale also attributed to Ives the brutal slaying of an unknown man. The assailant supposedly perpetrated the crime in broad day-light on the road near Cold Spring ranch, firing a double-barreled shotgun at his victim. But since the buckshot had been badly loaded, it did not even pass through an overcoat, and the highwayman coolly drew his revolver and shot the man through the head. The shoot-ing, however, was not reported to authorities, and Dimsdale did not state who witnessed it.[72]

Though Dimsdale's roster of crimes is based on hearsay, some pioneers have left firsthand accounts. The most condemning is that of Anton Holter, who on December 8, 1863, encountered two high-waymen in the Stinking Water Valley. One of them ordered Holter to hand over his purse, but after he complied, the robber fired at him. "Instantly I dodged as the shot went, receiving the full force of

the unexploded powder in my face," Holter wrote. "I regained my
senses and faced Ives, who had his pistol lowered, but raised it with
a jerk, pointing it at my breast. I heard the click of the hammer,
but it missed fire." Holter did not mention whether the highwaymen
wore disguises, but even if they did not, he would not have known
them. A native Iowan, Holter had arrived in Alder Gulch only one
day previous. He concluded later that the two men were Ives and
Irvin because the bartender who worked at Laurin's ranch told him
that the pair had that same day fired at his bottle display. On hearing Ives was on trial for robbery and murder, Holter rushed to
Nevada City to identify the defendant, but arrived after Ives had
been buried. Holter did not have the opportunity to view the man
he suspected of having robbed him two weeks earlier. Thus his
story does not conclusively prove Ives a robber, but it does support
the defense's contention that there had not been sufficient time before
the trial to summon witnesses.[73]

An early freighter also left a firsthand account of a holdup conducted by Ives. George W. Goodhart, who was traveling with the
Moody train when it was robbed in December 1863, wrote years
after that the party had noticed two suspicious riders trailing them.
"That was Dutch John and George Ives," a companion informed
Goodhart, "and they are the two worst road agents there are." The
assault soon followed. "George Ives sat on his horse," Goodhart
related, "and held his shotgun on us and waved it back and forth
and said that if we moved he would fill us with buckshot." After the
party successfully repelled the robbers, Goodhart received as his
share of the recovered booty Dutch John's saddle and a twenty-dol-
lar bill covered with blood.[74] It is to be hoped that Goodhart's mental image of Ives wielding a shotgun in his face is inaccurate, because
the Montana Vigilantes hanged Stephen Marshland for that crime!

Conrad Kohrs and C. A. Broadwater both told stories about
encounters with Ives, but since they are so similar, we will relate
only one. In February 1863, Broadwater rode from Bannack "with
$5,000 in gold dust in his belt." As he approached Deer Lodge Val-
ley, he came upon Ives and John Cooper seated at their camp fire.
They wanted to join him, but he was suspicious and hurriedly
returned to the trail. At the summit of a hill, he turned back and
observed them saddling their horses. From that point on, he "commenced a handicapped race for his life." Glancing back from time
to time, he noted that the two riders were gaining on him. Though

he expected his tired mount to collapse at any moment, he continued spurring it. Behind him came "the thunder of the hoofs"; each
moment he anticipated "the report of the gun which would end his
existence." But no report came. On reaching the Contway ranch,
Broadwater's horse "dropped from exhaustion," but Ives and Cooper rode up to the cabin "nonchalantly." When Contway's Indian
wife offered to prepare her guests a meal, Broadwater recounted,
"Ives said he would like some flapjacks for breakfast and if the squaw
would show him where the flour was he would mix the batter. 'I can
beat the champion flapjack carpenter in the territory,' " he boasted.
While Ives was turning flapjacks, Broadwater hurried to the pas-
ture, obtained a fresh horse, and sped to his own camp. Later Contway informed Broadwater that after breakfast they had spotted him
"riding at full speed" in the distance. "That feller seems to be in a
hurry," Ives commented "unconcernedly."[75] The reader must judge
whether such tales describe a robbery attempt.

In addition to his own story of a jaded horse outrunning Ives's
fleet, long-legged mount, Conrad Kohrs provided a second anecdote which not only illustrates Ives's generosity, but also includes a
confession to robbing the stages. Kohrs, whose January 1864 ride
with Montana Vigilantes revealed his individual bias, claimed that
he once met George and friends in a Virginia City saloon. They
treated Kohrs several times, and then he invited them to have a
drink on him. "George Ives," Kohrs remembered, "stepped in saying, 'No, Con, this is my way. When my money is gone we will
make the old stage coach come down with some more.' " Kohrs considered this remark "a rather frank admission of the source" of
George's income.[76]

Francis Goss's claim that Ives planned to rob the Sun River
farm, when actually George was on the western side of the mountains, demonstrates the necessity of approaching early accounts with
a certain amount of skepticism. It is difficult to assess a man's guilt
of a crime when he was never placed on trial. One accusation made
by Dimsdale, however, is *not* true. George did not send his mother
the false news that he had been killed by Indians. Almira Ives received
no such letter, nor did she receive the few lines George penned to
her just before his death. And despite her financial distress, Almira
did not receive any of her eldest son's estate. At Wilbur Sanders's
suggestion, the miners' court appropriated George's property to pay
those who conducted the trial and to reimburse guards for board

and room. Three and a half years after the Nevada City hanging, George's great-uncle, Edward Ives, was still attempting to locate his nephew through newspaper ads, probably to inform him of the deaths of Almira and Roland, Sr.[77]

George Ives's trial is of historical importance because it marks the point at which pro-vigilance forces came into power, but it did not establish who murdered Nicholas Tiebolt. Ives may or may not have killed Nick for a pouch of gold dust. Like his great-grandfather, Captain David Ives of the Southwick militia, George would "take his sentence in the world unknown." But if during the years spent in the West, George came to have more regard for gold than for human life, it was a decided departure from the future one would have predicted for the fair-haired boy who reared orphan cubs and worked like a man at his parents' inn in the Wisconsin wilderness.

SIX

OTHER DESPERADOES

OTHER DESPERADOES

To broaden the base of our study of desperadoism, we will make brief surveys of eleven other men: Brockey, Matt Bledsoe, Charley Harper, Nelson Scott, William Peebles, David English, James Crow, George Skinner, Charley Ridgley, Charley Reeves, and William Riley.

WILLIAM WINTERS, ALIAS "BROCKEY"

When James Marshall discovered gold at the Coloma mill, William was only ten years old. Ten years later, the New York boy's dream of becoming rich in California would culminate at San Quentin. While working as a laborer in San Francisco, he was convicted of an unnamed felony, receiving the minimal sentence of one year. The prison register describes the twenty year old as being five foot nine and having brown hair, blue eyes, "sharp" features, and a "light" build. His body was riddled with scars—suggesting that he had seen his share of knife fights—and his face was "much marked with small pox." Ironically, just above the right wrist he wore the tattoo "Hope."[1]

He entered state prison on November 27, 1858, escaped the following July, and, after two weeks of freedom, returned to serve his term. On release, Winters assumed the name Brockey and migrated to Washington Territory. In the spring of 1862 he joined the stampede to Florence, arriving before Cherokee Bob, Cynthia Williams, Bill Mayfield, and George Ives.[2] When a mid-August gambling spree ended in a sunrise brawl, Brockey fired his revolver at a man named Hickey. Though the shot missed the intended victim, it killed another man, and Brockey immediately surrendered himself to the peace officer. At the ensuing trial, he was acquitted, reportedly on grounds that "the shot was accidental and did not hit the person he intended to kill." One juror remarked that "good citizens" believed that "Brockey had done a good thing," but "if he had killed two of the ruffians instead of one, and then hung himself, good men would have been better pleased."[3]

Following his acquittal at Florence, Brockey established a ferry on Slate Creek, but soon became involved in another altercation. While making purchases at the store of Arthur Chapman, the son of Oregon's surveyor general, Brockey argued with the proprietor and drew his bowie knife. As Brockey advanced with the weapon in his hand, a Washington paper reported, Chapman "seized a hatchet and buried it in Brockey's skull. Brockey is said to be a notoriously bad man." At the news of his death, a Sacramento paper volunteered the information that "Brockey was an old California convict and his loss will be least regarded where he is best known."[4]

Winters's attempt to assume a new identity after leaving San Quentin had been no more successful than his efforts at the California goldfields. Though at his death at age twenty-four, the lean, pock-marked young man had not attained the wealth he had "hoped" for upon leaving his home in the East, the above obituaries reveal that during his years in the West, he had achieved notoriety.

MATT BLEDSOE

Like Brockey, Matt Bledsoe arrived at the Salmon River mines under stigma of being a bad man: a "bloody character" and "notorious freebooter," who had "killed several persons" in California and Oregon. The reputation may have arisen from his own boasting, because on arrival at Florence, the gray-eyed, pleasant-voiced young Texan had no criminal record. In fact, he was the second cousin of the much-respected Captain Bledsoe, a messenger for Wells Fargo. Matt usually behaved like a gentleman, but when aroused, he displayed a temper as fiery as his curly red hair.[5]

He reached Florence before the great stampede. Though by December the heavy snows had not yet arrived, the weather was still too cold to wash pay dirt. The realization that phenomenal profits awaited seemed to make the long, dull days drag by even more slowly, and the living expenses in the mountain camp were exorbitant: "Dr. Farber," one resident complained, "charged me $150 for three bottles of medicine." Searching for a little action, Matt descended the mountain and, at a camp at the mouth of Slate Creek, entered a card game in progress. His winning hands greatly provoked an Elk City packer named James Harman, but the two men parted that night without any outbreak of violence. On the following morning, however, Harman renewed hostilities, and, in the heat of the argument, Matt shot the packer in the head, killing him instantly. Believing he was innocent by reason of self-defense, Bledsoe rode to Walla Walla and gave himself up for trial. A jury acquitted him.[6]

A year and a half later he traveled to Boise Basin and there joined a volunteer company of Indian fighters. Captain Jefferson Standifer, who had met Matt in Florence, selected him as his lieutenant, and, under their leadership, the company won fame through a series of skirmishes with the natives on the Snake and Malheur rivers. During these battles, early residents claimed, Captain Standifer proved to be "brave as a lion," and though his men killed several enemy warriors, they themselves suffered but two minor casualties. One of the wounded was Madison Bledsoe, who received "a glancing shot across the forehead, knocking him down."[7]

On recovery, Matt journeyed to Eugene, Oregon, where, in a quarrel that reportedly was "caused directly by the whiskey traffic," he shot and killed one Hugh Feney. Again, a jury acquitted him, and he moved on to California to participate in what appeared to be his final affray: "Mat. Bledsoe was killed in Placerville last week by Dr. I. H. Harris," an Oregon paper reported. "Bledsoe shot at Harris, whereupon Harris stabbed him to the heart with a knife."[8]

Rather than dying, Matt made a quick recovery and returned to Oregon to open a gambling hall and saloon. While serving his customers, he frequently mentioned his Indian fighting experiences, but his Umatilla County listeners were not impressed. Because of the Civil War, antipathy for Southern sympathizers was quite strong. Residents could not forget the time Matt had passed Meacham's Hotel and noticed a small boy waving an American flag. Jerking the tiny flag from the child's hand, Matt snapped its staff in half, threw the banner to the ground, and trampled it in the dust. Also, rumor had it that Matt used marked cards at his gaming tables, and as for Standifer's Volunteers, they had been a "terror" to the law-abiding people of the Boise Basin. "Mat used to brag about killing Indians," one critic wrote, "but all he ever killed were old men,

squaws and papooses." And when they were not engaged in mas-
sacres, the detractor went on, the "infamous" Sagebrush Rangers "stole
horses."

The redheaded Rebel had at least one admirer, however. Unfor-
tunately, she was the wife of Mose Milner, who carefully guarded
his young bride. Despite his wariness of Mose's skill with a weapon,
Matt could not stay away from Mrs. Milner, who was described as
"plump as a quail, with dark eyes, abundant black hair, a wonderful smile and as pretty as a picture." One night, Matt dropped by
the Milner's house, stayed for supper, and afterwards invited Mose
to a game of cards. When Milner accused Matt of cheating, both
men drew revolvers, but the gambler was quicker. As on the other
occasions, a jury acquitted Matt. The plump, raven-haired widow
became Matt's "woman."[9]

Bledsoe's next scrape occurred on the streets of Portland. He
was accompanying two women to an oyster saloon one Friday night
when a bartender accosted him, claiming one of the women belonged
to him. As the bartender pulled a knife, Matt struck him on the
head with the butt of his pistol, knocking him to the boardwalk.
The injured man arose, entered the saloon and washed the blood
from his face and head, and then retired for the night. On Saturday
morning, friends discovered the bartender lying "lifeless" in his
bed.[10]

A jury found Matt guilty of murder in the second degree, and
the judge, after reviewing the defendant's past record, stated that it
was a "painful necessity" to pronounce a sentence of life imprisonment. On December 2, 1864, the night before he was to enter Oregon Penitentiary, Matt composed a letter in his jail cell: "I shall
always believe the act for which I was convicted was one entirely in
self-defense," he wrote. "I have received many marks of kindness
from the citizens of Portland, . . . hoping they will not view me in
the most discordant light, but will cast a mantle of charity over my
past conduct."[11]

He was twenty-four at the time of his conviction and was listed
on the prison register as having "dark red, inclined curly" hair,
"round, gray" eyes, and "sandy" complexion. His face was "thin,"
his carriage "straight," his speech "pleasant." He was five foot nine,
weighed one hundred forty-eight pounds, and wore a size seven
shoe.[12]

Despite the repentant tone of the letter written from the Portland jail, Matt escaped prison less than two years after his entry. Hindered by a thigh wound, he headed for Mexico, but got no farther south than Ashland, Oregon. There authorities placed him in heavy irons and shipped him back to prison on the stage. After having served six more years of his life term, he received a welcome Christmas gift from Governor S. F. Grover. On December 25, 1872, Bledsoe collected his "property" of one dollar cash and, with pardon in hand, walked through prison gates.[13]

The ex-convict returned to the Southwest, but only three and a half years after his departure, Oregonians again came across his name in the news: "Mat Bledsoe, who was well known over the northwest coast, was shot and killed a few weeks ago at a saloon in Prescott, Arizona." Madison Bledsoe was, as Mark Twain phrased it, "on the shoot" up until the moment of his death.[14]

WILLIAM BEST, ALIAS CHARLEY HARPER

Harper was known as "chief" of the goodly number of desperadoes who traversed the dogleg main street of Florence. And if the "dashing" young outlaw actually committed the crime for which he was lynched, he deserved his reputation for being "totally depraved."[15]

As defined in the *Compiled Laws of California* for 1853, robbery is the "violent taking of money, goods, or other valuable thing from the person of another, by force or intimidation," a crime punishable by a term of one to ten years, or death, at the discretion of the jury. William Best's jury chose not to execute him for committing robbery but to send him to prison for five years. The New York native entered San Quentin on June 30, 1855. He was twenty-six and had been working as a laborer. Only five foot six, he had fair complexion, blue eyes, and blond hair. His handsome features were slightly marred by a scar on the right nostril, and the skin of his right arm was badly disfigured by a burn, such as from scalding water.

It is not Best's appearance, but the violence of his first crime, that sets him apart from the other desperadoes examined in this study. His page of the prison register provides a random sample of the crimes and backgrounds of those who entered San Quentin the summer of 1855. Out of fifteen, Best was the only robber; two were guilty of manslaughter and twelve had committed nonviolent crimes

such as grand larceny, counterfeiting, forgery, and receiving stolen
goods. Two thirds of the convicts were in their twenties, and nearly
half were working as laborers at the time of their conviction. More
than half were foreign born, representing the following countries:
Chile, Ireland, East Indies, Mexico, and China.[16] This brother-
hood of international, mainly nonviolent criminals provided Best no
lessons in character building.

After serving his term, he left the state, using the alias of Charley
Harper. He spent the winter of 1861 in Walla Walla, and in the
spring rode to Florence. His story demonstrates the gulf between
the desperadoes' reputations and their actual exploits. Langford,
who wrote only thirty years after the events he described, perpetu-
ated the myth that Harper was a noted chief who, at the head of his
formidable robber band, made a grand entrance at Florence:

Mounted on strong, fleet horses . . . the criminal cavalcade with its chief
at the head dashed up the river valley, insulting, threatening, or robbing
every one so unfortunate as to fall in their way. . . . No crime was too
atrocious for them to commit, no act of shame or wantonness was
uncongenial to their grovelling natures. . . . They distributed themselves
among the saloons and bagnios, and by means of gambling and frequent
robberies, contrived to hold the community in fear.[17]

But during Harper's lifetime, he was not known as the leader of a
robber band. Instead, contemporary newspapers referred to him as
a lone horse thief who had the bad habit of sticking his nose in
"other peoples' business."[18]

In November 1862 the press announced a lynching near Lapwai:
"Another man is hanging to a tree, on the Florence road. His name
is supposed to be Chas. Harper."[19] Though the lynch party may
have been after Harper, he was not the man found hanging on a
limb near the Sweetwater forks; Charley was alive and well in
Colville. Two months later a correspondent dispatched an item regarding "one of the vilest, and most inexcusable murders" of which he
had ever heard. It had been committed in Colville, Washington
Territory, on the night of January 26, 1863. "A ball was given at a
house near the old fort, on the Columbia river," the reporter wrote,
"at which a large party of citizens from the surrounding neighborhood were present." As it neared midnight, "whiskey began to work
on a ruffian, known as Charlie Harper, who by the rowdy demon-
strations frequently interrupted the festivities." At 3:00 A.M. a young

housewife named Mrs. McRice left the hall to return home, but Harper followed after her, insisting she return and dance with him. When Mrs. McRice refused him, Harper followed her to her house and "there deliberately and without provocation shot her down like a dog. The ball entered the right side of the neck, ranging downwards toward the left shoulder, killing her instantly." The deceased, the article continued, "was a white woman, of a kind disposition, and an exemplary wife and mother."[20]

Mrs. McRice's murderer returned to the dance hall, retrieved his blankets, saddled his horse, and rode away. On the following day the local sheriff formed posses who went in pursuit. One of the groups tracked a man to a cabin situated on a hillside overlooking the Columbia. Since they were unable to approach without being fired upon, the posse members threatened to set fire to the cabin, whereupon its inhabitant surrendered. As they retraced their trail, with prisoner under heavy guard, they encountered a party of miners who by force took the prisoner into their own custody. There in the wilderness the miners gave the suspect a speedy trial, found a tree, and hanged him from a sturdy limb. Colville residents did not lament the lynching: "This fellow was an unmitigated villain and is known to have committed several murders."[21] Contrary to popular sentiment, it was lamentable that the miners did not return the suspect to Colville for trial in order to be certain that, this time, they were hanging the right man.

NELSON SCOTT, WILLIAM PEEBLES, AND DAVID ENGLISH

During the 1860s, H. H. Bancroft wrote, the highwaymen of the Salmon River mines used to paint their faces, "boldly and facetiously" proclaim themselves "knights of the road," and terrorize packers and merchants traveling between Florence and Lewiston. Among the road agents, Bancroft claimed, was a "mere boy" who ultimately "met violent death." The best known of the Florence robbers, however, was a trio of young men lynched more than a year prior to the execution of Renton, Romain, and Lowrey.[22]

None of the three men lynched in Lewiston in November 1862 had prison records, and all came from good families. Nelson Scott, born in 1835, was one of the younger children of an Illinois farm family. When twenty-one, he married a neighbor girl, age sixteen, and with his bride, aged parents, and teenage brother, migrated to Oregon. The first child of Nelson and his teenage wife — a son whom they named Francis — was born in Oregon. But soon after Francis's birth, Nelson, who had assumed the role of head of the extended household, relocated the family across the border to Siskiyou County, California. Here the Scotts settled into a farm home near the town of Callahan (located on the Scott River just west of the Scott Mountains), and the three adult males hired on as ranch hands for a wealthy Canadian. In 1860, Nelson's second child was born, a daughter whom the couple named Mary. Then the following year, the placer discovery at Pierce attracted the young father's attention. Leaving his wife and two small children in the care of his parents and brother, Nelson traveled to Washington Territory. During the "hard winter" of 1861–62, he and two new acquaintances named Peebles and English waited in Walla Walla for the late-breaking spring, whiling away the hours in the saloons.[23]

William Peebles was one year younger than Scott, having been born in Pennsylvania in 1836. When Bill was thirteen, William, Sr., joined the California gold rush, leaving his son in charge of the family. But after only three years, Bill, Jr., followed after his father, who was mining in Sacramento County. Though only sixteen, he staked out his own claim at Oregon Gulch in Trinity County. At the time he merged with the stream of miners and merchants rushing to the Washington goldfields, Peebles was twenty-five and, unlike his two companions, still unmarried.[24]

The youngest and most fascinating of the trio of alleged robbers was David English. Born in Missouri in 1839, he was the fourth child of a prominent family. The Englishes were among the twenty-seven devout Presbyterians who first organized a church on the border line between Clay and Platte counties in 1826. David, Jr.'s, father was a prosperous farmer, and his uncle a lawyer and mill owner. His aunt, Susan English, had married into the Todds, a prolific family who had pioneered the area. David's mother, Polly, was not only a Todd, but a sister to Aunt Susan's husband. Thus David, Jr., belonged to two highly respected, intermarried clans.[25]

The Todds had emigrated from England early in the 1700s, and in 1817 left Kentucky in search of new land. According to family tradition, David's Grandfather Todd and his brother had brought their wives and children "in wagons," and being attracted by "the lovely prairies and noble forests," homesteaded a fertile strip east of the Missouri River near present-day Platte City. They rolled and burned logs, replacing the timber with fields of golden wheat and orchards that produced "the finest apples grown in the West." Family members never left home without filling their saddlebags with fruit for their neighbors. Grandfather Todd, over six foot and weighing two hundred pounds, was known as an expert hunter and unerring rifleman. He possessed rare honesty and generosity, being the single farmer to offer to stand the loss for his grain when the mill flooded. On his death in 1851, he was buried in what the Todds called their "sacred graveyard."[26]

But even before Grandfather Todd's death, his daughter Polly and her husband, David English, Sr., had both died. The five English youngsters were separated, each going to live at the home of a different relative. At age two, the orphaned David, Jr., moved to the home of his mother's younger sister, Elizabeth Todd, who was married to Andrew Tribble. The couple had no living children at that time. The foster mother, only nineteen, was described as "intelligent, lively, and spirited, with a heart full of kindness for all." Her husband, age thirty-five, was a wealthy farmer and mill owner, and, as well, a "highly esteemed" elder of the church. The Tribbles provided David with a privileged yet religious upbringing, considering him the older brother of the four children later born to them.[27]

When but a teenager, the restless youth traveled West, taking up residence in Corvallis, Oregon, and there in 1860 marrying a girl from Illinois. David's bride, Elizabeth, was fourteen. Her new husband could not afford to buy her a home, and, since he could not find more suitable employment, was forced to settle for the job of a butcher. Still he was prudent enough to gradually accumulate savings amounting to four hundred dollars. With the news of the fabulously rich strike at Florence, he was off to Washington Territory, leaving wife and infant in Corvallis. But the long winter of 1861–62 kept the anxious gold seekers waiting at Walla Walla for much longer than they were prepared. Hoping to replenish his dwindling resources, David soon became known as a "desperate gambler." There is an unconfirmed rumor that the twenty-two-year-old husband and father fell in love with a Walla Walla woman and married her also. Thus when snow-packed trails were once more passable and David English rode for Florence with Scott and Peebles, he may have left behind a second bride.[28]

According to another rumor, the trio traveled with Charley Harper. If the following anecdote about a robbery they committed along the way was actually told by Nelson Scott, as Langford claimed, it reveals the former Illinois farm boy's idea of how a highwayman ought to behave. The robbers surrounded five miners, aimed cocked pistols at them, and gave the usual order: "Throw up your hands." As the miners handed over five purses, each holding as much as five hundred dollars, Scott noticed a boy sitting on a boulder and observing the action. "Come," Scott ordered the boy, "draw your weasel."

"How do you know I've got any?" the boy replied.

"Hand out your buckskin," Scott repeated.

"You wouldn't rob a poor little devil like me, would you?" the boy asked.

"Get off from that stone and shell out," Scott said, making a motion toward his gun, "or I'll blow your brains out."

At the final threat, the boy hopped up, dug into his pocket, and pulled out an empty purse. The robbers were so "pleased with the pluck and humor of the lad," that they "threw him a five-dollar piece" and then "galloped furiously on towards Florence." On reaching the basin at the top of the mountain, they "thundered" up main street, firing their pistols over their heads, and rode into the first saloon. Without dismounting, they ordered drinks all around, tossed a stolen purse on the counter for payment, and refreshed themselves. Then as quickly as they had come, they whirled their mounts about and galloped out of town.[29]

Their self-chosen title of "knights of the road" suggests a chivalric code which members of the order were expected to uphold, such as a constant display of courage, daring, and flamboyant generosity. George Ives had shown the latter trait while treating Kohrs in the Virginia City saloon. But the question of who created the image — the robbers by their actions or their chroniclers by their tales — remains unanswered.

Scott, Peebles, and English spent the summer of 1862 flitting back and forth across the 100-mile stretch between Florence and the supply center of Lewiston, their precise activities unknown. Then in October, the *Golden Age* reported, packers John and Joseph Berry left Florence, wound down the mountain, and with twelve hundred dollars in the bags slung over their saddle mules, started across Camas Prairie. There three masked men surprised them, demanding "their money or their lives." Though "well armed," the Berrys decided to hand over the gold dust.[30]

In this account of a documented robbery, there is no mention of subsequent revelry or displays of generosity. Instead, the three masked men rode from the area as fast as their horses could carry them. And rather than allowing the robbers to escape "unmolested," the Berrys enlisted help and rode in pursuit to recover their money. The brothers believed that the "one who stopped them" was Bill Peebles and that David English "was the one who kept his double barreled shot-gun on them." The identity of the third robber they ascertained later from other persons. Strange though it seems, the Berrys claimed that "they had known Nelson Scott for seven years," but he was the only one of the trio that they did not recognize. Instead, they identified the voices of Peebles and English, whom they had met "in Florence during the previous summer." The Berrys did not accuse Charley Harper, whom early historians labeled the robber chief of Florence, of any involvement.[31]

In Walla Walla a posse captured Peebles and Scott, but young Dave English had already departed for Corvallis, evidently hoping to make it back to his sixteen-year-old wife and small child with his share of the profit: four hundred dollars (the exact amount he had saved as a butcher before his venture to the mines). "Dave had got to Wallula," pioneer Reinhart recalled, "and was in a saloon gambling when Jim Buckley, the sheriff, had a man to go in and invite Dave to take a drink at the bar." When Dave stepped up to the counter and lifted the glass in his hand, the sheriff and a deputy handcuffed him, put him on the stage, and escorted him back to Walla Walla.[32]

On the three prisoners' arrival at Lewiston, residents met at the Luna House to discuss a trial, but the turnout was so large they had to reconvene at Arcade Hall. With the three suspects lodged in a vacant saloon under armed guard, thousands assembled and voted to allow the defendants counsel and a voice in selecting the jury. But on the following night, a hotelkeeper believed to be Peebles's friend attempted to free the prisoners. After receiving a shot in the arm, the hotelkeeper abandoned the attempt, but as the news spread through town, a mob commenced to form. Near midnight, three hundred men overpowered the guard, seized the three suspects, and hanged them from the ceiling joists.[33]

The editor of the *Washington Statesman* thought the lynching a just punishment since evidence obtained during the preliminary examination at Walla Walla was "most positive." However, he did not elaborate on the alleged evidence. Those who traveled the Florence road, the editor wrote, must "regard the lives of highwaymen as of no more value than that of the wild beast which awaits in his lair to spring upon the unwary." Historian John Hailey agreed with the Walla Walla editor that though there had been no trial, the "guilt" of the three men was "conclusive." Besides, Hailey added, "these three men had the reputation of having committed other robberies."[34]

The lynching left not only an unresolved question of guilt, but also two widows (possibly three, if Dave had two wives) and three fatherless children. Though the *Oregonian* reported that the bodies of Scott, Peebles, and English were carried to Florence and buried there on November 5, it seems doubtful that the three coffins made the long journey up the steep, winding trail to the mountain basin cemetery. In any case, the location of the graves is unknown. What is certain is that David English, twenty-three at the time of his death, was not laid to rest in the Todd's sacred burying ground with his Missouri ancestors.[35]

The lynching of Scott, Peebles, and English did not put an end to crime in the Lewiston area. An early history tells of another robbery on the Florence road the following month, more horse thievery on Camas Prairie, several known robberies and homicides, and "perhaps hundreds of which nothing was ever known." This pessimistic picture, however, must be balanced by the *Oregonian*'s claim that if robbery reports were limited to those that could be documented, few items would appear in the papers.[36]

JAMES CROW

Among the undocumented robberies of 1862 was the alleged holdup of "three travelers between Oro Fino and Lewiston" by Michael Mulkie, Jack McCoy, and James Crow. By the time Crow, a former resident of Texas, was arrested on some minor charge in Walla Walla in May 1863, he had already made a name for himself as a horse thief. Apparently, the characterization was accurate. Crow soon broke jail, traveling on foot and heading east. When two Indians from the Umatilla reservation passed him on horseback, he begged them to ride, just "until he was rested." One of the Indians kindly obliged him, dismounting and walking behind the two ponies. Later, the *Statesman* reported, "they came to a halt to light their pipes, and Crow rode leisurely off on the prairie without arousing the suspicion of the Indians." Then he suddenly "whipped up the horse and has not been heard from" since. The "irrepressible Crow," the editor remarked "is evidently at his old tricks and as full of inventions as he is of rascality."[37]

Riding the stolen pony, Old Tex — as acquaintances called him — crossed the Bitterroots and followed the June 1863 press to reach Alder Gulch. There he associated himself with several roughs he had known on the other side of the mountains. Thus when a passenger noticed Tex looking on as the Virginia City mail coach rolled out, he commented, "I am sorry to see that rascal watching us; he belongs to the gang. It bodes us no good." And when the stage pulled into Cold Spring ranch, some twenty miles distant, Tex was already there watching it roll in.

At 11:00 A.M. the following day, three masked and blanketed men surprised the stage just beyond Stone's ranch. The robbers relieved two passengers of a total of five hundred dollars and then suggested that the stage driver "Get up and skedaddle." Though none of the three robbers appeared to be Tex, it was rumored that he had acted as a spy. Still, no charges were preferred against him for having observed the stage's departure, or for having been on hand to witness its arrival at Cold Spring ranch.

But the following month, December 1863, Old Tex was once more at the wrong place at the wrong time. The posse who came to arrest Ives discovered Crow curled in a blanket outside Franck's wickiup. As Tex was "engaged in the highly necessary operation" of changing his undershirt, Dimsdale related, a posse member informed him that he was under arrest. "Tex denuded himself of his undergarment," Dimsdale went on, "and throwing it towards Tom Baume, exclaimed, 'There's my old shirt and plenty of graybacks. You'd better arrest them, too.'" Crow's lack of concern at the arrest was justified. After an examination, Nevada City officials released him, stating he had no connection to Tiebolt's murder.[38]

When he next encountered a posse, Tex was in a Deer Lodge saloon. On January 18, vigilante captain James Williams coaxed Tex into the street, pinioned his arms, and confined him for further questioning. But on the following day, the former Texan once more gained his freedom. Despite bitter cold and deep snow, he hurriedly departed, crossing the mountains to the safety of the Kootenai mines. During that January of 1864, few desperadoes were as fortunate as James Crow.[39]

GEORGE SKINNER, ALIAS WILLIAMSON AND WALKER

Among those the vigilantes hanged at Hell Gate was saloonkeeper Cyrus Skinner. Had George Skinner survived his California troubles, he might have swung from the corral fence alongside his brother. The Skinners' story bears some similarity to that of Edward and Charles Richardson — an older brother stumbling into a life of crime and a younger following in his footsteps. The Skinners, however, did not come from a prominent family. They were born on an Ohio farm — Cyrus in 1830 and George in 1832. Both were of medium build and had fair complexions, brown hair, and hazel eyes; Cyrus was five foot nine, George only five foot seven.[40]

When he accompanied his older brother West to acquire farmland, George was still a teenager. Cy settled in El Dorado County, California, but in 1851 received a two-year prison sentence for the crime of "Larceny and Burglary." He boarded the San Quentin brig as prisoner number 20. After his brother's imprisonment, George moved to town and found a job as a clerk, but it took him only a year to follow Cy's example. On November 20, 1852, prisoner 128 joined prisoner 20 on the brig, also charged with "Grand Larceny." He had without the use of "force or intimidation," stolen property valued at "fifty dollars or more." As Cy had done, George spared the family name by claiming that his surname was Williamson; perhaps authorities did not consider the initials "GDS," encompassed by an ornate wreath, which George wore on his left arm.[41]

At the time of his commitment, the brig was anchored off Point San Quentin, where the 100 inmates worked in the brickyard by day and by night crowded below deck into tiny compartments reeking of sweat, urine, and feces. George had the security of his older brother's presence for only nine months. In August 1853, Cy's term expired, and he moved to Yuba County, where he again acquired farmland. Within another nine months, however, he was back in prison, convicted of larceny for a second time. Prisoners now occupied the new facility, the Stones, but after putting in only a few months, Cy took advantage of the lack of an enclosing wall to make an escape. George, who had only one month to serve, wisely remained behind.[42]

On his discharge in November 1854, he assumed the alias Walker, the name Cy was using to conceal his identity. For nearly a year the two Skinners managed to stay out of trouble, but in the fall of 1855, George was arrested in connection with the Langton express robbery near Forest City. While awaiting trial at the Downieville jail, he escaped; both brothers were now fugitives from justice.[43]

Their luck ran out in the spring of 1856. In April Cy was accused of stealing thirteen mules and confined to the Auburn jail pending trial, and that same month George became a suspect in another stage robbery. On March 12, twelve disguised men had held up the Rhodes & Whitney express, making off with $16,000 worth of gold dust being transported from the Yreka mines. In hopes of receiving the reward offered for the robbers, three local officials searched an empty cabin situated on the bank of the American River about a mile from Folsom. In one bunk they discovered a gold watch taken from a Rhodes & Whitney passenger. Owners of the cabin were George Walker, a Swede named Adolph Newton, a teenage Mexican named Niconora Rodriguez, and an ex-convict named Bill Gristy, alias White. When officers found Adolph Newton at a restaurant in Folsom, he quickly surrendered, admitting he had stolen the gold watch from a stage passenger. The three reward seekers then donned disguises, armed themselves with double-barreled shotguns, and at 9:00 P.M., returned to the river cabin.

Details of the "desperate conflict" that followed came out during a coroner's inquest held on April 23, 1856, with George Walker's bloodied body lying in the next room. As policeman Robert Harrison and ex-officers Isaac Anderson and A. J. Barkley had approached the canvas-walled cabin, its inhabitants heard their footsteps and came outside with a lantern to search the bushes. Finding nothing, they reentered the cabin. The disguised officers crept closer, Barkley jerked open the door, and with shotguns cocked, Anderson and Harrison burst inside. "Now we have got you," Harrison cried, "surrender!" At the same time Anderson "gave a whoop" and leveled his gun at Walker. As George reached for his pistol, Harrison pulled the trigger. "I thought the whole contents of the gun went into his heart or side; he fell dead—do not think he even struggled,"

Harrison testified. George fell between the two officers, the blood from his wound "bespattering" their clothes. "I could see no one to shoot at then," Anderson added, "there was too much smoke."[44]

Gristy escaped in the smoke, but young Niconora, who was "running from one corner of the tent to another with a pistol in hand" was shot in the arm and thigh, handcuffed, and taken prisoner. The coroner reported that he had found "two porte-monnaies" containing "$240 in gold coin and sixty five cents in silver coin" on George's body. By his jewelry—"a gold ring with quartz specimen setting"—an officer identified Walker as the prisoner who had escaped the Downieville jail the previous year.[45]

George Skinner, alias Williamson and Walker, received a criminal's burial in Sacramento. While still incarcerated in the Auburn jail for mule theft, Cy learned of his younger brother's death. He claimed that authorities were wrong in thinking George had been involved in the March robbery, that his brother had only befriended Adolph Newton in order to enlist his aid in breaking Cy out of jail. Skinner's claim may have been true. A suspect named Carter confessed to the Rhodes & Whitney robbery and led officers to the cache. "In all about sixteen thousand dollars" in gold dust was recovered, the papers reported. Of the four men living in the canvas cabin, only Adolph Newton was convicted of "Highway Robbery."[46]

WILLIAM RIDGLEY

Though Cyrus Skinner and some twenty others fell victim to the Montana Vigilantes, one young man who had earned the reputation of a "gun-fighter" and "bad man" had departed the area just in the nick of time. William Ridgley was born in 1837 into a prolific Maryland family. At age thirteen, he ran away from home and, in New York, boarded the small brig *Orleans*, bound for California. Though in 1850 the usual passage time for the sixteen-thousand-mile route around Cape Horn ranged from four to eight months, the *Orleans* required nine. Disembarking in San Francisco on September 18, 1850, only nine days after California became a state, young Ridgley worked his way inland to Santa Clara County and there took advantage of his musical training to find work.[47]

His most likely place of employment was a saloon, a dire ambience for an impressionable adolescent. His first difficulty with the law came in Sacramento, where he was sentenced to several months aboard the brig, under jailer R. C. Gilchrist. During his brief imprisonment, the youth developed an intense hatred for his jailer, swearing to someday take revenge. Next he received a sentence of three years for burglary, an "offence against habitations and other buildings" committed "in the night time." Twenty-two at the time of his March 20, 1859, entrance into San Quentin, Ridgley was described as five foot six and having a "sallow" complexion, blue eyes, small mouth and nose, and light brown hair. His crime, plus the scar in the center of his forehead, seemed to belie a childlike innocence portrayed by the round blue eyes and features so softly formed as to appear "feminine." How unnatural the two years and seven months of enforced silence inside the prison were to a musician—dedicated to the world of sound—and how devastating the abuse a small, baby-faced youth might suffer from guards and fellow inmates can best be imagined by considering that with only five months left to serve, Ridgley risked severe punishment and increased sentence by attempting to escape.[48]

After making a successful getaway, he followed the usual pattern of fleeing to the territories. Using the given name Charley, rather than William, he arrived in Walla Walla and entered a saloon, only to encounter his former jailer leaning on the bar. Releasing the frustration built up during his imprisonment, the ex-convict fired six rapid shots at the hated man. Four balls ricocheted off Gilchrist's pistol and knife, and the two that entered his body left only slight wounds. "The shooter," a reporter wrote, "was recognized as a desperate character who was confined on the Sacramento brig. . . . The attack was, no doubt, caused by some old grudge which the man had harbored against Gilchrist ever since his imprisonment here."[49]

After the assault, a bystander heard Ridgley breathe, "That takes a load off my shoulders." Though Gilchrist survived to later become a San Quentin guard, Charley thought that he had "got his man." In order to avoid capture, he crossed the border into Oregon and from there worked his way up to Lewiston. Now wanted in both Washington and California, he sought anonymity by blending into the mass of humanity migrating to Florence. But like other disappointed gold seekers, he soon deserted that overcrowded camp, teaming up with Charley Reeves, Jim Harris, Henry Plummer, L. A. O. Payne, and James Wheeler. On August 23, 1862, the party signed in at Lewiston's Luna House, Reeves taking Room 32, Harris 33, and Plummer 34. Ridgley had no room number written opposite his name on the hotel register.[50]

When they learned that another hotel guest, a Mr. Patrick Ford, was on his way to Oro Fino to open a Spanish dance hall, Ridgley, Reeves, and Plummer followed after him. No one knows exactly how the intended spree developed into a fatal shootout. Patrick Ford, who has been classified "from a worthless adventurer to a real hero," was angry at Plummer for having broken up a lynch mob in Lewiston. Langford, however, blamed the affray on the three desperadoes:

Uttering a shout of exultation, the robbers dashed into the town of Oro Fino with the impetuosity of a cavalry charge. Reining up in front of Ford's saloon, which they entered, they called loudly upon the bar-keeper for liquor. . . . When they had drunk, they commenced demolishing the contents of the saloon. Decanters, tumblers, chairs, and tables were broken and scattered over the apartment. One of their number, more fiendish than the others, seized a lap-dog from one of the females and cut off his tail.[51]

Should there be any truth to Langford's account, Ridgley would make a likely candidate for the "more fiendish" one. Upon being ordered to leave—whether for rowdiness or for Plummer's anti-vigilance speech—the three walked to the corral where their horses were tied and were mounting when Ford commenced shooting from behind them. Their combined return fire killed Ford, but Ridgley had already taken two balls through the leg. Though the three considered their actions self-defense, they were in danger from angry Irishmen who were determined to lynch their countryman's killers. The gold dust Plummer was carrying—proceeds from Nevada mining claims—made the trio even more vulnerable. They fled town one step ahead of the aroused Irishmen and found a farm family willing to care for the wounded Ridgley. Then Reeves and Plummer rode for Elk City, with Jack Cleveland on their trail.[52]

As soon as he had recuperated, Ridgley traced Reeves to Bannack, arriving early enough to locate an excellent claim. On Plummer's appearance in December, he advanced the capital for a makeshift stamp mill, and employees commenced pounding the ore into workable dust. The profits were astounding. A correspondent who visited the Ridgley-Plummer claim saw $3,800 worth of gold dust in their retort, representing just one day's crushing.[53]

Other than his mining success, Ridgley made no news in Bannack. Shortly before the organization of the vigilance committee, he moved to the Boise Basin, where he again demonstrated his proclivity for getting involved in violence. Though in March 1864 the Idaho City newspaper had boasted of a low crime rate and warned "outcasts" that they would find no "asylum" for renewing "their outrages against law," the same issue listed the following indictments issued by the February district court: nine first-degree murder, three second-degree murder, one manslaughter, and twenty assault and battery with intent to murder.[54]

Charley Ridgley and two companions were among the twenty charged with assault and battery with intent to murder, but they pleaded guilty to reduced charges of assault and battery, receiving a fine of "$100 cash and costs." A year later, while visiting the remote camp of Rocky Bar, Ridgley shot and killed one Jonathan Ewing during a card game argument. A jury found that he had acted in self-defense.[55]

The following year brought more violence, but a kind the community condoned. In 1863 Standifer and Bledsoe had conducted successful Indian campaigns, but 1864 had seen a renewal of bloodshed. Prospector Michael Jordan, who had first discovered gold on the creek named for him, had settled on a ranch a few miles from his mine. When Indians stole his livestock, Jordan enlisted twenty-one volunteers, a pioneer recorded, and "started after the savages." They discovered the camp on a small flat fifty miles from Silver City, but on their approach, the Indians retreated to a canyon, scaled the banks, and fired, killing Jordan. Leaving their leader lying where he fell, his men fled "in disorder to Silver City, followed by the Indians."

Within twenty-four hours of the routing, one hundred forty armed and mounted men, leading forty pack mules, returned to engage the Indians. At 7:00 A.M. they reached the canyon banks and found Jordan's "charred and mutilated trunk." His arms and legs had been "severed at the joints and flung along the trail and hung in trees or thrown in mud holes." Outraged at the brutality, the volunteers gathered and buried Jordan's remains and then trailed the natives to the Owyhee River headwaters. Again the Indians awaited the enemy in a canyon, but this time their tactics were not as success-ful. The battle raged throughout one afternoon, the trapped war-riors fiercely defending themselves, but in the end, those Indians who had not been able to escape lay dead on the canyon floor.[56]

Despite the sporadic campaigns against them, the "savages" con-tinued what the settlers called "their depredations." In February 1866 citizens of Silver and Ruby cities met and voted to organize a company to go "after Mr. Indian, 'red-eyed.' " Those assembled resolved that "for every buck scalp be paid one hundred dollars, and every squaw scalp fifty dollars, and twenty-five dollars for every-thing in the shape of an Indian under ten years of age. . . . Each scalp shall have the curl of the head." Noting the citizens' fervor, the reporter concluded that the Snake Indians would "likely suffer some." Then he added, "It will test the wealth of Owyhee to pay for all those scalps though."[57]

In March the Ada County Volunteers left to "wage a war of extermination against bands of Indians that have so long infested" Owyhee country. They had voted ex-sheriff David Updyke as cap-tain and Charley Ridgley as lieutenant. In April another company reported the following "clean out: Loss of the enemy, 80 warriors and 35 squaws. The latter were dressed the same as the bucks and were fighting, and had to be killed, to ascertain their sex. We recov-ered 60 horses, captured 9 squaws and 10 children, and destroyed near three tons of dried beef."[58]

Ridgley's company, however, returned without having encoun-tered the enemy. Public opinion had turned against the slaughter of the natives, and the territorial governor was negotiating a treaty. Two weeks after the Volunteers' return, Boise Vigilantes hanged Captain Updyke, but just as at the Beaverhead mines, Ridgley had departed beforehand.[59]

He turned up two years later in Nevada, where he made news for one final time. Again his antagonist was Irish. "A shooting affray occurred here this morning," an Austin, Nevada, correspon-dent wrote on September 5. For some time "bad feelings" had existed between Ridgley and Irish Tom Carberry, and on the night of the fourth, they met and quarreled. The following morning, Carberry approached Ridgley, calling him "some vile names" and warning him to go arm himself. Ridgley hurried back to the International Hotel, where he had deposited his pistol, and stepped back into the street, gun in hand. Carberry, who had been waiting for him, "jumped into the street and the firing commenced." Both missed their first shots and fired again. Though Charley missed his second shot also, Irish Tom struck his opponent directly in the heart. The wounded man slumped to the ground, landing dead upon the very spot where an earlier Carberry victim had fallen that same year.[60] Like other desperadoes included in this volume, Charley Ridgley entered San Quentin in his early twenties and in his early thirties met violent death.

WILLIAM CHARLES REEVES

Ridgley was not the only desperado fortunate enough to escape both San Quentin sentence and vigilante wrath. Like Cherokee Bob and Ridgley, Charley Reeves ran away from home while a boy and ended up in state prison. He had left not to join the gold rush, however, but to escape an abusive stepmother. He was born in Sharon, Pennsylvania—near the Ohio border—in 1829, the son of a carpenter with nine children, eight of them daughters. When Charley was but a few years old, his mother died and the father remarried. The young stepmother's treatment of the lively, redheaded boy newly committed to her care was very harsh. At age nine, Charley could no longer endure his repeated punishments and ran away, heading for the sea.[61]

He ended up in Texas, and, after spending several years in that wild country, worked his way overland to Mariposa County, California, and found work on a farm. He arrived in Mariposa about the same time as Cherokee Bob, though there is no evidence they became acquainted then. As Charley admitted, in California "he fell into bad company and bad habits." His admission is something of an understatement; two days after Columbus Day of 1852, twenty-three-year-old Reeves became the one hundred twelfth convict to discover the ruthless world of San Quentin. Since his entrance fell between the admissions of the Skinner brothers, he lived on the prison brig with both Cyrus and George. His new home bore one resemblance to the home deserted in Pennsylvania—punishment was liberal and rigorous. Though the theft had been his first offense, he faced five years, a sentence he attempted to shorten by escaping from the unenclosed, new facility.

If Charley and Cherokee Bob had not met earlier, they had the opportunity in March 1854 when Bob entered prison and Charley reentered after his escape. Facing harsher treatment and a doubled term, Reeves enthusiastically joined in the December insurrection plans. During the futile attempt to take over the prison sloop, he was badly wounded, but, clutching his injuries and spitting blood, he ran toward the hills. Mounted guards followed the fleeing men. Able-bodied inmates hoisted two helpless men onto the two available horses, but Reeves and Cherokee Bob were left to hobble along as best they could on crippled limbs. Bob could not keep up, and at last collapsed, but Reeves continued running until he reached the safety of the trees. There he crouched, watching as guards scoured the timber where prisoners were vainly attempting to conceal themselves in the underbrush. After hours of searching the surrounding hills, the guards returned to the prison, reporting that seventeen men had escaped.[62]

Charley Reeves was among the desperate men — branded by half-shaven heads and ball and buckshot lesions — who "robbed every ranch as they came to it." The escapees, the *Alta* reported, took "first the arms, then horses, saddles, clothing, and everything else they fancied." The prison supervisor placed the entire countryside on alert, warning that "every good citizen should be on the watch for all suspicious strangers. . . . All strangers complaining of indisposition should be examined at once, and if gun shot wounds be found on them they are 'escaped convicts.' " He offered a "liberal reward" for "all apprehended."[63]

Despite the reward incentive and his own wounds and half-shaven head, Reeves successfully avoided capture. And despite his admitted bad habits of drinking and gambling, he stayed out of serious trouble for eight years. His success was due, at least in part, to his friendly, talkative nature and to his good appearance. He was described as five foot ten, "slender," and "handsome." As an adult, his eyes remained a clear blue, his hair darkened to a deep auburn, and his face was usually so tanned as to make him appear "dark-complected."[64]

He spent considerable time at Carson City, Nevada, but by August 1862 was at Lewiston. Following the Oro Fino corral shootout with Ford, he and Plummer crossed the mountain range on the Nez Perce Trail and then rode north and east to reach Hell Gate.

Frank Woody — later to become a Montana judge — was alone at Worden's store on that early September afternoon of 1862 when the two riders appeared. Woody's recollection of their arrival makes an interesting comparison to Langford's imaginative version of the reckless abandon with which desperadoes entered a settlement. The "well dressed" strangers, Woody noted, "did not look like laboring men" and "their horses appeared to be nearly worn out with travel." They entered the store, Woody went on, "and asked me if there was any chance to get something to eat. I told them we would not have dinner until about 6 o'clock, but that we had an old lady cook who probably could give them a little lunch. . . . They asked me if there was any show to get a drink of whiskey and said they needed a drink very much." Though Woody had no whiskey to sell, he found enough to "give each one of them a good drink." After the cook served them lunch in her cabin, the two men spent the afternoon resting and chatting with Woody.

The conversation preserved something quite rare in Idaho territorial history, an instance in which a desperado related his side of a story. "The eldest," Woody remembered, "told me his name was Henry Plummer and the young man was Charley Reeves." They said "that they had been over in a mining camp on the west side of the Bitter Root mountains, called Oro Fino, which at that time was quite a lively mining camp, having several saloons, dance halls . . . and quite a crowd of men." Though Plummer and Reeves did not explain how the trouble broke out, they mentioned a "difficulty," which resulted in "a fight and shooting." They were "compelled," they said, to kill the Irish proprietor. When Ford's friends began making threats, Plummer, Reeves, and Ridgley "were satisfied that if they did not get out of there that the Irish would rob them and perhaps kill them."[65] A correspondent who spent the year 1862 at the Salmon and Clearwater mines corroborated the story told to Woody, that the three men had killed Ford "on the defensive," but that nevertheless "the people might have executed" them.[66]

From Hell Gate, Reeves and Plummer rode to Gold Creek with Woody and Granville Stuart and separated, Plummer taking the Sun River trail and Reeves heading for Grasshopper Creek. At Bannack, Reeves operated a gaming table, probably having learned the trade in Carson City. Bannackites called him "Texas Charley" and took him to be a youth of about twenty-one. Though he may have looked that young, and acted it as well, he was actually thirty-two. Feeling himself ready to settle down to marriage, he acquired—for the price of two blankets—an Indian wife. Rumors that he abused his bride are in keeping with the brief years of home life he had known. His two salient childhood memories were his stepmother's beatings and a story about Indians killing a family member. His bitter resentment for the race who had brought sorrow to his family had a disastrous effect not only on his marriage, but also on his chances of staying alive.[67]

When the Indian girl returned to her own people, Reeves went after her, but she would not return nor would her father refund the two blankets. Reeves sought consolation at the Goodrich Hotel saloon. After a few drinks, he and his companion, Gus Moore, commented that "If the d — d cowardly white folks on Yankee Flats were afraid of the Indians, they were not, and that they would soon 'set the ball rolling.' " Removing their shotguns and revolvers from the bar, they walked to the Indian camp and fired into a tepee, wounding one occupant. Then they returned to the saloon, downed more drinks, headed back to the tepees, and fired more shots. Attorney William C. Rheem, who witnessed the attack, heard the "cries of the wounded" and saw the "prostrate dead": two Indians and a Frenchman, who had run to the camp at the sound of the shots.[68]

Though Reeves and Moore fled, a posse tracked them to Rattlesnake Creek and brought them back to stand trial. Attorney Rheem agreed to represent them. "When I first went in to see the men," he wrote, "they were sitting on a bench smoking their pipes. They had a defiant air, evidently expecting . . . they would be speedily lynched, and were determined to die game." The prisoners begged Rheem to use his influence to have them shot rather than hanged. "These border men," Rheem explained, "have such a detestation of the disgraceful noose, that they would rather commit suicide than be strangled." When Rheem told them they would have a jury trial, "looks of penitence took the place of their first appearance of boldness and defiance. They put away their pipes, pulled down the rims of their slouched hats and took decorous positions at the mourners' bench."

Since the only excuse Reeves could offer for the attack was that "the Indians had killed a relative of his some years before," Rheem had little hopes of an acquittal, especially with Nathaniel Langford serving as jury foreman. As their attorney had feared, the jury found the defendants guilty. Though Langford at first insisted on the death penalty, the other jurors eventually persuaded him to vote for banishment. Grateful their lives were spared, the two exiles mounted Moore's horse and set out for Deer Lodge.[69]

C. A. Broadwater was living in Deer Lodge Valley at the time and noted their arrival. Reeves and Moore, he said, built "a miserable wickyup for themselves, which afforded them but little protection from the wintry blasts. They had no food except beef and coffee." After a short time, Moore became so ill he was not expected to live, and the Bannack miners sent word that the convicts could return to town until warm weather. Since Indians had stolen Moore's horse, Broadwater donated a mount.[70]

At Bannack, Moore soon became well enough to join Reeves and the others about the saloon fires, but there was the constant risk of more trouble. One evening, Reeves and Ed Richardson were discussing "the good old days" in Carson City, when Sam Turner interrupted, doing his best to provoke a fight. Since Reeves's situation was too precarious to risk further involvements, he had to sit quietly and let Richardson deal with the intruder. Though Ed ended up taking a ball in the groin and shooting Turner, at least Reeves had not violated the terms of his reprieve.[71]

In April a California paper printed the news that Charley Reeves had been hanged "by the people," but in reality he was still frequenting the Bannack saloons as late as May. The date of his departure from the Grasshopper mines is not known, but on July 10 the Stuart brothers jotted down in their accounts book that Charley had left town owing them $69.20. Dimsdale thought that Reeves had headed for Mexico, but the possibility exists that on his way he may have stopped off at his former home in Texas and stayed. The 1870 census lists a Charles Reeves—a Pennsylvania native of the correct age—who was farming in Lamar County, Texas. He was married to a woman from Ohio, but they had no children. If Reeves did make the transition from gold camp desperado to family man and farmer, he was the only one in this study.[72]

WILLIAM RILEY, ALIAS BUCKSKIN BILL AND DICKERSON

The final desperado story demonstrates the near impossibility of a young man freeing himself from the tendrils of a desperate past. Like George Skinner, Riley did not live long enough to follow the gold camp circuit; he died in a fight near the entrance of a house of ill fame in Nevada City, California. He was born in Kentucky, was nearly five foot eleven, and had a "low forehead, long nose, small mouth, dimple on chin, scar on center of forehead, thin beard, . . . fingers long and bony, and shot wounds on left thigh and groin."[73]

He was first linked to crime in March 1859 when five robbers forced a Daneville, California, merchant to open his safe and hand over its contents. Then the robbers helped themselves to the store's gourmet food—oysters, bread, and wine—and selected new suits from the merchant's stock. Officers trailed the well-dressed robbers to French Ravine, near Grass Valley, and, at midnight of March 24, surrounded their cabin. But before the posse could approach, Riley and seven other men rushed out and commenced firing. Shooting then became general, and when it was over, Riley, dressed in buckskin, lay sprawled across a dead companion sporting a new suit.[74]

Though there was no evidence that Riley had participated in the Daneville robbery, a jury found him guilty of attempting to murder law officers at French Ravine and sentenced him to one year in prison. When he had only two months left to serve, he escaped, but instead of fleeing as wiser escapees had done, he returned to the same county where he had been convicted. Rather than resuming his former job as a laborer, he wandered from camp to camp, earning a reputation as quarrelsome and dissipated. On the Fourth of July he awakened to find himself in the small town of Gopher Hill. Suddenly the morning stillness was broken by a series of explosions. When the Secessionist went to investigate, he discovered two Yankees "firing an anvil" to commemorate the national birthday. Riley ordered them to stop the racket immediately, and when they refused, he hurled his bowie knife, striking one man in the head and slashing open the scalp. But the patriot brought no charge against his assailant, and Riley left the camp.[75]

Three months after the Gopher Hill incident, Riley encountered yet another Yankee and committed another assault. While roving the streets of Nevada City at 2:00 A.M., he met Henry Plummer. The cause of their quarrel was a mystery, but after an exchange of words, Riley pulled his knife and slashed through Plummer's hat, inflicting a three-inch scalp wound. As Riley raised his hand to strike again, Plummer fired his revolver, and the ball entered Riley's left side, killing him instantly.[76]

On the advice of Nevada City law officers, Plummer departed town before the inquest, becoming a fugitive himself and leaving

DRAWING OF HENRY PLUMMER BY C. M. CALLISON DIAZ. The artist based the above drawing on a photograph of a Plummer family member who resembled Henry, the gallows sketch, and written descriptions.

his altercation with Riley a mystery. The press speculated that heavy drinking had caused the fatal affray, and one resident claimed a woman was to blame. But the San Quentin Register provided yet another explanation. When Riley entered prison, he used the alias Dickerson; therefore, on his escape, no alert was issued for a William Riley, and he was able to reenter the community without arousing suspicion. Plummer, however, was experienced at recognizing suspects from their telegraphed description, and Riley's appearance was distinctive. As Plummer's arrest of Ten Year Smith illustrated, the ex-marshal could not shake his self-image as a law officer. Ironically, it was probably his attempt to arrest Riley as a suspected fugitive that brought about Plummer's own conversion to a desperado.[77]

During the eighteen months in which he followed the mining circuit, associating with other exiles, Plummer gained a thorough knowledge of desperadoism. Though Langford's portrayals of the outlaws offer little insight into their psyche, he once held a conversation with Sheriff Plummer which got to the heart of the matter. Plummer stated that his days in Florence, Lewiston, and Oro Fino were devoid of family and community ties, and therefore empty and meaningless. Throughout his period of alienation from society, the former lawman had felt that he had no reason to live. His revelation makes an appropriate closing for the desperado stories.[78]

CONCLUSIONS

Since the majority of the one hundred fifty-five convicts who escaped California's state prison between 1851 and 1858 did not go on to make names for themselves, and since our study deals mainly with those who did, it cannot be considered representative of all fugitives from justice in the decade following the gold rush. It is simply the biographies of twenty-one men known as outlaws in the mining camps. Yet these biographies illustrate quite well the nineteenth-century phenomenon of desperadoism and the environment in which it flourished.

Edward and Charles Richardson, Bob Durkin, David Renton, James Romain, Chris Lowrey, Cherokee Bob Talbot, Bill Mayfield, Jack Cleveland, George Ives, William Winters, Madison Bledsoe, Charley Harper, Nelson Scott, William Peebles, David English, James Crow, George Skinner, Charley Ridgley, Charley Reeves, and William Riley represent all regions of the United States—Connecticut, New York, Pennsylvania, Maryland, Ohio, Kentucky, Illinois, Missouri, Georgia, Louisiana, and California. Though it was not possible to obtain information about all of their families, more than half of the group came from respectable homes, thus supporting an earlier study which reported that the outlaws "were often men of good background," who "were alienated from the values of the community."[1] As for the outlaws' original occupations, there were three farmers, three miners, three laborers, three gamblers, and one each of the following: printer, business proprietor, building contractor, musician, clerk, blacksmith, and waiter. (Occupations of two are unknown.)

Thirteen served time in San Quentin. And though several of the others spent time in local jails, the thirteen San Quentin inmates had no previous criminal records. None entered state prison with the characteristic brands of having met with popular justice: a missing ear, a "T" on the chest, nor the telltale "scars of whip on back and arms."[2] Only one of the thirteen entered San Quentin for committing a violent crime, yet all perpetrated violence after release or escape. How six of the twenty-one outlaws met their end is unknown, but fifteen suffered violent death: four executed, four lynched, four killed in gunfights, two mortally wounded while committing an assault, and one shot during an arrest attempt.

The stories in this volume provide information not only about young men who became frontier outlaws, but also about life in the camps which sprouted up along the constantly shifting border between wilderness and supply communities. The desperadoes' tumultuous lives reflect a tumultuous society. Frederick Jackson Turner viewed the frontier as "a new field of opportunity, a gate of escape from the bondage of the past."[3] Yet as the young outlaws rushed to each new El Dorado, they found no escape from their pasts.

At times, Langford noted, stealing became a matter of survival: "Money and food were so scarce that robbery with the sporting community became an actual necessity." But those fleeing justice were not the only desperate members of the gold camp society. There were also what Langford called "mining vagabonds," unsuccessful miners who were "lost to all self-respect, ragged, uncombed, often covered with vermin." The overland trip had left others in a similar condition. Alfred Barstow reported needy immigrants and their starving livestock camped outside Sacramento: "Grass began to get short and they began to steal. Before that, there was no stealing." A Sacramento physician referred to the struggle for existence as the "Battle of Life." "All who are settled in business are making money," Dr. J. D. B. Stillman wrote home, "but, alas! for the many unfortunates. . . . The fallen are trampled into the mud, and are left to the tender mercies of the earth and sky." Stillman, who established the first hospital in Sacramento, was appalled at the lack of charity extended to those suffering from want of food, shelter, and medicine. "What can be expected from strangers when men's own friends will abandon them because they sicken and become an encumbrance?" he asked. "There are men here who would hang their heads at home at the mention of their heartless avarice." The "all-absorbing object" of the society is "money, money."[4]

Stillman's letters expose the darker side of the gold rush, a side we might prefer to overlook. Though gold fever brought productive results for the nation as a whole, it could also be described as a moral illness which infected the adventurers gathered at the mines. The lure of gold dust was so seductive — as in the Magruder party — that men came to hold it in higher esteem than human life. As a consequence, they not only killed their former townspeople in order to obtain gold, but also offered rewards for the scalps of Indian children inhabiting the gold-rich territories. In the balance between the value of life and property, the scales tipped toward the latter; thus legislators deemed it just to kill a human being for committing a crime against property.

Despite the high value placed on gold, miners squandered it in saloons and wagered it on every event imaginable. "There was a great deal of money and a great deal of gambling it," Barstow attested. "The first billiard table that was brought into Downieville ran for seventy-two hours without a moment's cessation, night or day, at a dollar a game." A Grass Valley editor decried the extent to which gambling was practiced in California. The laws preventing gambling, he contended, "are and have always been a dead letter upon the Statute book of our state, and they will remain so as long as those occupying high official and social positions, . . . worship themselves at its shrine thereby setting an example fraught with the most evil consequences."[5]

The editor's prediction — that passing antigambling legislation and then winking at violations would promote disrespect for the law — proved correct. The fledgling justice system did not need any more problems; it was already burdened with poor juries, unfair trial procedures, and inequitable sentences that created injustices where none need exist. Furthermore, in the remote camps, lynch mobs mocked the forms of justice by holding a trial before hanging their victims. Such abuses hindered the growth of true lawfulness.

The foregoing observations are not intended as argument that there was no charity, morality, or justice on the mining frontier. There are abundant examples of all three. But rounding out the picture by including society's negative aspects is essential in determining the social environment in which decent young men became criminals. The life-style of the desperadoes — seeking gold, drinking, gambling, and joining stampedes — was the life-style of the mining camps. As Langford observed, "In the presence of vice in all its forms, men who were staid and exemplary at home laid aside their morality like a useless garment . . . for lives of shameful and criminal indulgence." And though Langford charged that desperadoes "settled all difficulties with bowie-knives and revolvers," his own admired "enemies of the outlaws," such as Jakey Williams, settled their difficulties in the same manner. Barstow claimed that prostitutes were "wholly supported by married men, and the young men were the only moral ones in the community!" So if our desperadoes disgraced themselves by chasing after gold, drinking, gambling, visiting bagnios, and settling disputes with weapons, apparently such behavior was more the norm than the exception.[6]

As for the myth of the robber gangs, the preceding stories lend it no support. California had its loosely formed groups headed by Tom Bell and Rattlesnake Dick, but the roving gold camp outlaws were not loyal members of an Ali Baba-type band with passwords, secret signs, and omnipotent leaders. Though there are examples of three men conducting a robbery, one did not stand out as a band leader. There is no evidence that Charley Harper directed a single holdup, and even in the case of the Magruder murderers, no one person seemed to be in charge. Instead, Lowrey informed Page that both Romain and Howard wished to talk to him about robbing and murdering the rest of the party, and on one occasion, Romain countermanded Howard's orders by insisting that Page "gut shoot" Phillips.

Many of our twenty-one subjects were merely alleged robbers. Talbot, Scott, Peebles, English, Crow, Reeves, Ridgley, Skinner, and Riley fall into this category. Since ten of the entire group were originally convicted of the nonviolent crimes of grand larceny or burglary at the time of their conviction, they were thieves rather than highway robbers. It is impossible to predict how some might have fared had they stood trial for robbery.

When we compare romanticized tales of robber gangs with a realistic account — such as Judge Woody's recollection of Reeves and Plummer arriving at Hell Gate — we discover the desperadoes' entrance to be rather pale. Rather than racing into town, spurring skittish horses through a saloon door, and pitching gold-filled pokes on the bar, Reeves and Plummer wearily dismounted from fatigued horses and humbly requested food and drink. Langford's charming paragraph in our introduction notwithstanding, any horse with the stamina to launch a cavalry charge on Florence's main street after having just tackled the challenging mountain trail leading to the basin belongs to myth, not history. But despite Langford's embellishments and exaggerations, he and other early historians do not deserve credit for inventing the myths; in most instances, they were only recording stories in circulation. The *Oregonian* warned that the number of robberies reported on the Florence-Lewiston road was greatly exaggerated: "We have had several of these contradicted by letter and information," the editor advised, "and have got so that we are doubtful about anybody being robbed, unless we know they have something to be robbed of."[7] Apparently, the citizens themselves fostered desperadoism by perpetrating the myth that being a desperado was not only romantic, but also lucrative.

Author Jack Burrows blames such historical inaccuracies for lowering the quality of our western novels and movies. In a speech delivered at the Fifteenth Rendezvous of NOLA (National Association for Outlaw and Lawman History), Burrows postulated that our histories of the West, infiltrated by stereotype and myth, have produced poor literature and a body of writing that does not rely on authentic tradition. But if stereotypes have proven fatal to western fiction in the present century, during the 1850s and 60s they proved equally fatal to the young men lured into the outlaw life.[8]

One early writer claimed that rather than being regarded as "deep-dyed criminals," desperadoes were "treated more like heroes." Yet existing side by side with the outlaw's glorified image was the stigma attached to being a convict. For example, when young Cyrus Skinner first escaped from a California jail, authorities issued the following description of the wanted man: "complexion dark, low forehead, very narrow between the eyes, and stoop-shouldered."[9] Yet officials who later examined Cyrus on his three entrances in San Quentin found none of those features. In the absence of concrete data, those who posted the reward had fallen back on standard physical traits associated with criminality. They had done exactly what Burrows claims western writers have done in a similar absence of adequate historical basis — they had relied on stereotype.

In writing up the material researched, we have attempted to avoid the common pitfalls of myth and stereotype as much as possible. Our goal has been to present as much information as we could uncover about the young men examined — their heritage, their lives, and their times. They were times when greed for gold dust was a prime motivator, when riotous habits were general, and when violence—either racial, sectional, criminal, or judicial—was sporadic. The Mountain Code, which asserted the right of self-defense, guided the intrepid pioneers through these turbulent times, but gradually the right to survival broadened to include the right to defend dignity, thus making an insult a capital offense. Containing anger within legal confines was unnecessary; instead, those who displayed their manhood by refusing to accept the stain of dishonor proffered by an antagonist became heroes. All in all, the social environment was conducive to the creation of desperadoes.

Still, the individual outlaw cannot place the full blame on society; each was responsible for his own actions. His crimes brought immeasurable suffering to his own family as well as to the families of his victims. And by failing to live up to his own potential, he also victimized himself. In addition, the "terrible curse" of desperadoism took its toll on society, depriving the young nation of contributions the alienated citizens could have made. For example, George Ives was a "born leader," a man of potentially heroic stature; Edward Richardson was a gifted writer; and Judge Parks characterized Renton, Romain, and Lowrey as men of "more than ordinary energy and intelligence" who could have been influential in their day and generation.[10] The alienation of energetic, intelligent, courageous young men represented a national loss. Like the Todds' and Iveses' log rollings and burnings, and like the Yellowstone expedition's "free" and "exciting" buffalo slaughter, the young men who became gold camp desperadoes were a national resource wasted during our pioneering period.

NOTES

INTRODUCTION (pp. 1-7)

1. *Webster's New Collegiate Dictionary*.
2. Rewards Offered by State of California Executive Department, California State Archives, Sacramento.
3. *Boise News*, 26 March 1864. Reprinted from *Times* (Aurora, Nev.), n.d.
4. Richard Maxwell Brown, "The American Vigilante Tradition," in *The History of Violence in America*, eds. Hugh D. Graham and Ted R. Gurr (New York: Frederick A. Praeger, Publisher, 1969), 168.
5. John Hailey, *The History of Idaho* (Boise: Syms-York, 1918), 49.
6. John Paul Dart, "A Mississipian in the Gold Fields," *California Historical Society Quarterly* 35 (1956) 3:215.
7. William Shaw, *Golden Dreams and Waking Realities* (New York: Arno Press, 1973), 88.
8. Henry B. Maize, "Early Events," Handwritten MS., Bancroft Library, University of California, Berkeley, 7.
9. William Shaw, 114.
10. David Augustus Shaw, *El Dorado or California as Seen by a Pioneer* (Los Angeles: B. R. Baumgardt & Company, 1900), 143-44.
11. *Compiled Laws of the State of California, Sessions of 1850-51-52-53* (Boston: Franklin Printing, 1853), 647.
12. Thomas J. Dimsdale, *The Vigilantes of Montana* (Butte: McKee Printing Company, 1945), 13.
13. Ibid., 250.
14. Mark Twain, *Roughing It* (New York: Holt, Rinehart and Winston, 1966), 253-54.
15. William J. McConnell, *Early History of Idaho* (Caldwell, Idaho: Caxton Printers, 1913), 56.
16. Nathaniel Langford, *Vigilante Days and Ways* (New York: A. L. Burt Company, 1912), xii.
17. Twain, 254.
18. Martha Edgerton Plassmann, "Judge Edgerton's Daughter," MS. 78, Montana Historical Society Archives, 119.
19. Langford, 47.

CALIFORNIA GOLD COUNTRY (pp. 9–40)

1. *Nevada National* (Grass Valley, Calif.), 14 July 1860.
2. Ibid., 12 February 1859.
3. Ibid., 14 July 1860; *Morning Transcript* (Nevada City, Calif.), 26 September, 15 October, 20 November, and 15 December 1860.
4. *Nevada National*, 14 July 1860 and 22 October 1859.
5. Ibid., 27 August 1859; U.S. Bureau of the Census, *Eighth Census of U.S.: 1860 Population Schedule of Nevada County, California.*
6. *Sacramento Bee*, 12 November 1861; *Register and Descriptive List of Convicts Under Sentence of Imprisonment in the State Prison of California*, California State Archives, Sacramento.
7. *Nevada National*, 30 June 1860.
8. State of California, *Census of 1852*; *Register and Descriptive List of Convicts*; *Sacramento Daily Union*, 25 and 27 May 1864.
9. *Sixth Census of U.S.: 1840 Population Schedule of Livingston County, Louisiana*; State of California. Census of 1852; *Eighth Census of U.S.: 1860 Population Schedule of Nevada County, California.*
10. Ibid.; Louis J. Rasmussen, *San Francisco Ship Passenger Lists* (Baltimore: Dedford, 1965), 2:128.
11. *History of Nevada County*, Reproduction of Thompson & West's *History of Nevada County, California, 1880* (Berkeley: Howell-North, 1970), 64–65.
12. Ibid., 155; *Nevada Democrat* (Nevada City, Calif.), 10 October 1860 and 22 April 1862; *Morning Transcript*, 10 December 1860 and 21 November 1862; *Nevada National*, 19 December 1859.
13. Alonzo Delano, *Pen-Knife Sketches or Chips off the Old Block* (San Francisco: Grabhorn Press, 1934), 51–52.
14. *Nevada National*, 5 March 1859.
15. Ibid., 23 April 1859.
16. *History of Nevada County*, 154.
17. Ibid.
18. Ibid.
19. Ibid., 153.
20. *Nevada National*, 5 May 1860. As this article attests, the rubbish problem was still unresolved by 1860.
21. Ibid., 30 April and 17 September 1859.
22. Ibid., 10 September 1859.
23. Ibid., 12 November 1859 and 7 January, 10 March, and 21 April 1860.
24. *Nevada Democrat*, 4 December 1866.
25. Governor's File on Francis Van Moore, California State Archives, Sacramento.
26. *Nevada National*, 12 and 26 November 1859.
27. Ibid., 21 January 1860.
28. John David Borthwick, *The Gold Hunters* (Cleveland: International Fiction Library, 1917), 67; *Eighth Census of U.S.: 1860 Population Schedule of Nevada County, California.*
29. Dimsdale, 77; Helen F. Sanders, ed., *X. Beidler: Vigilante* (Norman: University of Oklahoma Press, 1957), 27; *Register and Descriptive List of Convicts.*
30. *Nevada National*, 27 August 1859 and 21 January 1860.
31. Ibid., 24 December 1859 and 7 January 1860.
32. Ibid., 10 March 1860.

33. Ibid., 27 January 1860.

34. Ibid., 6 June 1860.

35. *Eighth Census of U.S.: 1860 Population Schedule of Nevada County, California*; *Register and Descriptive List of Convicts*.

36. *Nevada National*, 7 and 14 July 1860.

37. Ibid., 14 July 1860.

38. *Nevada Democrat*, 15 August 1860.

39. *Nevada National*, 17 September 1859 and 6 June 1860; *Nevada Democrat*, 8, 15, and 22 August 1860; *Morning Transcript*, 6 September 1860.

40. Ibid., 12 September 1860; *Nevada Democrat*, 19 September 1860.

41. Ibid., 13 November 1860; *Morning Transcript*, 14 November 1860.

42. *Nevada National*, 10 November 1860.

43. *Register and Descriptive List of Convicts*.

44. *Nevada Journal* (Nevada City, Calif.), 23 November 1855.

45. "An Act Creating a Board of State Prison Commissioners, and Defining Their Duties," 21 March 1856, California State Archives, Sacramento.

46. Ibid.; Governor Weller's Address to State Legislature, 10 March 1859, in *Journal of the Senate*, Ninth Session; Hubert Howe Bancroft, *California Inter Pocula* (San Francisco: History Company, 1888), 422.

47. Ibid.

48. *Nevada Democrat*, 15 August 1860; *Alta California* (San Francisco), 12 and 22 July 1858; *Morning Transcript*, 13 December 1860.

49. *Grass Valley National* (Grass Valley, Calif.), 7 September 1861.

50. *Sacramento Bee*, 12 November 1861.

51. Governor's File on Edward Richardson.

52. Ibid., *Sacramento Bee*, 26 October 1861.

53. Governor's File on Edward Richardson.

54. Governor's File on Charles Richardson.

55. Ibid.

56. Ibid.; Governor's File on Edward Richardson.

57. *Grass Valley National*, 14 December 1861. Reprinted from S. C. Richardson's Card in *Times*, n.d.

58. *History of Nevada*, Reproduction of Thompson & West's *History of Nevada, 1881* (Berkeley: Howell-North, 1958), 401–4, 418; *Sacramento Bee*, 10 November 1861.

59. *Sacramento Daily Union*, 29 November 1862.

60. *Nevada Daily Transcript* (Nevada City, Calif.), 20 February 1863.

61. *Sacramento Daily Union*, 6 January 1863.

62. Ibid., 12 January 1863; *Daily Appeal* (Marysville, Calif.), 18 March 1863.

63. *Nevada Daily Transcript*, 27 February 1863.

64. *Sacramento Daily Union*, 7 March 1863.

65. *Nevada Daily Transcript*, 20 March 1863.

66. *Daily Appeal*, 18 March 1863.

67. *Nevada Daily Transcript*, 29 March 1863.

68. Ibid., 28 May 1863; *Register and Descriptive List of Convicts*.

69. Dimsdale, 77.

70. *Sacramento Daily Union*, 17 June 1863. Any suspicions that Ed Richardson might have written and dispatched the article himself are allayed by the correspondent's references to the days when he used to set type for the *Union*. Ed was never an employee of the *Sacramento Daily Union*.

71. Ibid.

72. Dimsdale, 78; Langford, 215.

73. Langford, 207–14; Dimsdale, 72–81; Sanders, *Beidler*, 25–29.

74. Dimsdale, 77–78; Sanders, *Beidler*, 28.

75. Langford, 214, 219.

76. Dimsdale, 24.

77. *Boise News* (Idaho City), 2 January 1864.

78. Ibid., 6 and 17 February, 19 March, 20 May, and 23 July 1864.

79. *Nevada Daily Transcript*, 8 May 1863.

80. Cotton Mather, *Diary* (New York: Frederick Ungar Publishing, n.d.), 2:484, 489, 611, 753, 760.

CLEARWATER RIVER MINES (pp. 41–80)

1. *Washington Statesman* (Walla Walla, Wash.), 6 February 1864.

2. *Seventh Census of U.S.: 1850 Population Schedule of Independence County, Arkansas*; *Idaho Statesman* (Boise), 11 October 1942. *Eighth Census of U.S.: 1860 Population Schedule of Klickitat County, Washington Territory*; Langford, 334.

3. *Elmore Bulletin* (Mountain Home, Idaho), 14 April 1894.

4. *Daily Oregonian* (Portland), 9 November 1863.

5. *Boise News*, 30 April 1864; *Idaho Statesman*, 27 May 1875; *Sacramento Daily Union*, 4 December 1863.

6. Ibid.; *Oregon Statesman* (Salem), 7 December 1863.

7. Ibid.

8. Hubert Howe Bancroft, *History of Washington, Idaho, and Montana* (San Francisco: History Company, 1890), 454.

9. *Boise News*, 18 January 1864.

10. Cornelius J. Brosnan, *History of the State of Idaho* (New York: Charles Scribner's Sons, 1948), 140.

11. *Elmore Bulletin*, 5 May 1863; *Washington Statesman*, 6 February 1864; *Boise News*, 18 January 1864; Francis Thompson, "Reminiscences of Four Score Years," *Massachusetts Magazine* 6 (July 1913) 3:122–23; 6 (October 1913) 4:162–63.

12. "Marysville Correspondence," *Boise News*, 26 March 1864; *Register of Missouri Penitentiary Inmates, 1841–1851*, Missouri State Archives, Jefferson City.

13. Herman Francis Reinhart, *The Golden Frontier* (Austin: University of Texas Press, 1962), 238: Dimsdale, 124; *Eighth Census of U.S.: 1860 Population Schedule of Klickitat County, Washington Territory*; *Daily Oregonian*, 6 November 1863; *Elmore Bulletin*, 14 April 1894.

14. "Marysville Correspondence," *Boise News*, 26 March 1864; *Daily Oregonian*, 6 November 1863; Thompson, 6 (July 1913) 3:123.

15. William S. Shiach and Harry B. Averill, *An Illustrated History of North Idaho* (n.p.: Western Historical Publishing, 1903), 38; *Daily Oregonian*, 6 November 1863. Reprinted from *Dalles Mountaineer* (The Dalles, Oreg.), n.d.; *Washington Statesman*, 12 March 1864.

16. *Sacramento Daily Union*, 24 February 1864. Reprinted from *Golden Age* (Lewiston, Idaho), 23 January 1864.

17. *Fifth Census of U.S.: 1830 Population Schedules of Lancaster and Beaver Counties, Pennsylvania*; Jerome H. Wood, Jr., *Conestoga Crossroads, Lancaster, Pennsylvania 1730–1790* (Harrisburg: Historical and Museum Commission, 1979), 113–14.

18. Francis Parkman, *The Oregon Trail* (Garden City, N.Y.: Doubleday, 1946), 56.

19. Wood, 115, 170.

20. *Boise News*, 18 January 1864.

21. *Register and Descriptive List of Convicts*; Langford, 328.

22. *Fifth Census of U.S.: 1830 Population Schedule of Lancaster and Beaver Counties, Pennsylvania.*

23. *Register and Descriptive List of Convicts*; Bancroft, *History of Washington, Idaho, and Montana*, 453.

24. Ibid.; *Weekly Oregonian*, 12 March 1864; *Register* (Rockford, Ill.), 2 February 1861.

25. *Sixth Census of U.S.: 1840 Population Schedule of New York City, New York*; Governor's File on David Renton; *Sacramento Daily Union*, 22 December 1863.

26. *Register and Descriptive List of Convicts*; Bancroft, *History of Washington, Idaho, and Montana*, 453.

27. "Marysville Correspondence," *Boise News*, 26 March 1864; Governor's File on David Renton.

28. Ibid.

29. Ibid.

30. Ibid.

31. Ibid.

32. "Marysville Correspondence," *Boise News*, 26 March 1864; *Weekly Oregonian*, 26 January 1864; Bancroft, *History of Washington, Idaho and Montana*, 453.

33. Thompson, 6 (July 1913) 3:122-23; 6 (October 1913) 4:162-63.

34. *Washington Statesman*, 12 December 1863. The truth of this article is confirmed by Caroline Magruder's granddaughter in *Idaho Statesman*, 11 October 1942.

35. *Boise News*, 2 January 1864.

36. *Elmore Bulletin*, 14 April 1894; Shiach and Averill, 35.

37. *Fifth and Sixth Census of U.S.: 1830 and 1840 Population Schedules of Montgomery County, Maryland*; *Idaho Statesman*, 11 October 1942.

38. *Seventh Census of U.S.: 1850 Population Schedule of Independence County, Arkansas*; *Idaho Statesman*, 11 October 1942.

39. Ibid.

40. Ibid.

41. *Seventh Census of U.S.: 1850 Population Schedule of Independence County, Arkansas*; *Idaho Statesman*, 11 October 1942.

42. *Elmore Bulletin*, 14 April 1894; *Idaho Statesman*, 11 October 1942; *Seventh Census of U.S.: Population Schedule of Independence County, Arkansas.*

43. Peter J. Delay, *History of Yuba and Sutter Counties* (Los Angeles: Historical Record Company, 1924), 126-28, 139, 165.

44. Ibid., 122.

45. Ibid., 127; *Eighth Census of U.S.: 1860 Population Schedule of Yuba County, California.*

46. Shiach and Averill, 35; Byron Defenbach, *Idaho: The Place and Its People* (Chicago: American Historical Society, 1933), 1:329; *Idaho Statesman*, 11 October 1942.

47. Victor Goodwin, "William C. Beachey, Nevada-California-Idaho Stagecoach King," *Nevada Historical Society Quarterly* 10 (1967) 1:8.

48. *Golden Age*, 5 September 1863.

49. Ibid.

50. Ibid.

51. *Idaho Statesman*, 11 October 1942; *Boise News*, 25 June 1864.

52. Thompson, 6 (October 1913) 4:163.

53. Langford, 335.

194   *NOTES*

54. *Sacramento Daily Union*, 24 February 1864, Reprinted from *Golden Age*, 23 January 1864.

55. Ibid.; *Boise News*, 26 December 1863.

56. Langford, 345–46. Langford claimed to have obtained his information directly from Hill Beachey. See Langford, 336.

57. Ibid., 345–46.

58. *Sacramento Daily Union*, 24 February 1864, Reprinted from *Golden Age*, 23 January 1864; "Lewiston Correspondence," *Washington Statesman*, 30 January, 6 February, and 12 March 1864.

59. "Lewiston Correspondence," *Washington Statesman*, 6 February 1864.

60. *Sacramento Daily Union*, 24 February 1864, Reprinted from *Golden Age*, 23 January 1864.

61. "Lewiston Correspondence," *Washington Statesman*, 30 January 1864.

62. Ibid., 6 February 1864.

63. *Oregon Statesman*, 7 December 1863; *Sacramento Daily Union*, 24 February 1864, Reprinted from *Golden Age*, 23 January 1864.

64. "Lewiston Correspondence," *Washington Statesman*, 30 January 1864.

65. *Sacramento Daily Union*, 24 February 1864, Reprinted from *Golden Age*, 23 January 1864. The excerpts from Page's testimony are presented in the same chronology as the events he described.

66. Ibid.

67. Ibid.

68. Ibid.

69. "Lewiston Correspondence," *Washington Statesman*, 30 January 1864.

70. Ibid.

71. *Sacramento Daily Union*, 24 February 1864, Reprinted from *Golden Age*, 23 January 1864.

72. "Lewiston Correspondence," *Washington Statesman*, 6 February 1864.

73. *Sacramento Daily Union*, 24 February 1864, Reprinted from *Golden Age*, 23 January 1864.

74. *Weekly Oregonian*, 26 January 1864.

75. *Boise News*, 20 February 1864.

76. "Lewiston Correspondence," *Washington Statesman*, 6 February 1864.

77. *Boise News*, 20 February 1864.

78. "Lewiston Correspondence," *Washington Statesman*, 6 February 1864.

79. *Washington Statesman*, 12 March 1864.

80. Shiach and Averill, 38.

81. *Weekly Oregonian*, 12 March 1864, Reprinted from *Golden Age*, n.d.

82. "Lewiston Correspondence," *Washington Statesman*, 13 March 1864.

83. Ibid., 6 February and 13 March 1864; *Weekly Oregonian*, 12 March 1864, Reprinted from *Golden Age.*, n.d.; Shiach and Averill, 38.

84. "Lewiston Correspondence," *Washington Statesman*, 12 March 1864.

85. *Weekly Oregonian*, 12 March 1864, Reprinted from *Golden Age*, n.d.

86. Ibid.

87. "Lewiston Correspondence," *Washington Statesman*, 12 March 1864.

88. *Idaho Statesman*, 11 October 1942.

89. "Lewiston Correspondence," *Washington Statesman*, 12 March 1864.

90. *Weekly Oregonian*, 12 March 1864, Reprinted from *Golden Age*, n.d.; "Lewiston Correspondence," *Washington Statesman*, 12 March 1864.

91. Ibid.

92. Ibid.

93. *Boise News*, 25 June 1864, Reprinted from *Golden Age*, 11 June 1864.

94. *Sacramento Daily Union*, 3 November 1863; Hubert Howe Bancroft, *Popular Tribunals* (San Francisco: History Company, 1887), 2:663.

95. "List of Early Settlers," *Contributions to the Historical Society of Montana* 1 (Helena: Rocky Mountain Publishing, 1876), 298, 300; Granville Stuart, *Prospecting for Gold*, ed. Paul C. Phillips (Lincoln: University of Nebraska Press, 1977), 174, 189, 214, 245.

96. *Union Vedette* (Camp Douglas, Utah), 12 March 1864.

97. Reinhart, 239.

98. *Daily Oregonian*, 3 February 1863.

99. *Idaho Statesman*, 11 October 1942; McConnell, 154.

100. Early Ada County Records, Idaho State Historical Society Library, Boise; "Death of Hill Beachy," *Idaho Statesman*, 27 May 1875.

101. *Eighth Census of U.S.: 1860 Population Schedule of Yuba County, California*; *Ninth and Tenth Census of U.S.: 1870 and 1880 Population Schedules of Idaho Territory*.

102. *Boise News*, 26 December 1863; *Idaho Statesman*, 11 October 1942.

103. *Idaho Statesman*, 28 July 1870.

104. *Boise News*, 2 April 1864.

105. Langford, 325; Thompson, 6 (October 1913) 4:163–64.

106. *Sacramento Daily Union*, 24 February 1864, Reprinted from *Golden Age*, 23 January 1864.

107. *Union Vedette*, 21 March 1864.

108. *Sacramento Daily Union*, 24 February 1864, Reprinted from *Golden Age*, 23 January 1864; "San Francisco Correspondence," *Boise News*, 30 April 1864.

109. Ibid.

110. "Lewiston Correspondence," *Washington Statesman*, 30 January 1864.

111. *People v. Williams*, Idaho Territory Supreme Court, August 1866.

SALMON RIVER MINES (pp. 81–106)

1. Langford, 41.

2. Eliza A. Bowen, *The Story of Wilkes County, Georgia* (Marietta, Ga.: Continental Book Company, 1950), 54.

3. Robert Marion Dillingham, Jr., *We Have This Heritage: The History of Wilkes County, Georgia* (Washington, Ga.: Wilkes Publishing, 1969), 5, 10, 11.

4. Virgil Talbot, *The Talbots* (Calcord, Okla.: Author, 1983), 16, 17.

5. Mary Bondurant Warren, ed., *Chronicles of Wilkes County, Georgia* (Danielsville, Ga.: Heritage Papers, 1978), 52, 53.

6. Dillingham, 127.

7. Janet Harvill Standard, *Wilkes County Scrapbook* (Washington, Ga.: Wilkes Publishing, 1970), 20.

8. *Sixth Census of U.S.: 1840 Population Schedule of Wilkes County, Georgia*; Probate Records and Wills, Wilkes County, Georgia.

9. Talbot, 7–12; "The Talbot Heraldry," Item one of Film Number 249475, Church of Jesus Christ of Latter-day Saints Genealogical Library, Salt Lake City; Warren, 4.

10. *Register and Descriptive List of Convicts*; Governor's File on Cherokee Bob; Talbot, 17; "The Talbot Heraldry."

11. Alfred Barstow, "Statement of Alfred Barstow, A Pioneer of 1849," MS., H. H. Bancroft Collection, Bancroft Library, University of California, Berkeley, 2.

12. Paris S. Pfouts, *Four Firsts for a Modest Hero, The Autobiography of Paris Swazy Pfouts* (Portland, Oreg.: Dunham Printing, 1968), 85.

13. Robert K. DeArment, *Knights of the Green Cloth: The Saga of the Frontier Gamblers* (Norman: University of Oklahoma Press, 1982), 21–24. DeArment does not specifically mention Henry Talbot in his book, but does provide excellent descriptions of professional gamblers and gaming establishments. Physical descriptions of Talbot come from sources mentioned in note 10.

14. Twain, 250; Borthwick, 70; Dimsdale, 14, 18; Langford, 27.

15. James J. Sinnott, *Downieville: Gold Town on the Yuba* (Volcano, Calif.: California Traveler, 1972), 48.

16. Governor's File on Cherokee Bob; *Weekly Oregonian*, 6 February 1864; Bancroft, *Popular Tribunals*, 1:130; Twain, 252–53.

17. *Register and Descriptive List of Convicts*; *Compiled Laws of the State of California, Sessions of 1850-51-52-53*, 647; Governor's File on Cherokee Bob.

18. *Alta California*, 14 May 1855; *Register and Descriptive List of Convicts*; Governor's File on Cherokee Bob.

19. *Alta California*, 29 December 1854.

20. Ibid., 14 May 1855.

21. Ibid., 29 December 1854; *Register and Descriptive List of Convicts*; *Mariposa Democrat* (Mariposa, Calif.), 5 August 1856.

22. Governor's File on Cherokee Bob.

23. *Register and Descriptive List of Convicts*.

24. *Star* (Mariposa, Calif.), 1 March 1859.

25. *History of Placer County, California* (Oakland: Thompson & West, 1882), 332.

26. *Register and Descriptive List of Convicts*.

27. Reinhart, 186.

28. *Sacramento Bee*, 18 November 1861.

29. *Washington Statesman*, 3 October 1863.

30. *Sacramento Bee*, 12 October 1861.

31. Ibid., 11 October 1861.

32. Langford, 41.

33. *Pacific Tribune* (Olympia, Wash.), 16 May 1862.

34. Reinhart, 205–6.

35. "Address by Justice Robert D. Leeper," in Defenbach, 1:325n.

36. Cecille Owens Foster, *The Owens Family Through Sedalia* (Kansas City, Mo.: Nat and Lisa Cassingham, 1981), 35.

37. *San Francisco Chronicle*, 24 January 1892.

38. Ibid.; *Eighth Census of U.S.: 1860 Population Schedule of Utah Territory*.

39. *Nevada National*, 26 November 1859.

40. *San Francisco Chronicle*, 24 January 1892.

41. Ibid.

42. *Sacramento Bee*, 26 November 1861.

43. *Nevada Democrat*, 2 January 1862.

44. *San Francisco Chronicle*, 24 January 1892.

45. Ibid.

46. Ibid.

47. "Walla Walla Correspondence," *Weekly Oregonian*, 9 June 1862; *Washington Statesman*, 5 July 1862.

48. *Sacramento Daily Union*, 19 June 1862.

49. "Florence Correspondence," *Nevada Democrat*, 12 July 1862.

50. *Washington Statesman*, 25 January 1862.

51. *The Overland Press* (Olympia, Wash.), 24 February 1862; "Florence Correspondence," *Argus* (Oregon City, Oreg.), 31 May 1862.

52. Pfouts, 99.

53. Defenbach, 1:326.

54. Betty DeVeny, "Slate Creek History," 1974, TS., Slate Creek Ranger Station, White Bird, Idaho, 14.

55. *Sacramento Daily Union*, 1 November 1862.

56. *Weekly Oregonian*, 1 January 1863 and 6 February 1864; *Sacramento Daily Union*, 24 November 1862.

57. Ibid., 17 June 1863.

58. *Nevada Daily Transcript*, 17 January 1863.

59. *Sacramento Daily Union*, 2 March 1863, Reprinted from *Golden Age*, n.d.

60. Defenbach 1:325n; Bancroft, *History of Washington, Idaho, and Montana*, 452n.

61. State of California, *Census of 1852*; Reinhart, 223; Defenbach, 1:327.

62. Langford, 70; Defenbach, 1:327.

63. *Washington Statesman*, 17 January 1863; Twain, 249–50; Langford, 72.

64. *Washington Statesman*, 17 January 1863.

65. *Boise News*, 10 November and 26 December 1863.

66. *Idaho World*, 16 September 1865. Orlando "Rube" Robbins died in 1908, James H. Hawley, ed., *History of Idaho* (Chicago: S. J. Clarke Publishing, 1920), 128.

67. McConnell, 127–28; Defenbach, 1:328.

68. *Weekly Oregonian*, 12 November 1864.

69. Reinhart, 204.

GRASSHOPPER CREEK MINES (pp. 107–22)

1. James Henry Morley, "Diary," SC. 533, Montana Historical Society Archives, 72.

2. *Seventh Census of U.S.: 1850 Population Schedules of Sacramento County, California and Jo Daviess County, Illinois*; *Register and Descriptive List of Convicts*; Governor's File on Henry Plummer; *Nevada Democrat*, 2 and 9 October 1860.

3. Ibid., 24 October 1860.

4. Ibid., 23 September 1859.

5. Ibid., 29 October 1861; Langford, 131.

6. James Harkness, "Diary," *Contributions to Historical Society of Montana* 2 (Helena: State Publishing, 1896), 356; Dimsdale, 27–28.

7. Ibid., 28; *Sacramento Daily Union*, 17 June 1863.

8. Brosnan, 124–26.

9. *Boise News*, 25 June 1864.

10. Stuart, *Prospecting for Gold*, 223n.

11. Thomas Francis Meagher, "A Journey to Benton," *The Montana Magazine of History* 1 (October 1951) 4:49–50.

12. Ibid., 50.

13. Harkness, 350, 351, 356.

14. "Letter from John Strachan," *Register*, 6 April 1861.

15. Ibid.

16. Ibid.

198 NOTES

17. Thompson, 6 (July 1913) 3:124; *Deseret News* (Salt Lake City), 21 September 1859.

18. Thompson, 6 (July 1913) 3:116, 120.

19. *Glasgow Courier* (Glasgow, Mont.), 4 March 1924: Dimsdale, 26.

20. Thompson, 6 (October 1913) 4:160.

21. *Grass Range Review* (Grass Range, Mont.), 19 May 1919.

22. *Washington Statesman*, 13 June 1863.

23. *Grass Range Review*, 19 May 1919.

24. *River Press* (Benton, Mont.), 29 November 1882. Maurice Kildare summarizes the numerous stories of the Sun River treasure in "Henry Plummer's Golden Loot," *Frontier Times*, April–May 1965, 6–58.

25. Stuart, *Prospecting for Gold*, 231; Morley, 72.

26. Langford, 130–31; Dimsdale, 25.

27. Conrad Kohrs, *An Autobiography* (Deer Lodge, Mont.: Platen Press, 1977), 22.

28. Dimsdale, 28; Stuart, *Prospecting for Gold*, 235n.

29. Morley, 72.

30. Langford, 131–32; Dimsdale, 28–29.

31. Langford, 132; Dimsdale, 28.

32. Kohrs, 24; Langford, 133.

33. Langford, 156.

34. Kohrs, 25.

35. Morley, 72.

36. Harmon Graeter, Letter to R. E. Mather, 8 March 1988.

37. Frank Marryat, *Mountains and Molehills* (Philadelphia: J. B. Lippincott, 1962), 144; Borthwick, 122.

ALDER GULCH MINES (pp. 123–52)

1. Alfred Minot Copeland, ed., *A History of Hampden County, Massachusetts* (n.p.: Century Memorial Publishing, 1902), 203, 208; Arthur C. Ives, *The Ives Family* (Watertown, N.Y.: Hungerford-Holbrook, 1932), 128–30.

2. Ives, 14–18.

3. Ibid., 21.

4. Copeland, 199, 208; Ives, 20, 129.

5. Ives, 128–29.

6. Records of Congregational Church, Southwick, Massachusetts; *First, Second, Third, Fourth, and Fifth Census of U.S.: 1790, 1800, 1810, 1820, and 1830 Population Schedules of Hampshire and Hampden Counties, Massachusetts.*

7. *Sixth Census of U.S.: 1840 Population Schedule of Racine County, Wisconsin*; Wisconsin Genealogical Society, *History of Racine and Kenosha Counties* (Chicago: Western Historical Company, 1879), 304.

8. Probate Records of Racine County, Wisconsin; *The Grassroots History of Racine County* (n.p.: Racine County Historical Museum, Inc., 1978), 281.

9. Mary D. Bradford, "Memoirs," *Wisconsin Magazine of History* 14 (September 1930) 1:4.

10. Wisconsin Genealogical Society, 302, 304.

11. Ibid., 304; *Seventh Census of U.S.: 1850 Population Schedules of Jefferson and Racine Counties, Wisconsin*; *The Grassroots History of Racine County*, 18, 133.

12. Ibid., 30–31, 281.

13. Ibid., 31.

14. Ibid., 281.

15. Ibid.; *Seventh and Eighth Census of U.S.: 1850 and 1860 Population Schedules of Jefferson and Racine Counties, Wisconsin.*

16. Ibid., Probate Records of Racine County, Wisconsin.

17. *The Grassroots History of Racine County*, 281-82.

18. State of California, *Census of 1852.*

19. Wilbur F. Sanders, "The Story of George Ives," in Sanders, *Beidler*, 40, 45; Langford, 307.

20. Sanders, "The Story of George Ives," 40.

21. Dimsdale, 116; Langford, 306-7.

22. Ibid., *Nevada Daily Transcript*, 21 April 1863; "List of Early Settlers," 301.

23. Sarah Wadams Howard, "Reminiscences of a Pioneer," *Souvenir Booklet Commemorating Bannack, First Territorial Capital of Montana, Dedication and Pageant, 15 August 1954*, Montana Historical Society Archives, n.p.

24. Dimsdale, 30-31, 264; Langford, 133-34.

25. Dimsdale, 14.

26. Federal Writers' Project of the Work Projects Administration, *Montana: A State Guide Book* (New York: Hastings House, 1939), 40.

27. James Stuart, "Journal," *Contributions to the Historical Society of Montana* 1 (Helena: Rocky Mountain Publishing, 1878), 149, 154-55, 166.

28. Ibid., 157-63, 181; Sanders, "The Story of George Ives," 44; *Western News* (Westby, Mont.), 27 October 1918.

29. Stuart, "Journal," 176-80; Granville Stuart, *Pioneering in Montana*, ed., Paul C. Phillips (Lincoln: University of Nebraska Press, 1977), 122.

30. Stuart, "Journal," 182-87.

31. Ibid., 194, 190.

32. Ibid., 191, 197.

33. Ibid., 200-203.

34. Ibid., 207, 213, 216, 233; Sanders, "The Story of George Ives," 44.

35. Ibid., 45; Promissory Note of George Ives, Montana Historical Society Archives; Stuart, *Pioneering in Montana*, 122.

36. Sanders, "The Story of George Ives," 44-45, 49-50; Dimsdale, 91.

37. Probate Records of Racine County, Wisconsin.

38. Dimsdale, 96.

39. Margaret Ronan, *Frontier Woman: The Story of Mary Ronan* (Missoula: University of Montana, 1973), 19-20.

40. George A. Bruffey, *Eighty-One Years in the West* (Butte: Butte Miner Printers, 1925), 34-35; Sanders, "The Story of George Ives," 44.

41. Ibid., 50; Langford, 285-86; Dimsdale, 90, 106; Reginald Stanley, Letter to James U. Sanders, 29 August 1903, SC. 781, Montana Historical Society Archives.

42. Dimsdale, 98; Ronan, 26; William Y. Pemberton, "Notes of Lecture Before Unity Club, May 12, 1908," William Y. Pemberton Papers, Handwritten MS., SC. 629, Montana Historical Society Archives, 31.

43. Dimsdale, 94-97; John W. Grannis, "Diary-1863," TS., Montana Historical Society Archives, 22-23.

44. Dimsdale 96-97; Jerome Peltier, ed., *The Banditti of the Rocky Mountains and Vigilance Committee in Idaho* (Minneapolis: Ross and Haines, 1964), 103.

45. Dimsdale, 101-2; Lew L. Callaway, *Montana's Righteous Hangmen* (Norman: University of Oklahoma Press, 1982), 30.

46. Stanley Letter, 1903; Sanders, "The Story of George Ives," 51.

47. Dimsdale, 98, 104; William Y. Pemberton, "Early Day Courts and Judges," *Glentana Reporter* (Glentana, Mont.), 12 November 1917; Sanders, "The Story of George Ives," 60.

48. Ibid., 61.

49. Ibid., 65; Bruffey, 36, 37; Stanley Letter, 1903.

50. Sanders, "The Story of George Ives," 64; Dimsdale, 93; Bruffey, 37; Pemberton, "Early Day Courts and Judges"; Kohrs, 34.

51. Sanders, "The Story of George Ives," 67, 68; Callaway, 31; Dimsdale, 105.

52. Pemberton, "Early Day Courts and Judges."

53. Langford, 300.

54. Ibid., 304; "Nelson Story Sr.," *Fergus County Argus* (Lewistown, Mont.), 18 April 1918.

55. Sanders, "The Story of George Ives," 71-72.

56. Ibid., 74-75; Langford, 97; Dimsdale, 113.

57. Reginald Stanley, Letter to James U. Sanders, 25 February 1905, SC. 781, Montana Historical Society Archives.

58. "Nelson Story Sr.," *Fergus County Argus*, 18 April 1918.

59. Stanley Letter, 1903; Langford, 304.

60. Dimsdale, 115; *Seventh Census of U.S.: 1850 Population Schedule of Fairfield County, Connecticut.*

61. Sanders, "The Story of George Ives," 57; Dimsdale, 106; William Herron, Unidentified Newspaper Article, in Sanders, *Beidler*, 35.

62. Sanders, "The Story of George Ives," 54; Callaway, 31.

63. Stanley Letter, 1903.

64. Bruffey, 37.

65. "Nelson Story Sr.," *Fergus County Argus*, 18 April 1918; *Daily Oregonian*, 13 April 1864.

66. Langford, 304; Sanders, "The Story of George Ives," 65.

67. Dimsdale, 115-16; Reinhart, 240; Shiach and Averill, 30.

68. Dimsdale, 91; Sanders, "The Story of George Ives," 49-50.

69. Dimsdale, 65-67, 69; Langford, 240.

70. Dimsdale, 54; Langford, 275-77, 261; Plassmann, 121-22.

71. Dimsdale, 83; Langford, 250-51.

72. Dimsdale, 91-92.

73. Anton M. Holter, "Pioneer Lumbering in Montana," *Contributions to the Historical Society of Montana* 8 (Helena: Independent Publishing, 1903), 251-52.

74. Abraham C. Anderson, *Trails of Early Idaho: The Pioneer Life of George W. Goodhart* (Caldwell, Idaho: Caxton Printers, 1940), 281, 284, 290.

75. "How Colonel Broadwater Outrode George Ives, Saved His Own Life and a Fortune," *The Leader* (Piniele, Mont.), 2 September 1918.

76. Kohrs, 30.

77. Sanders, "The Story of George Ives," 73; *Montana Post* (Virginia City, Mont.), 6 July 1867; *Seventh Census of U.S.: 1850 Population Schedule of Fairfield County, Connecticut.*

OTHER DESPERADOES (pp. 153-82)

1. *Register and Descriptive List of Convicts.*

2. Ibid.; Langford, 45.

3. *Sacramento Daily Union*, 22 January 1863; Langford, 55.

4. *Sacramento Daily Union*, 22 January 1863; *The Overland Press*, 5 January 1863.

5. Langford, 56; *Convict Record Oregon Penitentiary*, Oregon State Archives, Salem.

6. "Correspondence from Florence," *Daily Oregonian*, 31 December 1861, Reprinted from *Washington Statesman*, n.d.

7. Hiram T. French, *History of Idaho* (Chicago: Lewis Publishing, 1914), 135–36.

8. *Daily Oregonian*, 20 February 1866 and 4 August 1863.

9. *Oregon Journal* (Portland), 26 April 1914, Reprinted from *Chicago Evening Post*, n.d.

10. *Weekly Oregonian*, 5 November 1864.

11. *Daily Oregonian*, 3 December 1864.

12. *Convict Record Oregon Penitentiary*.

13. *Oregon Statesman* (Salem), 8 October 1866; *Convict Record Oregon Penitentiary*.

14. *Daily Oregonian*, 11 April 1876; Twain, 254.

15. Langford, 40, 45.

16. *Compiled Laws of the State of California, Sessions of 1850-51-52-53*, 647; *Register and Descriptive List of Convicts*.

17. Langford, 40, 45, 47.

18. *Daily Oregonian*, 15 November 1862.

19. *Washington Statesman*, 17 November 1862.

20. "Colville Correspondence," *Washington Statesman*, 28 February 1863.

21. Ibid.

22. Bancroft, *History of Washington, Idaho, and Montana*, 452n; Shiach and Averill, 30.

23. *Eighth Census of U.S.: 1860 Population Schedule of Siskiyou County, California*; Langford, 45.

24. *Seventh and Eighth Census of U.S.: 1850 and 1860 Population Schedules of Sacramento and Trinity Counties, California*; *The Overland Press*, 24 November 1862.

25. W. M. Paxton, *Annals of Platte County, Missouri* (Kansas City, Mo.: Hudson-Kimberly Publishing, 1897), 133; *History of Clay and Platte Counties, Missouri* (St. Louis: National Historical Company, 1885), 508–9, 839, 990.

26. Paxton, 129, 131, 134, 135.

27. Ibid., 129, 134; *Seventh Census of U.S.: 1850 Population Schedule of Platte County, Missouri*.

28. *Eighth Census of U.S.: 1860 Population Schedule of Benton County, Oregon*; Reinhart, 239; *Daily Oregonian*, 15 November 1862.

29. Langford, 46–47.

30. *Washington Statesman*, 18 November 1862, Reprinted from *Golden Age*, Special Edition of November 1862.

31. Ibid.; McConnell, 107.

32. Reinhart, 239.

33. *Washington Statesman*, 18 November 1862, Reprinted from *Golden Age*, Special Edition of November 1862.

34. *Washington Statesman*, 18 November 1862; Hailey, 35.

35. *Daily Oregonian*, 11 November 1862.

36. Shiach and Averill, 30; *Daily Oregonian*, 1 January 1863.

37. Shiach and Averill, 30; *Washington Statesman*, 16 May 1863.

38. Langford, 244; Dimsdale, 84, 98.

39. Ibid., 175, 176.

40. Dimsdale, 266; *Register and Descriptive List of Convicts*.

41. Ibid., *Compiled Laws of the State of California, Sessions of 1850-51-52-53*, 647.

42. *Register and Descriptive List of Convicts.*

43. *Sacramento Daily Union*, 24 April 1856; Dudley T. Ross, ed., *The Golden Gazette* (Fresno, Calif.: Valley Publishers, 1978), 93.

44. "Coroner's Inquest," *Sacramento Daily Union*, 24 April 1856.

45. Ibid.

46. *Sacramento Daily Union*, 24 April 1856; *Placer Herald* (Auburn, Calif.), 12 April 1856; *Register and Descriptive List of Convicts.*

47. McConnell, 102; Rasmussen, 2:38; *Register and Descriptive List of Convicts.*

48. *Compiled Laws of the State of California, Sessions of 1850–51–52–53*, 646, 647; *Register and Descriptive List of Convicts.*

49. *Sacramento Bee*, 2 January 1862.

50. McConnell, 102; *Luna House Register*, Luna House Museum, Nez Perce County Historical Society, Lewiston, Idaho.

51. Defenbach, 1:321; Langford, 38.

52. Ibid.; *Madisonian* (Virginia City, Mont.), 1 January 1915.

53. *Sacramento Daily Union*, 17 June 1863.

54. *Boise News*, 19 March 1864.

55. Ibid., 9 April 1864; *Weekly Oregonian*, 4 November 1865.

56. Maize, 4–5.

57. *Idaho World*, 24 February 1866.

58. *Owyhee Avalanche* (Silver City, Idaho), 24 March 1866; *Idaho World*, 14 April 1866.

59. *Washington Statesman*, 27 April 1866.

60. *Daily Oregonian*, 8 September 1868.

61. *Seventh Census of U.S.: 1850 Population Schedule of Mercer County, Pennsylvania*; "Moore and Reeves," *Herald* (Helena, Mont.), 3 January 1882.

62. *Register and Descriptive List of Convicts.*

63. *Alta California*, 29 December 1854.

64. *Register and Descriptive List of Convicts*; "Moore and Reeves," *Herald*, 3 January 1882.

65. *Luna House Register*; *Madisonian*, 1 January 1915.

66. *Sacramento Daily Union*, 17 June 1863.

67. "Moore and Reeves," *Herald*, 3 January 1882.

68. Dimsdale, 34; *Washington Statesman*, 2 May 1863; "Moore and Reeves," *Herald*, 3 January 1882.

69. Ibid.

70. "How Colonel Broadwater Outrode George Ives, Saved His Own Life and a Fortune," *The Leader*, 2 September 1918.

71. *Sacramento Daily Union*, 17 June 1863.

72. *Nevada Daily Transcript*, 21 April 1863; "James and Granville Stuart Account Book," William Andrews Clark Memorial Library, Los Angeles; Dimsdale, 24; *Ninth Census of U.S.: 1870 Population Schedule of Lamar County, Texas.*

73. *Register and Descriptive List of Convicts.*

74. "Coroner's Inquest," *Nevada National*, 26 March 1859.

75. *Nevada Democrat*, 6 July and 29 October 1861.

76. Ibid., 29 October 1861; *Morning Transcript*, 29 October 1861.

77. *Register and Descriptive List of Convicts*; *Nevada Democrat*, 29 October 1861; *Morning Transcript*, 29 October 1861.

78. Langford, 187.

CONCLUSIONS (pp. 183–88)

1. Brown, 168.

2. *Register and Descriptive List of Convicts.*

3. Frederick Jackson Turner, "Statement of the Frontier Thesis," in Ray Allen Billington, ed., *The Frontier Thesis* (Huntington, N.Y.: Robert E. Krieger Publishing, 1977), 19.

4. Langford, 32, 191; Barstow, 3; J. D. B. Stillman, *The Gold Rush Letters* (Palo Alto, Calif.: Lewis Osborne, 1967), 38.

5. Barstow, 2; *Nevada National*, 10 March 1860.

6. Langford, 53, 176, 71; Barstow, 3.

7. *Daily Oregonian*, 1 January 1863.

8. Jack Burrows, Speech Delivered at Fifteenth Annual Rendezvous of National Association for Outlaw and Lawman History, 27 July 1988; Jack Burrows, Letter to R. E. Mather, 13 January 1989.

9. Michael Leeson, *History of Montana 1739–1885* (Chicago: Warner, Beers & Company, 1885), 265; *Morning Post* (San Jose, Calif.), 4 October 1851.

10. *Boise News*, 20 February 1864.

BIBLIOGRAPHY

BOOKS

Anderson, Abraham C. *Trails of Early Idaho: The Pioneer Life of George W. Goodhart.* Caldwell, Idaho: Caxton Printers, 1940.

Bancroft, Hubert Howe. *California Inter Pocula.* San Francisco: History Company, 1888.

———. *History of Washington, Idaho, and Montana.* San Francisco: History Company, 1890.

———. *Popular Tribunals.* 2 vols. San Francisco: History Company, 1887.

Borthwick, John David. *The Gold Hunters.* Cleveland: International Fiction Library, 1917.

Bowen, Eliza A. *The Story of Wilkes County, Georgia.* Marietta, Ga.: Continental Book Company, 1950.

Bradley, James H. "Journal." *Contributions to the Historical Society of Montana* 8. Helena: Historical and Miscellaneous Library, 1917.

Brosnan, Cornelius J. *History of the State of Idaho.* New York: Charles Scribner's Sons, 1948.

Brown, Richard Maxwell. "The American Vigilante Tradition," In Hugh D. Graham and Ted R. Gurr, eds., *The History of Violence in America.* New York: Frederick A. Praeger, Publishers, 1969.

Bruffey, George A. *Eighty-One Years in the West.* Butte: Butte Miner Printers, 1925.

Callaway, Lew L. *Montana's Righteous Hangmen.* Norman: University of Oklahoma Press, 1982.

Compiled Laws of the State of California, Sessions of 1850-51-52-53. Boston: Franklin Printing, 1853.

Copeland, Alfred Minot, ed. *A History of Hampden County, Massachusetts.* N.p.: Century Memorial Publishing, 1902.

DeArment, Robert K. *Knights of the Green Cloth: The Saga of Frontier Gamblers.* Norman: University of Oklahoma Press, 1982.

Defenbach, Byron. *Idaho: The Place and Its People.* 2 vols. Chicago: American Historical Society, 1933.

Delano, Alonzo. *Pen-Knife Sketches or Chips off the Old Block.* San Francisco: Grabhorn Press, 1934.

Delay, Peter J. *History of Yuba and Sutter Counties.* Los Angeles: Historical Record Company, 1924.

Dillingham, Robert Marion, Jr. *We Have This Heritage: The History of Wilkes County, Georgia.* Washington, Ga.: Wilkes Publishing, 1969.

Dimsdale, Thomas J. *The Vigilantes of Montana.* Butte: McKee Printing Company, 1945.

Federal Writers' Project of the Work Projects Administration. *Montana: A State Guide Book.* New York: Hastings House, 1939.

Foster, Cecille Owens. *The Owens Family Through Sedalia.* Kansas City, Mo.: Nat and Lisa Cassingham, 1981.

French, Hiram T. *History of Idaho.* Chicago: Lewis Publishing, 1914.

Gard, Wayne. *Frontier Justice.* Norman: University of Oklahoma Press, 1949.

Graham, Hugh D., and Ted R. Gurr, eds. *The History of Violence in America.* New York: Frederick A. Praeger, Publishers, 1969.

The Grassroots History of Racine County. N.p.: Racine County Historical Museum, Inc., 1978.

Hailey, John. *The History of Idaho.* Boise: Syms-York, 1918.

Harkness, James. "Diary." *Contributions to the Historical Society of Montana* 2. Helena: State Publishing, 1896.

Hawley, James H., ed. *History of Idaho.* Chicago: S. J. Clarke Publishing, 1920.

Herron, William. Unidentified Newspaper Article. In Helen Sanders, ed. *X. Beidler: Vigilante.* Norman: University of Oklahoma Press, 1957.

History of Clay and Platte Counties, Missouri. Kansas City, Mo.: Hudson-Kimberly Publishing, 1897.

History of Idaho Territory. San Francisco: Wallace W. Elliott, 1884.

History of Nevada. Reproduction of Thompson & West's *History of Nevada, 1881.* Berkeley: Howell-North, 1958.

History of Nevada County. Reproduction of Thompson & West's *History of Nevada County, California, 1880.* Berkeley: Howell-North, 1970.

History of Placer County, California. Oakland: Thompson & West, 1882.

Holter, Anton M. "Pioneer Lumbering in Montana." *Contributions to the Historical Society of Montana* 8. Helena: Independent Publishing, 1903.

Ives, Arthur C. *The Ives Family.* Watertown, N.Y.: Hungerford-Holbrook, 1932.

Kohrs, Conrad. *An Autobiography.* Deer Lodge, Mont.: Platen Press, 1977.

Langford, Nathaniel. *Vigilante Days and Ways.* New York: A. L. Burt Company, 1912.

Leeper, Robert D. Address by Justice Robert D. Leeper. In Byron Defenbach. *Idaho: The Place and Its People.* 2 vols. Chicago: American Historical Society, 1933.

Leeson, Michael. *History of Montana 1739–1885.* Chicago: Warner, Beers & Company, 1885.

"List of Early Settlers." *Contributions to the Historical Society of Montana* 1. Helena: Rocky Mountain Publishing, 1876.

Marryat, Frank. *Mountains and Molehills.* Philadelphia: J. B. Lippincott, 1962.

Mather, Cotton. *Diary.* 2 vols. New York: Frederick Ungar Publishing, n.d.

McConnell, William J. *Early History of Idaho.* Caldwell, Idaho: Caxton Printers, 1913.

Parkman, Francis. *The Oregon Trail.* Garden City, N.Y.: Doubleday, 1946.

Paxton, W. M. *Annals of Platte County, Missouri.* Kansas City, Mo.: Hudson-Kimberly Publishing, 1897.

Peltier, Jerome, ed. *The Banditti of the Rocky Mountains and Vigilance Committee in Idaho.* Minneapolis: Ross and Haines, 1964.

Pfouts, Paris S. *Four Firsts for a Modest Hero: The Autobiography of Paris Swazy Pfouts.* Portland, Oreg.: Dunham Printing, 1968.

Rasmussen, Louis J. *San Francisco Ship Passenger Lists.* 2 vols. Baltimore: Dedford, 1965.

Reinhart, Herman Francis. *The Golden Frontier.* Austin: University of Texas Press, 1962.

Ronan, Margaret. *Frontier Woman: The Story of Mary Ronan.* Missoula: University of Montana, 1973.

Ross, Dudley T., ed. *The Golden Gazette.* Fresno, Calif.: Valley Publishers, 1978.

Sanders, Helen F., ed. *X. Beidler: Vigilante.* Norman: University of Oklahoma Press, 1957.

Sanders, Wilbur F. "The Story of George Ives." In Helen F. Sanders, ed. *X. Beidler: Vigilante.* Norman: University of Oklahoma Press, 1957.

Shaw, David Augustus. *El Dorado or California as Seen by a Pioneer.* Los Angeles: B. R. Baumgardt & Company, 1900.

Shaw, William. *Golden Dreams and Waking Realities.* New York: Arno Press, 1973.

Shiach, William S. and Harry B. Averill. *An Illustrated History of North Idaho.* N.p.: Western Historical Publishing, 1903.

Sinnott, James J. *Downieville: Gold Town on the Yuba.* Volcano, Calif.: California Traveler, 1972.

Standard, Janet Harvill. *Wilkes County Scrapbook.* Washington, Ga.: Wilkes Publishing, 1970.

Stillman, J. D. B. *The Gold Rush Letters.* Palo Alto, Calif.: Lewis Osborne, 1967.

Stuart, Granville. *Pioneering in Montana.* Edited by Paul C. Phillips. Lincoln: University of Nebraska Press, 1977.

Stuart, Granville. *Prospecting for Gold.* Edited by Paul C. Phillips. Lincoln: University of Nebraska Press, 1977.

Stuart, James. "Journal." *Contributions to the Historical Society of Montana* 1. Helena: Rocky Mountain Publishing, 1878.

Talbot, Virgil. *The Talbots.* Calcord, Okla.: Author, 1983.

Turner, Frederick Jackson. "Statement of the Frontier Thesis." In Ray Allen Billington, ed. *The Frontier Thesis.* Huntington, N.Y.: Robert E. Krieger Publishing, 1977.

Twain, Mark. *Roughing It.* New York: Holt, Rinehart and Winston, 1966.

Warren, Mary Bondurant. *Chronicles of Wilkes County, Georgia.* Danielsville, Ga.: Heritage Papers, 1978.

Webster's New Collegiate Dictionary. Springfield, Mass.: G. & C. Merriam, 1975.

Wisconsin Genealogical Society. *History of Racine and Kenosha Counties.* Chicago: Western Historical Company, 1879.

Wood, Jerome H., Jr. *Conestoga Crossroads, Lancaster, Pennsylvania 1730–1790.* Harrisburg: Historical and Museum Commission, 1979.

ARTICLES AND NEWSPAPERS

Alta California (San Francisco). 1854–58.

Argus (Oregon City). 1862.

Boise News (Idaho City). 1863–64.

Bradford, Mary D. "Memoirs." *Wisconsin Magazine of History.* 14 (September 1930) 1:4.

Daily Appeal (Marysville, Calif.). 1863.

Daily Oregonian (Portland). 1861–76.

Dart, John Paul. "A Mississipian in the Gold Fields." *California Historical Society Quarterly* 35 (1956) 3:205–16.

Deseret News (Salt Lake City). 1859.

Elmore Bulletin (Mountain Home, Idaho) 1863–94.

Fergus County Argus (Lewistown, Mont.). 1918.

Glasgow Courier (Glasgow, Mont.). 1924.

Glentana Reporter (Glentana, Mont.). 1917.

Golden Age (Lewiston, Idaho). 1863.

Goodwin, Victor. "William C. Beachey, Nevada-California-Idaho Stagecoach King." *Nevada Historical Society Quarterly* 10 (1967) 1:3–46.

Grass Range Review (Grass Range, Mont.). 1919.

Grass Valley National (Grass Valley, Calif.). 1861.

Herald (Helena). 1882.

Idaho Statesman (Boise). 1870, 1875, 1942.

Idaho World (Idaho City). 1865–66.

The Leader (Piniele, Mont.). 1918.

Madisonian (Virginia City, Mont.) 1915.

Mariposa Democrat (Mariposa, Calif.). 1856.

Meagher, Thomas Francis. "A Journey to Benton." *The Montana Magazine of History* 1 (October 1951) 4:48–57.

Montana Post (Virginia City, Mont.). 1863.

Morning Post (San Jose, Calif.). 1851.

Morning Transcript (Nevada City, Calif.). 1860–62.

Nevada Daily Transcript (Nevada City, Calif.). 1862–63.

Nevada Democrat (Nevada City, Calif.). 1859–66.

Nevada Journal (Nevada City, Calif.). 1855.

Nevada National (Grass Valley, Calif.). 1859–60.

Oregon Journal (Portland). 1914.

Oregon Statesman (Salem). 1863–66.

The Overland Press (Olympia, Wash.). 1862–63.

Owyhee Avalanche (Silver City, Idaho). 1866.

Pacific Tribune (Olympia, Wash.). 1862.

Pemberton, William Y. "Early Day Courts and Judges." *Glentana Reporter* (Glentana, Mont.), 12 November 1917.

Placer Herald (Auburn, Calif.). 1856.

Register (Rockford, Ill.). 1861.

River Press (Benton, Mont.). 1882.

Sacramento Bee. 1861–62.

Sacramento Daily Union. 1856–64.

San Francisco Chronicle. 1892.

Star (Mariposa, Calif.). 1859.

Thompson, Francis. "Reminiscences of Four Score Years." *Massachusetts Magazine* 6 (July 1913) 3:116–24 and (October 1913) 4:114–90.

Times (Aurora, Nev.). 1864.

Union Vedette (Camp Douglas, Utah). 1864.

Washington Statesman (Walla Walla, Wash.) 1862–66.

Weekly Oregonian (Portland). 1862–65.

Western News (Westby, Mont.). 1918.

UNPUBLISHED MATERIAL

Barstow, Alfred. "Statement of Alfred Barstow, A Pioneer of 1849." MS., H. H. Bancroft Collection, Bancroft Library, University of California, Berkeley.

Burrows, Jack. Letter to R. E. Mather. 13 January 1989.

_____. Speech Delivered at Fifteenth Annual Rendezvous of National Association for Outlaw and Lawman History, 27 July 1988.

DeVeny, Betty. "Slate Creek History." 1974, TS., Slate Creek Ranger Station, White Bird, Idaho.

Grannis, John W. "Diary–1863." TS., Montana Historical Society Archives.

Graeter, Harmon. Letter to R. E. Mather. 8 March 1988.

Howard, Sarah Wadams. "Reminiscences of a Pioneer." *Souvenir Booklet Commemorating Bannack, First Territorial Capital of Montana, Dedication and Pageant, 15 August 1954.* Montana Historical Society Archives.

"James and Granville Stuart Account Book." William Andrews Clark Memorial Library, Los Angeles.

Luna House Register. Luna House Museum, Nez Perce County Historical Society, Lewiston, Idaho.

Maize, Henry B. "Early Events." Handwritten MS., Bancroft Library, University of California, Berkeley.

Morley, James Henry. "Diary." SC. 533, Montana Historical Society Archives.

Pemberton, William Y. "Notes of Lecture Before Unity Club, May 12, 1908." William Y. Pemberton Papers. Handwritten MS., SC. 629, Montana Historical Society Archives.

Plassmann, Martha Edgerton. "Judge Edgerton's Daughter." MS. 78, Montana Historical Society Archives.

Promissory Note of George Ives, Montana Historical Society Archives.

Stanley, Reginald. Letters to James U. Sanders. 29 August 1903 and 25 February 1905. SC. 781, Montana Historical Society Archives.

"The Talbot Heraldry." Item one of Film number 249475, Church of Jesus Christ of Latter-day Saints Genealogical Library, Salt Lake City.

PUBLIC DOCUMENTS

California. "An Act Creating a Board of State Prison Commissioners, and Defining Their Duties." California State Archives, Sacramento.

California. *Census of 1852.*

California. Governor's Files on Cherokee Bob, David Renton, Charles Richardson, Edward Richardson, Francis Van Moore, and Henry Plummer. California State Archives, Sacramento.

California. Governor Weller's Address to State Legislature, 10 March 1859. In *Journal of the Senate*, Ninth Session. California State Library, Sacramento.

California. *Register and Descriptive List of Convicts Under Sentence of Imprisonment in the State Prison.* California State Archives, Sacramento.

California. Rewards Offered by State of California Executive Department. California State Archives, Sacramento.

Georgia. Wilkes County Probate Records and Wills.

Idaho. Early Ada County Records. Idaho State Historical Society Library, Boise.

Idaho. *Reports.* Idaho Territory Supreme Court Term 1866. Idaho State Historical Society Library, Boise.

Massachusetts. Southwick Congregational Church Records.

Missouri. *Register of Missouri Penitentiary Inmates, 1841–1851.* Missouri State Archives, Jefferson City.

Oregon. *Convict Record Oregon Penitentiary.* Oregon State Archives, Salem.

Wisconsin. Racine County Probate Records.

U.S. Bureau of the Census. *First Census of U.S.: 1790 Population Schedule.*

———. *Second Census of U.S.: 1800 Population Schedule.*

———. *Third Census of U.S.: 1810 Population Schedule.*

———. *Fourth Census of U.S.: 1820 Population Schedule.*

———. *Fifth Census of U.S.: 1830 Population Schedule.*

———. *Sixth Census of U.S.: 1840 Population Schedule.*

———. *Seventh Census of U.S.: 1850 Population Schedule.*

———. *Eighth Census of U.S.: 1860 Population Schedule.*

———. *Ninth Census of U.S.: 1870 Population Schedule.*

———. *Tenth Census of U.S.: 1880 Population Schedule.*

INDEX